MW00424355

Praise for S

"Drawing from various religious traditions, particularly Christianity, Carl McColman shows us that spirituality is a way of life in which we encounter and respond to the Sacred through all aspects of our lives. As he dialogues with many resources—books, song, films, life stories—McColman illustrates the daily and varied dynamics of spirituality."

Mary Reuter, O.S.B., Ph.D.
Associate Professor of Theology
College of Saint Benedict, St. Joseph, Minnesota

"A most gentle book filled with nuggets of spiritual wisdom that will help bridge the reader to a new spiritual dimension."

Gerald G. Jampolsky, M.D.
Author, *Love Is Letting Go Of Fear*

"Carl McColman's *Spirituality* is a basic resource book in the best sense. It invites the reader into a life of real spirituality, one that avoids mistaking ourselves for lofty angelic beings or for merely materialistic mechanisms."

Gene R. Thursby, Ph.D.
Associate Professor
Department of Religion, University of Florida

"Whether the reader prays regularly or prays seldom; whether her spiritual tradition is Charismatic or Celtic; whether theist or atheist; whether [readers] worship in tongues, contemplate in silence, or not at all, the heart is strangely warmed and inexplicably changed by this insightful study. I strongly recommend this book. It is a richly rewarding read."

Rev. Colin G. Garvie
Methodist Minister, MCSA
Durban, South Africa

"At a time when words are twisted by 'spin doctors' and used narrowly and flippantly, Carl McColman paves a path that universalizes spirituality. The spirituality that McColman unfolds is not one of asceticism and separateness, but of community."

Rabbi Gerald Schuster
Chaplain
Weiss Memorial Hospital, Chicago

" . . . lucid and down-to-earth without sacrificing substance and depth. McColman may be articulating the secret thoughts of millions of baby-boomers in finding spiritual meaning in such 'unlikely' places as the lyrics of the music of the Grateful Dead, Led Zeppelin, and The Clash. *Spirituality: Where Body and Soul Encounter the Sacred* finds itself in the venerable company of the relatively few books on spirituality that are authentic and sound."

Brother Hugh Goforth
Oblate of New Creation Monastery
Boonville, North Carolina

SPIRITUALITY

SPIRITUALITY

*Where Body and Soul
Encounter the Sacred*

Carl McColman

NORTH STAR PUBLICATIONS
Georgetown, Massachusetts

North Star Publications
P.O. Box 10
Georgetown, MA 01833
(508) 352-9976 • fax (508) 352-5586
http://www.ReadersNdex.com/northstar

Cover design: Salwen Studios, Keene, NH

Printed in the United States of America

For further copyright information see page 238.

Publisher's Cataloging in Publication
McColman, Carl.
    Spirituality : where body and soul encounter the sacred / Carl
McColman.
    p. cm.
    Includes bibliographical references and index.
    ISBN: 1-880823-16-0

    1. Spiritual life—Christianity. 2. Conduct of life. I. Title

BV4501.2.M33 1997   248
                                     QBI97-40312

Acknowledgments

Part of the spiritual life involves exploring the sacred dimensions of relationships. Over the years, I have been blessed with many soul friends who have accompanied me on my divine journey. While I cannot list all the wonderful people who have befriended me, five in particular—Lin Ludy, Bob Hughes, Mary Avram, Vince Malatesta, and Emmett Jarrett—have given much to me in terms of time, energy, and prayer. Their love, challenge, and support have nurtured me deeply as I've sought intimacy with God.

As a writer, I especially wish to thank Meg Anderson, David Bottoms, Jim McNew, Don Rausch, Susan Strauss, Sylvia Sultenfuss, and Caroline and John Westerhoff for ideas, encouragement, and support. My agent, Linda Roghaar; my publisher, George Trim; and my editor, John Niendorff, each deserve an extra special "thank you," both for their willingness to believe in this book and for the hard work they put into helping me prepare the manuscript for publication.

Thanks to my dearest and closest friends—my wife, Fran, and my stepdaughter, Rhiannon—both of whom have been amazingly patient over the months I've spent writing this book. Finally, thanks to my folks, John and Sylvia McColman. Their love and care provided me with my first hint at the reality of Divine love—which, after all, is what spirituality is all about. As a token of gratitude for that gift of love, I dedicate this book to Mom and Dad.

Contents

. . . if you study the logistics and heuristics of the mystics
you will find that their minds rarely move in a line.

Brian Eno
"Backwater"

Prologue

We live in a time when more and more of us think of ourselves as "spiritual." We read books on living soulfully, or on the history of God, or on the lost wisdom of ancient peoples. We listen to meditative Gregorian chants and soothing, "spacious" instrumental music. We explore the transpersonal dimensions of psychology and the metaphysical dimensions of health and business. More and more, we seem to respond to an inner, "soul-level" longing for living life according to meaningful beliefs, values, and experiences beyond the mundane and the everyday affairs of the world. We understand "spirituality" as distinct from just plain "life"—but what does that mean?

This is a book for seekers, for persons who are willing to ask questions and explore possibilities and imagine many ways of seeing and being. I consider myself such a seeker, and I hope everyone who reads this will allow the "seeker within" to come out and play. I write as someone who simply wishes to present his thoughts and his findings to other seekers and travelers on the spiritual path. My inspiration as a spiritual writer comes from the ancient Celtic idea of the *anamchara*, or "soul friend." An *anamchara* (pronounced "ahn-im-kár-uh") is a person who befriends you as you journey through life, providing companionship and guidance as you seek to encounter the Divine. I hope that my writing can be the words of an *anamchara*, a friend of the spirit who accompanies each reader at this particular moment in his or her sacred journey. I see this book as a friendly contribution to a dialogue—the ongoing conversation of persons attempting to live a deep and soulful life filled with radiant imagination, passion, and wonder.

In looking at the images, practices, concepts, and experiences that underlie spirituality, our inquiry will meander into different forms of culture and different religious traditions. The inspiration to write this book actually came from popular culture—popular music, to be exact. That's why, in the pages that follow, I've drawn several examples from the music

1

and musicians of recent years as ways of illustrating various aspects of spirituality. Performers as diverse as the Grateful Dead, The Clash, John Coltrane, and Tori Amos have written and performed music and lyrics that are perceptive and imaginative in their treatment of spirituality. I once knew a minister who insisted that the best theology was found not in scholarly books, but in novels. A similar conviction leads me to look for lessons about spirituality in popular music.

As a teenager in the Bible-belt south, I discovered that, in the minds of many people, rock music and religion did not mix—at least, not on the surface. Even though this music had its roots in the Christian gospel music tradition, by the 1970s the split between fundamentalist (ultra-conserva-tive) Christianity and rock 'n' roll—"the devil's music"—appeared to be irreconcilable. Of course, the hostility that Christian fundamentalists showed toward popular music was returned in kind by the rockers. A disdain for religion was expressed sometimes in ironic ways (as in John Lennon's offhanded comment that the Beatles were more popular than Jesus Christ) and sometimes with blatant sarcasm (as in the mock-evil posturing of heavy metal bands like Black Sabbath, who proclaimed, "We sold our soul for rock 'n' roll").

This split between rock music and religion led me, while still a teenager, to begin questioning the relationship between culture and spirituality. So the concept that resulted in this book began as an experi-ment—to see if spirituality could be explained in a way that would make sense both to open-minded Christians and thoughtful fans of popular music. I hoped to show that spirituality does not require a rejection of popular culture, because spirituality is something that indeed lives and breathes *through* culture. Religious culture, popular culture, indeed any form of culture, can be an icon—a window onto the resplendent beauty of the Divine. One can "find God" not only in church, but in art and music and other aspects of human creativity as well. Of course, we also can find God in "nature"—the world beyond human culture—as evidenced by a commonly held idea that "it's easier to find God in a forest than in church."

A difficult task

As we explore spirituality, we face a difficult task—to honor the real differences in beliefs, values, and practices among the various religions and other forms of spirituality even while we search for their real similarities. I have attempted to avoid two traps in the course of this book:

the trap of advocating only one spiritual tradition at the expense of all others and the trap of smoothing over differences among traditions, pretending that "all religions are really just the same."

Spirituality takes many forms. It includes Catholic contemplation along with the Jewish mystical tradition and the tradition of Sufism within Islam. Likewise, spirituality includes the devotional practices of Hinduism, the meditative disciplines of Buddhism, and the "watercourse way" of Taoism. Various religious ceremonies, from the prayer and praise meetings of Pentecostal Christians to the steam-filled sweatlodges of Native Americans such as the Lakota, all nurture and cultivate the spiritual life among their participants.

Meanwhile, many persons (regardless of religious affiliation) find spiritual sustenance in nature, or in art, music, or other forms of culture. For some, spirituality comes through political activism, socially responsible business, or community living. I want to acknowledge all of these various (and sometimes incompatible) forms of spirituality. As our world increasingly becomes a smaller and smaller place, we cannot escape the diversity of religious traditions and spiritual practices. To understand spirituality, we cannot ignore these differences.

I believe that a healthy spiritual seeker matures by learning from many different traditions. This has certainly been true for me, as my path has been enriched by my exploration of the great religions of the world, along with some of the alternative religions that have appeared in recent years. However, I also believe a seeker needs to make a commitment to a specific path and to some form of spiritual community—a community of persons traveling the same path. For me, such a commitment has meant an opportunity to mature spiritually—much like marriage has meant an opportunity for me to mature emotionally. Thus, while I have learned (and continue to learn) from Buddhism, Judaism, Neopaganism, and other paths, my "home" path is Christianity. In my experience, my faithfulness to Christ and my openness to the wisdom of other traditions are two aspects of my spiritual journey that have enhanced and enriched each other.

To live a spiritual life without some sort of commitment to a specific path or community, merely dabbling in a variety of religions or traditions, is to risk being a spiritual dilettante—exploring many forms of spirituality but always avoiding the hard lessons that come with commitment, such as dealing with conflict, disillusionment, and doubt. On the other hand, to refuse to learn from unfamiliar paths or traditions is to risk becoming a fundamentalist—an ultra-conservative, self-righteous person suspicious of anyone who is "different." Such a person runs the risk of spiritual stagnation, by being less open to growth and learning that often come from people and cultures different from our own.

One Source, many paths

Exploring different forms of spirituality, for me, has meant learning to perceive the common wisdom that exists among many diverse traditions. I believe our unity originates in an infinite and loving Divine Source and that the deep wisdom of the world's religious and spiritual traditions testifies to this. That unity exists whether our "home spirituality" honors the Divine as "God" or "the Goddess" or "Allah" or "the Great Mystery" or "Mind" or "the Higher Self" or some other name or names for That-Which-Is-Beyond-All-Names.

After giving this matter a great amount of thought, I've come to believe the most truthful and helpful way for me to approach spirituality is this: to write honestly from my own perspective, using the language and imagery of my own experience. For example, I refer to the One Source as "God," and I refer to the process of opening oneself to the Sacred as "prayer." I understand the Divine as both transcendent (greater than the universe) and immanent (intimately present in people's lives), so I talk about God in ways that may seem abstract and mysterious one moment, then personal and loving the next. While I also use titles such as "the Divine" or "the Sacred" or "the Source," I like "God" because it reminds me of the personal aspect—that I can actually encounter, and have a relationship with, this Divine source.

I considered using many different names for the Divine in this book, but I ultimately decided that wasn't a good idea. If I blithely interchange words like "God" and "Goddess" and "Allah" and "Great Spirit," the book will not only be very confusing, but it will also misrepresent my conviction that commitment to a specific faith tradition is important. I want to plumb the depths of my personal path in a way that can speak to the depths of all mature and life-affirming forms of spirituality, without implying that they are all "just the same."

My purpose is not to convert anyone to "my way." I trust that the individual who carefully and lovingly seeks the Sacred will be led to the path that is right for her, so I am not going to argue for the "rightness" of my path—or any specific path. I do intend, however, to make a positive statement about spirituality in general. I believe in the values and attitudes and practices I call "spiritual," and I believe that persons who engage in spiritual practices live a richer and more meaningful life. To that extent, I hope this book not only explains spirituality, but also makes it attractive enough for you to explore further—by yourself and within your chosen faith community.

Overview of the book

I believe spirituality is as simple as breathing, and therefore I've tried to write an uncomplicated book. I've endeavored to keep it free of jargon, technical terms, foreign words, and esoteric footnotes. I believe strongly in the relationship of spirituality with the earth, the body, and nature, although I also believe spirituality entails the search for transcendence of our physical limitations. Therefore, I try to give down-to-earth examples and illustrations of my ideas whenever possible. Sometimes, however (as in chapter 1, when I'm exploring different ways to think about God), the discussion becomes unavoidably abstract.

My method of studying spirituality relies heavily on etymology. I think we can learn a tremendous amount about the wisdom and knowledge of our traditions simply by tracing words back to their earliest meanings. So, as part of this book's exploration, I'll define words like "culture" or "wonder" or "contemplation" in an attempt to find, in the history of the words themselves, clues about the nature of spirituality.

The pages that follow are written not so much in a linear, logical way as in a spiraling, free-association way. Each chapter explores a variety of concepts, not only literally but poetically as well, following my conviction that spirituality cannot be defined so much as it is evoked. Topics and themes appear and reappear throughout the course of the book.

Of course, reading this book in the normal way makes perfect sense: starting at page 1 and then simply going on. But I think skipping around is just as valid, dipping in here and there at whatever points seem interesting. Spirituality is not very linear, so neither is my exploration of it! To create an artificial structure, strapping spirituality down in a safe "beginning, middle, end" format doesn't seem to make much sense—since many concepts and characteristics of the spiritual life appear and reappear as this text meanders along. It's not too different from the way spirituality actually plays in our lives.

Happy exploring. I wish you all the blessings of the Sacred.

1

Breathing

A few years after Elvis Presley died, a comedy-music duo named Mojo Nixon & Skid Roper recorded a song called "Elvis Is Everywhere," which became something of a college campus hit. The song lampooned the so-called "sightings" of Elvis—not unlike the alleged sightings of UFOs or aliens that some people find so fascinating. Only in the case of Elvis, folks from all over the place kept insisting (usually in the tabloid press) that they saw him, still alive and well, involved in such incognito activities as eating in fast-food restaurants. But more than just lampooning the "Elvis lives" mentality, the Nixon & Roper song celebrated in an ironic way how much of a fixture Elvis Presley had become in American popular culture of the late twentieth century. For whether we're talking about roadside artists selling their black velvet paintings, musicians like Paul Simon writing songs in honor of Graceland, or the U.S. Postal Service's celebrated Elvis stamp, it was evident that, dead or alive, Elvis indeed *was* everywhere!

Spirituality is a lot like Elvis Presley—for spirituality, too, is everywhere. From churches and synagogues to crystal shops and New Age bookstores, and from Promise Keeper rallies to Buddhist meditation classes, American culture is permeated by organizations, institutions, and businesses devoted to fostering the spiritual quest—a quest for meaning or belief or experience that transcends the daily grind, that transcends the world of such mundane affairs as science and technology, or government and business. The transcendent, nonrational, soulful realm of spirituality seems to be increasingly popular in our day. Never mind that some of the leading philosophers of the last two hundred years have predicted the

7

demise of faith. Never mind that Friedrich Nietzsche declared God to be dead, Karl Marx called religion an opiate, and Sigmund Freud deemed it neurotic. As the twentieth century winds to a close, opinion polls repeatedly reveal that most people still believe in some sort of deity, some sort of angelic or noncorporeal beings, and some sort of persistence of life after death. Spirituality is everywhere.

Elvis's death did not deter his credulous fans for a moment. Likewise, the alleged "death of God" has not slowed down the spiritual impulse of humanity. Although Elvis's "believers" seem limited to readers of the tabloid press, the followers of God can be found in all walks of life and at all levels of intellectual and emotional development. By the 1960s, Nietzsche's ominous portent made the mainstream—*Time* asked if God was dead. Yet as the twentieth century comes to a close, God appears to be having quite a resurrection. This is not the first time.

A few sentences back, I said many people have "some sort" of spiritual belief. The words "some sort" are of crucial importance. Spirituality may be omnipresent, but it's hardly uniform—and in the world of the 1990s, dominated by multiculturalism, ethnic diversity, and pluralistic values, the multifaceted characteristics of spirituality are more visible all the time. Some people kneel in mosques. Others dance and raise their arms in "Holy Roller" churches or sing old-fashioned Victorian hymns in mainline churches. Still others chant in synagogues, meditate in ashrams, or bow silently in zendos. Practitioners of Native American forms of spirituality pray in such places as dark sweatlodges, where water poured over red-hot rocks creates steam and heat, purifying the body while inspiring the soul. Other Americans seek spiritual sustenance by rediscovering the tradition of their ancestral homeland—ranging from the joyful optimism of Celtic Christianity to the shamanic and tribal spiritualities of Yoruba and other African religions. Then there are the Neopagan folk— from reconstructionist Druids and Wiccans (witches) to ecofeminist Goddess worshipers—who dance around bonfires to the primal throb of drumbeats or engage in elaborate rituals of ceremonial magic. Meanwhile, channelers and astrologers and other types of occultists can be found everywhere, from metaphysical bookstores and psychic fairs to roadside establishments ("Madam Rosaria reads palms and tells the future—only $5"). In addition to being everywhere, spirituality presents many different faces to the world.

Defining "spirit"

So, then, what is spirituality?

Etymology—the history of a word's origin—is an enlightening place to begin our exploration. "Spirituality," of course, comes from "spirit," or, in Latin, *spiritus*, related to the Latin word for breath, *spirare*—from which we get "respiration." Just as air moves in and out of our lungs when we respire, so is spirit associated with the movement of air—with the wind. Not only are "breath" and "spirit" related in Latin, but other languages, such as Greek (*pneuma*) and Hebrew (*ruach*), have similar words that suggest a link between spirit and breath.

The scriptures of the Jewish and Christian traditions abound in imagery of breath and wind as metaphors for spirit. The creation story in Genesis describes the Spirit of God as moving over the chaos before creation "like a mighty wind" (Gen. 1:2). In the Gospel of John, we read that "Jesus breathed on them and said to them, 'Receive the Holy Spirit'" (John 20:22). We can see another connection between spirit and breath in Biblical descriptions of death. Consider these different translations of the same verse, Mark 15:37 (which in the original Greek uses the word *pneuma*). Where the New Revised Standard Version reads, "Then Jesus gave a loud cry and *breathed his last*," the Living Bible states, "Then Jesus uttered another loud cry, and *dismissed his spirit*" (all italics are mine). A dying person breathes his last *and* dismisses his spirit.

When considered along with other ways in which the word "spirit" is commonly used, the breath and wind imagery certainly makes sense. As a synonym for "ghost," "spirit" refers to a being without a body—a creature with no more substance than a breath. When we say someone is spirited, we are commenting on her level of energy or self-confidence—as if she were someone who breathes powerfully and deeply, filled with aerobic energy. Just as "courage" literally means "hearty," suggesting a person with a strong heart, so does "spirit," in a parallel sense, suggest a person with deep, confident respiration! A courageous, spirited person is one who is fully alive, so much so that she can feel her aliveness in her heart and in her lungs.

Of course, breath—and breathing—are prominent aspects of various forms of spirituality and spiritual practice. Many forms of meditation, from Zen to TM, emphasize conscious, relaxed breathing as the portal into the meditative state. The Chinese practice of Qi Gong and the Indian practice of Pranayama are two disciplines that seek to cultivate spiritual and physical well-being through controlled, proper breathing. Nor is the spirituality-breathing connection only an Eastern characteristic, for in the Greek Orthodox tradition of Christianity, the hesychasts—a monastic movement that flourished in the fourteenth century—practiced a form of praying that involved specific breathing techniques. What all these traditions share is a common recognition of the role that breathing plays in nurturing spiritual health and vitality.

I do not mean to suggest that "spirit," and thus "spirituality," can or ought to be reduced through etymology to no more than a synonym for the breath. I do think the value in learning the etymology of a word is that, as in this case, it often sheds poetic or metaphorical light on the word's meaning. Indeed, "breathing" and "wind" are useful, appropriate metaphors for "spirit," but spirit is something far deeper. Spirit refers to the source of life within us—that which animates the body so it can breathe in the first place. As our living breath is a symbol for spirit, so also is spirit itself the quality in a human body that separates the living from the dead. My spirit is the part of me that gives me my life and sustains that life.

What is the difference between spirit and soul? Do the two words have the same meaning? After consulting several dictionaries, including two etymological dictionaries, I am at a loss to find a difference between "soul" and "spirit" (with a lowercase "s"). The *Oxford English Dictionary*'s primary definitions of "soul" and "spirit" are virtually identical— "soul" is defined as the "principle of life" in humans and animals, and "spirit" as "the animating or vital principle" (*COED*, 2927, 2967). Since "vital" means "manifesting life" (think of "vital statistics"), the two words clearly refer to the same thing. So, for our purposes, "soul" and "spirit" (with the lowercase "s") are synonymous. Of course, I am suggesting that there *is* a difference between "spirit" and "Spirit"—a difference we'll attend to shortly.

Body and soul

When a person dies, he or she stops breathing. Likewise, death is the point at which the spirit ceases to give and sustain the body's life. Since our body continues to exist materially after our death but our soul is no longer present in the body, one common way of understanding spirit is that it is somehow fundamentally distinct from the body. "Dualism" is a philosophical term for seeing any category as involving two parts. Here, a dualistic view regards human nature in terms of a distinct body and spirit. Even the English language incorporates this dualism, for we say "I have a body" rather than "I am a body"—suggesting that the body is my possession rather than simply "me." I may think of "me" in terms of my mind, my consciousness, or my soul, but I have to overcome the bias of the English language to recognize "me" as including my body as well.

Indeed, attempts to explain the relationships among body, mind, and soul have been perennial topics for creative thinkers, from ancient philosophers and mystics down to modern-day channelers. However, while many people are dualists, others reject the idea that a spirit exists separate from the body. Some people believe that a fundamental unity exists between body and soul—that the body is a manifestation of the soul, which implies that "spirit" has both a material and a nonmaterial element. Others think of matter and spirit as "polarities" rather than as fundamentally distinct or fundamentally unified.

The dualistic idea that the body and spirit are distinct and separate has had many consequences, some of which are clearly toxic. An obvious problem has been the tendency to see "spirit" as sacred and holy, and "body" as profane and sinful. This extreme form of dualism has led to such ideas as the notion that sexuality is shameful or evil, which among other things has contributed to the oppression of women (who were thought to be more sexual than men) and gay and lesbian persons.

Another consequence of seeing the body as bad is a tendency to justify physical suffering—as the basis of a belief that persons who suffer physically (such as the poor or the victims of war) will be comforted in a spiritual way after death. This offers little relief for those who do suffer or are bereaved, yet it seems to persist as a glib way of explaining—or explaining away—the unfairness of life. No wonder Marx dismissed religion as an opiate—a drug—for such dualistic thinking not only belittles the reality of physical pain, but it also has an ominous political implication. It can be a justification for allowing appalling conditions, such as poverty or unjust war, to persist. To exalt the soul and denigrate the body is not unlike exalting the rich and oppressing the poor. Such ways of thinking have an essential quality of unfairness about them.

Although the notion of a split between body and soul is prevalent in Western thinking, not all religious or spiritual traditions hold that the body and the spirit are distinct and separable. Some people hold that spirit is as much a part of the body (and vice versa) as the act of breathing is a part of the lungs. An analogy could be taken from quantum physics, which asserts that light is both a particle and a wave, even though such a statement is a contradiction of "normal" physics. As we cannot separate the particle from the wave in the physics of light, so we cannot separate *the act of breathing* from *the lung* that is animated by that act—and likewise, according to this view, we cannot separate the soul from the body it animates.

A person's spirit animates his body, not unlike the way breath powers the lungs. It's an imperfect analogy, for breathing is an act and spirit is an aspect of life—but it's close enough to suit our purposes. The exact relationship between the body and the soul is a matter open to debate. We can nevertheless affirm that spirit and body are at least deeply linked, so much so that to take care of one mandates taking care of the other. I need my lungs in order to breathe, but without the breath, my lungs will die. Each depends on the other. Dualistic ways of thinking about body and spirit are not useful, since such views imply the inferiority of the body. No matter how much importance we place on the spiritual life, we must be careful not to deny or ignore the demands of the material world— including such needs as those for nurturing a healthy, fit body and balancing the inner aspects of spirituality (such as prayer and meditation) with outer activities (such as volunteering in a homeless shelter or speaking out in opposition to discrimination against gay people). Not only do such actions take care of our individual bodies, but they take care of the "body" of society, as well.

Defining "spirituality"

If "spirit" refers to the life-principle that animates and is in some mysterious way related to the human body, what, then, is "spirituality"? To answer that question, we also need to consider the definition of the adjective "spiritual."

"Spiritual" is constructed by taking the noun "spirit" (or its Latin form, *spiritus*) and adding the suffix *-al*. The adjective "spiritual" means something *related to spirit,* or something *of the spirit.* For example, a spiritual leader is a person whose leadership involves the spirit—whose leadership involves the heart or source of life.

Then, to this adjective, another suffix (*-ity*) is added, making a new and different noun. This suffix means that something has the "quality of being like" its root word (Barnhart 1995, 17, 401). For example, we see that "practicality" is the quality of being practical. "Spirituality" involves *the quality of being spiritual*—in other words, *the quality of being like spirit* or, put another way, *the quality of being related to spirit.*

This definition of spirituality makes even more sense when we capitalize Spirit—for doing so brings God into the equation. Earlier I suggested that a difference exists between "spirit" and "Spirit." The difference is between a finite human (or other creature) and the infinite Source of all life, which in my tradition is called God. In light of this, we may say that spirituality involves being like, or being related to, God.

I believe that the Source of all life—God—is also the Source of love. Although I'm stating that as my opinion, it certainly comes with the endorsement of more than a few of the world's great religions! As the Bible bluntly puts it, "God is love" (I John 4:8). So I'd like to round out my definition of spirituality by emphasizing the concept of relationship and putting that in the context of love. In short, *spirituality is the process of falling in love with, and seeking to become more like, God.*

God, the "Divine Spirit"

If spirituality involves being in some form of a relationship with God, then forming a way of understanding God will be central to the spiritual life. Just as I cannot form a relationship with another person without having some sense of who that person is, so I require a similar sensibility regarding the Sacred.

But if the Divine is the ultimate *Spirit*, then God does not have a body, at least not one that manifests in our world of space and time. With no body, God has no specific location and no certain way to be found. God is "located" both nowhere and everywhere. Practically speaking, God is found only within our mind—within our ability to "see" the Divine using the mind's eye. Finding God depends on our imagination, our ability to envision possible ways of existence beyond the limitations of the physical universe.

But if we can only find God in our mind, how then can we truly know God? Do we encounter God—or just a figment of our imagination? Here is a question that is even more salient: can the human community come to consensus about God?

Some persons argue that knowing God is not possible. In the fourteenth century, an anonymous English soul wrote a treatise called *The Cloud of Unknowing*, asserting that while God may be loved, God can never be apprehended by human reason or understanding. The situation is very simple. A human mind can no better comprehend the creator of the universe than an amoeba can comprehend the fullness of human experience. Can a mind ever fully comprehend its creator? Many mystics and saints of the Western mystical tradition have stressed a "negative theology"—God is only knowable by what we know is *not* God. Thereby, we know God is not finite, we know God is not limited to a body or a location in space and time, we know God is not limited by the confines of the universe, and so forth. Images of God that enable us to relate to the Divine may be useful for the purposes of spirituality, but they are ultimately inadequate for truly understanding the fullness of the Deity.

This view of God stresses God's *transcendence*. "To transcend" literally means "to climb beyond," a concept that refers to God as existing beyond the physical universe of matter and energy, of space and time; and therefore beyond the limits of human reason, understanding, and ability to know or experience. God ultimately is wholly "other" to humankind—a "Great Mystery," not unlike the way the Sacred is conceived in Native American culture. While the concepts of God's unknowability and transcendence are useful in emphasizing the majesty and splendor of God, such concepts are, by themselves, limited ways of thinking about the Divine. To stress God's otherness is to suggest that no relationship with God may be possible. Then, like deists or atheists, we can relegate the notion of God to a philosophical problem, without any real bearing on the lives of women and men, either individually or communally. A God who is wholly transcendent is a God who makes no difference.

How can we conceive of God in ways other than—or in addition to—those of such an unknowable transcendence? A number of possibilities exist. First, one way to envision God is as a "first principle." Here, God is the Source: the source of life, the source of love, the source of justice and goodness and consciousness and creativity. As the first principle, God functions like a compass, providing direction and orientation to human existence and experience.

If we think of Spirit in terms of the Source, then spirituality, regardless of its religious or cultural context, involves nurturing a relationship with that Source. According to this idea, spirituality involves the process of relating deeply and powerfully to "Life with a capital L."

Another, more personal way to envision God may be as the Spirit that resides in and radiates through the "body" of the entire universe, in a way similar to how the human spirit animates and resides in the human body. Earlier I suggested that God, as the ultimate Spirit, does not have an ultimate body—but I think it's reasonable to regard the entire universe as "God's body." Just as a relationship exists between the body and soul, so a relatedness exists between Creator and creation. My spirit relates to God's Spirit in the same way that my body relates to the universe. Just as my body exists within the universe, so my spirit exists within the Divine

Spirit. My body and spirit remain interrelated, just as the Divine Spirit and the universe are interrelated.

This takes us from transcendence to *immanence*—"immanence" meaning "remaining in or near" and signifying the idea that God is as fully present in the universe (and in people's lives) as God is beyond them. God is present in the universe, and God is greater than the universe. Each of these statements requires the other—for without both assertions, we would have only a limited concept of the Sacred.

Probably the most common way to conceive God, at least in Judeo-Christian culture, is to rely on tradition and on anthropomorphic (human-like) images. Tradition usually means any historical or ancestral way of relating to or talking about God, chiefly the revelations of the great religions. The testimony of generations of people in many different religious and cultural contexts is that God is indeed present in creation and that the Sacred does make a real difference in people's lives. Much of the sacred wisdom of the world also depicts God as personally loving, attentive to creation, interested in the lives of women and men, demanding loving and just behavior, and so forth. Closely connected to this, both in the ancient traditions and in many common present ways of thinking, is the attribution of human characteristics to the Divine: God may be seen as a loving father or a nurturing mother—or, for that matter, as a stern judge or a remote king.

If we do in fact glimpse God in the "first principles" and in the patterns of energy in the universe, then these humanlike images of a personal God serve as ways to make sense of those highly abstract glimpses. But given the claim that the Divine is ultimately unknowable, is it wrong to believe that God may be known in a personal way or through anthropomorphic images? Of course not—as long as we remember that our images of God are only that: images, partial and incomplete, incapable of capturing the fullness of the transcendent splendor of the Sacred. We need to remember that the human community does not have a consensus about God, and we need to accept the fact that our knowledge of God is finite and limited, and colored by our human experience. For example, the children of loving parents may envision God as loving, while the children of abusive parents may think of God as wrathful. However, if God is present in the universe the way a spirit is present in a living body, then God is knowable, however imperfectly—and since our knowledge of the Sacred is imperfect, we are wise to remain open to letting our image of God grow, as we grow and mature in our own spiritual lives.

The Quaker tradition has a wonderful way of talking about God. To Quakers, God inspires an "inner light" within every human being, and part of the task of spirituality is to learn to recognize and nurture "that which is of God" in every person. To assert that the Sacred resides in every human being is a powerful statement—and it provides the foundation for the Quaker commitment to nonviolence (for how can killing be justified when every person, even an enemy, contains God's inner light?).

The Quaker tradition of the inner light is lovely, but not all ways of thinking about the Divine are so optimistic. Some religious traditions emphasize God as a demanding parent or stern judge—an image of God that seems more furious than friendly and suggests that God is perfectly willing to destroy that which does not fit in. Perhaps one reason why many individuals abandon religion—and spirituality—is that the idea of relating to such a toxic God is unbearable.

Recalling that such images are just that—images—we need to consider that different images of God have different value. Some images of God are simply toxic or abusive or absurd. I, for one, have never understood how people reconcile a concept of God as "all-loving" with a concept of God as also "condemning sinners to hell." I grew up in the South, where the wrathful God looms large in the cultural religious consciousness; as an adult, I struggled for years to relate to God in ways other than fearfully trying to please this implacable authority figure. Learning to trust God's love has been a profound spiritual experience for me and has taught me this important lesson: spiritual growth involves allowing my understanding of the Divine to change.

In a successful marriage, a husband and wife learn to allow their relationship to grow and change over the years. Spirituality likewise works better when we allow our images of the Sacred to change and to grow. Keeping a sense of God's transcendence is helpful in this respect. When a specific humanlike image of God does not work, or no longer works, for you, one way to move beyond that image is to be mindful of God as "moving beyond" the universe and therefore limited by no images.

I began this section with the question, "How, then, can God be known?" For me, the best answer includes holding both transcendent and immanent ways of envisioning the Sacred in creative tension. The immanent God, the God we often understand in human terms, is the primary "lover" to whom the spiritual life is oriented. However, God's transcendence—the mystery beyond the limits of human reason—reminds us that our images of the Divine are *only* images, incomplete and prone to error, but necessary and meaningful nonetheless.

Alternative images of the Sacred

Now, what about persons who simply do not believe in God? Are such persons of necessity unspiritual? Or what about persons who reject a masculine God, but worship the Great Mother Goddess—or the Neopagans who, although very much in the minority in America, worship "the gods," rejecting monotheism in favor of polytheism? If we define spirituality as involving a relationship with God, what do we make of such traditions as Buddhism or Wicca, traditions that are manifestly "spiritual," but have a radically different understanding of the Sacred than the view I've presented?

I don't think a general definition of spirituality would be complete without acknowledging the fact that diverse traditions exist, including traditions that either do not emphasize God at all or else teach ways of understanding the Divine that are at odds with the monotheistic idea of one God (usually seen as masculine). Meanwhile, persons who participate in some nonreligious organizations or communities, such as twelve-step groups or the Rainbow Family, may consider themselves spiritual, but without emphasizing the Sacred at all.

Can we envision a way of understanding the Divine that is big enough to include many different paths, without glossing over the differences in beliefs? I think so. For spiritual seekers whose paths do not emphasize believing in one God, let me suggest the idea that "God" stands for a first principle, such as supreme Consciousness, or Creativity, or Love.

As for envisioning the Divine as a maternal Goddess, let me suggest that "God" means a transcendent Source greater than our biological division of male and female. The Divine is greater than gender and includes all aspects of gender in Divine existence. For us, attributing masculinity or femininity to God is simply a way to make God more accessible to our finite minds. The male God and the female Goddess are equally useful—and equally incomplete—images of the Sacred. The One who loves us, the One Who Is Beyond All Names, is beyond all gender limitations as well.

On the Internet, a number of persons have adopted the word "Godde" for the Sacred, reflecting a Middle English spelling of God. "Godde" falls in between "God" and "Goddess," and so may be a particularly useful way of naming the Sacred in a gender-inclusive way.

I want to talk about the Sacred in a way that feels comfortable and familiar for the majority of readers who believe in God—but I also want to be open and gracious enough to acknowledge those with alternative viewpoints, who nonetheless take seriously a commitment to spirituality in some form. Whether we like it or not, humankind does not have consensus on God. The concept of God, like so many aspects of spirituality, must remain open-ended.

The problem of pluralism

Obviously, efforts to articulate a universal understanding of the Sacred can easily get bogged down in the many different points of view I have just alluded to: Is there one God or many? Is there a personal God or an impersonal essence? Is the Sacred a gendered God or Goddess, or an inclusive Godde? The question of how we can know the Divine has brought us up against a central problem in trying to approach spirituality— the problem of pluralism.

We live in a pluralistic society, a society where members of different religions and adherents of different philosophies and value-systems live together and work and play together—or at least in close proximity to one another. Those of us who are Christians (still the majority religion in the United States, although it's losing its "market dominance") often forget that for our grandparents, meeting a Muslim or a Buddhist would have been a very odd thing indeed, and encountering a Goddess-worshiper would have been absolutely unheard of. But a number of factors, including sociological, technological, political, and cultural changes in the world over the last fifty years, have led to a much more diverse population existing in much closer quarters than ever before. Furthermore, church-going is itself much more of an option today than it was fifty or seventy-five years ago. Our grandparents and great-grandparents often felt a social pressure to participate in religious activities, a pressure no longer present in many people's lives. So, pluralism means not only the existence of different traditions in close proximity, but also the freedom to choose or reject these different paths.

Pluralism is not always easy to accept or live with. Even those of us who pride ourselves on our social and religious tolerance will sometimes wish that everyone saw things the "right" way—with the "right way" naturally being the way we ourselves see things! Obviously, one result of living in a pluralist culture is the social reality of not seeing eye-to-eye with many of our neighbors. No matter how psychologically sophisticated or mature we are, pluralism can be a challenge and can be a source of anxiety in our everyday effort to make sense of life.

One way of responding to the challenge of religious pluralism—of having to deal with Buddhists and Sikhs and Neopagans and Mormons and Pentecostals living on the same street—is to adopt the idea that all religions are really "the same" deep down inside. This idea may be connected with spirituality—a notion that, while the religions may be different ("religions" includes teachings, art and architecture, worship and ritual, and other forms of culture designed to foster spirituality), the spirituality that exists at a "deeper level" than the religions is the same for everyone. So, while our Buddhist and Neopagan and Christian neighbors may have radically different beliefs and ritual practices and ways of expressing their religions, the "spirituality" that lies at the bottom of the different traditions is presumed to be identical.

If we accept the idea of "one Source, many paths," then this idea of underlying unity may be helpful. But it is only helpful if we also acknowledge the many real differences that exist among different religious or cultural traditions. Claiming that all religions are in essence the same is like saying that horses and cows and whales all have the exact same kinds of lungs. They breathe the same oxygen, but obviously their lungs are very different.

This "same-in-essence" claim may sound good on a sentimental or romantic level, but it's just not true. The Buddhist path, which is often world-renouncing and nontheistic, is simply different on core levels from Christianity's path of devotion to God and engagement with the world. In other words, Christians believe in God and believe that the sensual world was created good; Buddhists do not necessarily believe in God and often view the world as an illusory source of suffering. But both traditions seek to end suffering and increase compassion in the world—both traditions serve the purposes of Love. One Source, many paths—and important differences do exist.

The pluralistic notion that "all religions are really the same" stems from a desire to avoid conflict and to affirm religious tolerance—good enough of an incentive, for a pluralistic world must have religious tolerance to prevent the possibility of widespread persecution, discrimination, or even worse evils. History has shown that large, dominant religious groups often attempt to destroy or assimilate smaller groups. Here in America, despite our proud guarantee to protect freedom of religion, many small religious groups find themselves constricted and even persecuted by political authorities. The Church of the Iron Oak, a Neopagan religious body in Florida, fought for years against an unfair zoning ordinance that the local government tried to use to prevent them from worshiping in members' homes. As the Iron Oak personnel pointed out, such an ordinance would never have been used to stop a Christian gathering in people's homes.

We need a better argument for religious tolerance than "all religions are the same," and for two reasons. First, it's just not true. Although all forms of spirituality point to the same Source, the religions of the world differ from one another in terms of values, practices, and doctrines. Second, the reality of religious *differences* underscores the reality of religious *intolerance* in our world. Each religion has members who think their religion is the best and that other religions are inferior if not downright evil. These people are not affected by any appeals to tolerance on the basis of a wished-for sameness. We need religious tolerance for its own sake, not because it arises out of a fuzzy way of seeing things. A healthy understanding of spirituality will both celebrate the commonalities and acknowledge the differences among the diverse traditions in the world.

The context of spirituality

Spirituality does not exist in a vacuum. A breath cannot exist without a lung to perform the breathing; a heart cannot survive without the safe structure of a skeleton. Likewise, a relationship with God cannot exist apart from some sort of context or supporting structure.

Throughout the chapters to come, we will dance between two realms that provide the context of spirituality—the inner realm of experiences such as wonder and vulnerability, and the outer realm of culture, community, and materiality. Just as a relationship between husband and wife requires both the inner experience of being in love and the outer experience of physical intimacy and togetherness, so the encounter with the Sacred requires both inner experiences of spiritual feelings and awareness and an outer grounding in culture and community.

Culture especially plays a central part of the spiritual life, for culture helps us to make sense of our inner experience. The language, ideas, and values that enable us to interpret and find meaning in our inner experiences are all aspects of culture. To understand spirituality, we need to honor the importance of culture in providing an outer context for the encounter with the Sacred. In the next chapter, we'll take a closer look at culture, seeing it as the soil out of which spirituality grows like a beautiful and majestic tree.

2

Tillage

S t. Teresa of Avila, a sixteenth-century Spanish Carmelite nun, wrote several books on the life of prayer. Probably the best known of her works is *The Interior Castle*. She wrote it following a vision she had of her soul progressing through a series of "mansions" in a sparkling castle, with each mansion taking her closer and closer to the center, where God resides. Teresa has been important enough in the Roman Catholic tradition that, today, she is one of only two women who have been awarded the title "Doctor of the Church," honoring her as an exemplary teacher of spiritual wisdom. Her teachings presenting spirituality as an interior process have been accepted as authoritative. Indeed, Teresa's idea of the interior castle places her squarely in a tradition that regards spirituality as an inner experience. We see this again and again. Evelyn Underhill, a twentieth-century authority on mysticism, gave one of her books the title *Concerning the Inner Life*. Indeed, spirituality often seems to be wholly an inner, subjective experience.

The inner dimension of spirituality is essential; however, before we can meaningfully look at spirituality from the inside, we need to find its secure ground. An airplane is not built in the air—it's designed and assembled on the ground, and only after it has been constructed can it take off into the vast atmosphere. Spirituality requires a similar groundedness before it can soar. Just as air needs lungs in order to become breath, so spirituality needs a way to be grounded and centered before it can fly free in the universe within—and beyond—the body and soul. To find that grounding, let's begin with culture—an earthy subject indeed.

Understanding culture: it starts with the soil

Kansas, one of the best-known rock groups of the mid-1970s, was typical of the bands popular in the years before punk rock exploded on the scene. Their music was convoluted and complex, having been influenced by the "acid rock" and "art rock" music of the late 1960s and early 1970s. Their lyrics were often self-consciously philosophical and spiritual in nature. One of their most popular songs, "Dust in the Wind," paired a haunting acoustic guitar melody with a mournful, almost cynical lyric that considered human mortality and concluded by asserting that people are nothing more than dust in the wind.

Several of the more traditional Christian churches commemorate that same sense of mortality every year during winter—a time when the earth is "dead." Ash Wednesday, the first day of Lent, is a time for religiously marking that same sense of mortality. At the Ash Wednesday service, according to Episcopal usage (other churches have similar wording), the words "Remember that you are dust, and to dust you shall return" are spoken as ashes are imposed upon the recipient's forehead. We come from dust—from the earth, the soil, the ground—and, like it or not, we (or at least our bodies) will someday return to the earth.

To understand culture and the web of relationships linking it to the environment, religion, and spirituality, there's no better place to begin than with the soil. Spirituality has a humble, earthy foundation, which we can see as we begin to understand the roots of culture. (Humility, by the way, means "of the earth"—of the soil.)

A precedent for this link between soil and spirit comes from the creation myth in Genesis, which recounts that God created human beings "from the dust of the ground," giving life to the first human by "breathing into his nostrils the breath of life" (Gen. 2:7). The spirit, or soul, is linked with the breath, and the body is linked with the soil, which comes from the earth. Thus, the spirit has its material identity in the body. In a similar way, spirituality has its material foundation in nature, culture, and religion. Just as the body is formed from the earth, so indeed the entire sweep of culture begins with the soil.

The soil and the roots of culture

Culture's origins are in the soil, arising from the earliest efforts of humans to shift their means of sustenance from hunting and gathering to gardening and, subsequently, farming. The words "horticulture" (for gardening) and "agriculture" (for farming) represent the origins of culture.

Both of these primal forms of culture stem from the development of tools for tilling the soil. Gardening arose from the invention of the hoe, agriculture from the invention of the plow. Culture, or cultivating, thus begins at the dawn of history with tools for digging into the earth, uncovering the soil that will give life by nurturing plants grown for human consumption.

Gardening gave way to farming with the invention of the plow. But gardening did not die out—instead, gardens increasingly took on a recreational or ornamental role. The farms produced the main supply of food, and gardens became the source of herbs to make the food tastier and of flowers to add beauty and color to life. This development represents the division of culture into two broad categories. The primary purpose of culture is to ensure human *survival*—to make sure there's enough food on the table. The secondary purpose of culture is to enhance the *quality* of human life—to add spice and color and beauty to the experience of living. Another way of seeing the basic division of culture is in terms of science and art. Science, or human knowledge, serves the quest for survival and mastery of the environment. Art, or human creativity, serves the quest to articulate beauty, enjoyment, and meaning in life.

Even today, all aspects of culture—philosophy and religion, art and music, science and technology, agriculture and government, architecture and medicine—fulfill one of these two basic human needs: the need to survive or the need to enjoy. Every form and object of culture serves either human survival or the quest for a better life. "Better life" is a broad topic, which includes the quest for meaning, for beauty, for entertainment, and for justice. It also includes the search for enlightenment or salvation—in other words, the quest for encountering the Sacred or for relationship with God. We cultivate our world—not just the soil anymore, but any and every part of the environment—to serve human efforts to secure survival and health as well as meaning, beauty, and enjoyment.

If the "roots" of culture are the quest for survival and enjoyment, then what is the "soil" in which these roots grow? Naturally, the basic forms of culture—gardening and farming—involve planting into the real soil. Primal culture was an earthy, physical affair. But culture has come to embody a much broader range of human endeavor. Fine art, dance, music, literature, and theater are all forms of culture but have little to do with the soil. Mathematics, philosophy, theology, and political and literary theory are all examples of culture that are purely abstract and not in the least bit materialistic. If culture originally meant managing the soil, how has the word come to refer to such abstract things as well?

The answer to this question may involve the concept of tilling. The original forms of culture—horticulture and agriculture—involved tilling the soil. Using the hoe or the plow, gardeners and farmers literally broke the surface of the earth, digging in to find the riches underneath that allowed plants to grow. Put another way, culture involved *interacting with the environment* to provide either survival or enjoyment. From the time the first hoe broke the skin of the earth to yesterday's latest triumph of high technology, culture has always involved tilling—or interacting with—some aspect of the human environment to produce results that will improve survival or enjoyment. When a scholar does research in the library, she is "tilling" the wisdom of humankind to cultivate her new theory. When a sculptor chips away at a block of marble, he is "tilling" the stone to create a statue. When a contractor builds a house, he uses wood and stone "tilled" from the earth to shape the new structure.

It's easy to see how physical forms of culture, such as sculpture or masonry, involve "tilling" the environment. By using raw materials from nature, humankind has been able to create cultural objects ranging from statues to buildings, from the wheel to the microchip. Resources from the environment provide the foundation for making clothing, weapons, tools and utensils, and sacred or religious objects. The wheel made possible the first machinery, then machinery anticipated the advent of electronics, and now electronics is paving the way to artificial intelligence. From the crudest implement to cyber-intelligence, all culture is the product of human hands, using the material of the natural environment. The joining of human imagination and resources from nature resulted in the creation of all the sciences and the arts. As always, culture's purpose remains to promote human security or human fulfillment.

Probably from the beginning, the most mysterious "ground" to be tilled was—and is—the human mind itself. Within the depths of mind, we began to cultivate the imagination, the ability to develop abstract concepts, and the capacity to reason and to make value-based judgments. Here is the foundation of abstract culture, culture that is not *materialistic* in the sense of being an "object out there" but is nevertheless *real* in the sense of having a genuine existence, even if only as concepts within the mind. This cultivation of the human mind has led up to the highest pinnacles of thought—philosophy (the love of wisdom) and theology (the language of God). Human interaction with the environment has journeyed from cultivating the food that nurtures our bodies to cultivating a relationship with wisdom and the Sacred that nurtures our souls. Culture takes the human race in a grand sweep from the soil to the heart of God.

In the words of Georg Langemeyer, "Culture is the specifically human way through which persons perceive and shape their reality, that is, their own selves, their fellow human beings, and the world they share" (Langemeyer 1995). Any element of culture, whether it is as solid and huge as the pyramids of Egypt or as fleeting and ethereal as the random thoughts of a brilliant philosopher, involves some sort of shaping or changing of reality, whether it's a material change in the environment or a change in the ideas of a creative person. Culture results from human efforts to adapt our natural habitat to our purposes—including the "inner habitat" of the mind. The smallest of such changes can have world-transforming repercussions. Siddhartha sat under the Bodhi tree, and Buddhism was born. Jesus broke bread and shared wine with his closest friends, and Christianity was born. When one person changes, all may be subtly affected. The philosopher's random thought might set off a process of reflection that will result in a new theory that changes the course of history.

Creativity and cherishing

How do these concepts of tilling and culture relate to spirituality?

To answer this question, let's consider the etymology of *culture*. The word comes from the Latin *colere*, a splendid word that means "to till" as well as "to attend to" and "to cherish." *Colere* suggests that culture represents not only the products of human creativity (tilling/cultivation), but also the products of human cherishing (love/worship). An obvious illustration for this would be the great cathedrals of medieval Europe. These towering buildings are awesome works of art, masterpieces of architecture, masonry, engineering, and stonecarving. The cathedrals likewise are monuments of worship, created for the love of God—resplendent buildings created not for financial gain or personal glory, but the fruits of labor lovingly given for the Divine. The cathedrals are pinnacles of culture, both in the sense of "works of art" and in the sense of "works of cherishing." The cathedral artisans cherished the Sacred, and so created the ineffable beauty of the cathedrals, cultivating heavenly beauty out of raw materials from the earth.

The roots of culture include both creativity and cherishing, both work and worship. Cultural creativity, as previously noted, served either human survival or human enjoyment. Cherishing applies to both aspects of culture—I certainly cherish the fruits of agriculture and the conveniences of science, as well as the music and art that fill my life with beauty. But cherishing does not stop there, for I am capable of cherishing the Sacred—the first principle, the source of all life and all love. From the Source come all things—the mystery of nature's existence, the gift of consciousness and reflective thought, the ability to survive through cultivated food, and the pleasure of a life enhanced by the arts. Having received all these gifts, humankind is faced with the invitation to bow in worship. Cherishing and worshiping—this response to the mysteries and the gifts of life—is the foundation of spirituality. Spirituality represents humankind reaching out —with cherishing, worship, and love—toward the mysterious Divine Spirit, the God who gives us the natural environment we live in, the food we eat, and the inspiration to create our culture.

Place and time

Culture is specific to place and time—different locations and different eras produce different cultures. Consider how many people cherish a particular place and time as a source of meaning for their lives. Some people revere Ireland and Scotland, others Jerusalem, and still others China or Tibet. Some live according to the ideas of the Middle Ages, others the Age of Enlightenment, and still others the 1960s. This cultural reverence may be religious in form: Catholics revere Rome while the Lakota revere the Black Hills. Or it may be secular, as in Deadheads who revere Haight-Ashbury and the Summer of Love, or gays and lesbians who revere the Stonewall uprising. What they all have in common, however, is that all of them relate to a specific culture in order to find meaning, purpose, and value in their lives. In each of these examples, culture plays a spiritual role in people's lives—it helps them encounter the Sacred, whether that is understood as "God" or as "justice" or as "beauty" or some other first principle.

Culture and cult

Colere can mean both "to till" and "to cherish." We saw in chapter 1 that spirituality involves loving (cherishing) the Sacred. Cultivating, creating, worshiping, and believing—all have in common an element of cherishing. Thus, I believe that spirituality and culture are deeply and profoundly linked. This is not just a matter of religion, although religion is a form of culture—the part of culture most explicitly "spiritual." Since culture is linked with cherishing, *all* forms of culture—science as well as art, business as well as religion, politics as well as charity—function as possible arenas for encountering the Sacred—potential "lungs" for the breath of the Spirit.

The link between culture and spirituality may become more obvious when we consider another word derived from *colere*—"cult." Although its contemporary usage suggests a dangerous or exotic minority religion, the word originally had a neutral connotation. *Cult* originally referred to any system of worship or homage, good or bad. For example, the "cult of the Virgin Mary" in medieval Europe consisted of persons who actively cherished, and perhaps even worshiped, the mother of Jesus.

To understand "cult" in its original sense, consider the sense of awe and even reverence we sometimes feel when we encounter magnificent beauty in nature—a vast, cloudless, starlit sky or a view of a lush valley from a mountaintop overlook. We call such beautiful vistas "breathtaking" —a clue that *spiritus* is involved. We cherish places like this—we travel hundreds of miles to visit them, and once we're there, we take photographs, we linger over them, and sometimes we're even moved to silence or to tears. Nature is the object of a "cult," in the purest and best sense of the word—for we honor and cherish its glorious beauty. Beautiful places in nature are sources of wonder and happiness and also can evoke a sense of awe that may even be unsettling and anxiety-producing. (As we will see in chapter 3, wonder and awe are dispositions central to the spiritual life.)

The "cult" of nature consists of the ways in which we honor and revere the breathtaking beauty of the wilderness (or of anything not created by humankind)—and the efforts we make to encounter and experience such beauty. This reverence of nature is so meaningful because it is one way in which we cultivate spiritual dispositions like wonder and awe. Just as agriculture and the arts are attempts to cultivate security and beauty, so any "cultic" activity is an attempt to cultivate spirituality—to create concepts, images, and practices that are as helpful as the starlit sky or the mountaintop vista for cultivating wonder, belief, prayer, and other characteristics that nurture and support a relationship with the Sacred.

Culture, religion, and spirituality

Without lungs, breath does not exist. A slight breeze in the air is not the same as a breath, which empowers and animates a living body. If spirituality is the "breath" of our relationship with the Sacred, then what are the "lungs"—the structure that provides shape to the Divine encounter?

I believe that culture—including but not limited to religion—functions as the "lungs" for the "breath" of the spirit. Spirituality depends on the "body" of human culture to exist! This may seem to be an outrageous statement, but when we contemplate the pervasiveness of culture, we can easily see that a cultural component is part of every encounter with the Sacred. Consider these points:

- In order for a person to differentiate between "Sacred" experiences and "mundane" experiences, that person needs to have language skills, along with a basic conceptual understanding of the notion of "Sacred." A baby, for all we know, lives life purely in the presence of God—but since the baby lacks the linguistic and conceptual skills to identify the experience, the baby has no way to consciously understand the Sacred, and certainly no way to communicate the experience.
- Religions universally depend on culture. This includes sacred writings (the Bible, the Qu'ran, the Sutras, and so forth), sacred art (icons, stained glass windows, statues of the Buddha), architecture (churches, mosques, synagogues, ashrams, zendos), music (Gregorian chants, Bach fugues, shamanic drumming), and ceremonies (the Holy Eucharist, the sweatlodge, the Wiccan circle).
- The possibility of uniting with the Sacred is transmitted through culturally based teachings and traditions that may be oral or written, religious or nonreligious in nature.

Language, tradition, art, architecture, music—these are all are forms of culture. Even experiences of the Sacred in nature, a topic to be explored more fully in chapter 8, are still indirectly mediated through culture. Although we may not be accustomed to consciously regarding it as such, our common understanding of "nature" is, in essence, that it is "the absence of culture"! Culture is exemplified by the city, while nature is exemplified by the wilderness. A person who prefers to find God in nature rather than in a church is taking a stand of protest against culture—but without culture to shape her understanding of nature, she would not be able to view nature as a special place for encountering the Sacred. Furthermore, a spiritual experience in nature still requires language and abstract thinking if one is to recognize the experience as being "of the Sacred."

Especially important in terms of spirituality is language. Like a hoe, language is the tool we use to till the soil of our minds. We know that deaf children who do not learn sign language or lip reading are sometimes diagnosed as mentally handicapped, not because they really *are* handicapped, but because their minds are devoid of language.

Language is both a tool for survival and a tool for the increased enjoyment of life. I'm not suggesting that the entire sweep of spirituality can be neatly packaged in a linguistic box. Indeed, practically every saint and holy person who ever lived talks about how God's presence is ineffable (beyond the ability to be fully expressed in words). Nevertheless, the very fact that "ineffable" is a word reveals the extent to which we rely on language to make sense of our experience of spirituality.

Spirituality requires context; it doesn't exist in a vacuum. We are not accustomed to thinking of spirituality as requiring a cultural context, let alone a material context—thanks to the legacy of centuries of thinking that divided "spirit" and "matter" into hostile camps. But just as culture is born of the natural world, so is spirituality born of culture. Spirituality is related to materiality in the same mysterious way that the soul is related to the body, or that God is related to the universe. Spirit and matter may not be identical, and the exact nature of their relationship may always be a mystery—but we cannot separate them, either. Spirituality is embedded in the transcendent grandeur of cathedral architecture, the sublime poetry of sacred writings, and the breathtaking glory of ecstatic music. Spirituality is embedded in the culture of the human mind—the conscious realms of beliefs, values, feelings, and theological or philosophical concepts, and the subconscious realms of dreams, forgotten memories, and unfaced conflicts. Spirituality is embedded in the "culture-in-process" of religious behavior, such as praying, feeding homeless persons, or participating in a sweatlodge. Whether material, mental, or behavioral, all spiritual experiences have some kind of cultural element.

Spirituality requires a cultural context the way the soul requires a body, but that cultural context does not have to be a congenial one. Many aspects of our culture seem hostile to spirituality—a topic we'll examine in greater detail shortly. Men and women have had experiences of God's presence while cleaning a sewer or engaged in combat—hardly situations we normally consider to be conducive to spirituality. Spirituality will emerge even in the most unlikely contexts for one simple reason— spirituality involves an encounter with the presence of the Divine. God's presence is revealed according to God's own will—not according to our human designs. Just because we think a context is "unspiritual" makes no difference to the Divine. I once heard an Episcopal priest mention in a sermon how she had a sudden sense of the Holy while in the midst of cleaning out her cat's litterbox! The Sacred, filled with a Divine whimsy, is always capable of surprising us in just that way.

"Meta-culture"

Because *colere* means both "to till" and "to cherish," I believe that culture's origins involve a deep and primal link with worship. However, over the last few centuries, Western society has increasingly lost sight of that foundational relationship between reverence and culture.

In most cultures, the agricultural cycle was once marked by a series of seasonal festivals, but today farming is only a matter for profit-driven agribusiness. The arts, once almost exclusively concerned with singing praises of and to the Sacred, now often express our society's hostility toward religion and spirituality.

Losing the link between spirituality and culture has mirrored the loss of a sense of connection between spirit and matter. Religion, the aspect of culture devoted to spirituality, is no longer considered by many to be part of the "real world." The attitude of much contemporary culture and society is that religion, and therefore spirituality, is implicitly "unreal"—merely a pie-in-the-sky, ethereal activity totally unrelated to the practical concerns of a world dominated by business, government, the media, and education. In this regard, I call our culture a "meta-culture," for we have moved beyond culture's origins in worship and cherishing. Where culture's primary existence was once linked with cherishing—whether cherishing the soil, cherishing nature, or cherishing the Sacred—the primary purpose of Western culture now appears to be linked with private profit. When spirituality and religion are seen to be separate from the "real world," spiritual values such as love, forgiveness, peacemaking, and justice are at risk of being absent from the "real world" as well.

Another characteristic of the meta-culture is the marginalization of religion and spirituality as purely private affairs. Our culture seems to operate under the assumption that spirituality is "a private matter," which means that no place exists in the public realm for the application of spiritual values. This parades under the guise of "separation of church and state"—but as Stephen Carter points out in his book *The Culture of Disbelief*, the separation of church and state was intended originally to protect religion from governmental tyranny. However, in the last few decades, our society has come to see the separation of church and state as meaning that religion—and by implication spirituality—only belongs in the private sphere of individual personal choice, almost as if spirituality were nothing more than a hobby.

What has caused the shift from a culture with its roots in cherishing the Sacred and tilling the soil, to a meta-culture based on profit, where spirituality is only a personal preference? It's a vast and complex question, too broad to be addressed fairly in this brief book. It involves the triumph of science, the rise of democracy, and the expansion of technology, along with numerous theological and philosophical developments. The times when religion and worship were public certainly could not be called superior to our own, for those were times when heretics and witches suffered capital punishment for their "crimes." However, I don't think we should applaud our own time as being superior, either. A world where spirituality is private is a world where belief in the Sacred is extraordinarily difficult. Even more ominous, a world of privatized spirituality is a world where powerful people and organizations can be free to exercise their power in unjust ways. Spiritual concerns inspired the civil rights movement as well as much of the protest against the Vietnam War; much activism on behalf of the environment comes from a spiritual perspective as well. But if we trade spirituality for profit-oriented living, who will lead the next movement for liberation? Even today, with an American government extraordinarily indifferent toward the poorest members of society and business increasingly more concerned about profits than people, we live in a society desperately in need of creative protest. But such protest can only arise from a spiritually inspired vision that seeks to make the world a better place—in public as well as private ways.

All is not bad news, however. Despite the breakdown of reverence in the public or official aspects of our meta-culture, vestigial remains of the primal link between culture and spirituality persist. "Cultural centers" like art museums, libraries, and cathedrals continue to command from most thoughtful people a sense of reverence (and a similar custom of silence, although that is breaking down). "Spiritual" themes—involving such matters as angels and heaven and miracles—continue to crop up again and again in the arts, especially in popular literature, music, and television. People still willingly adore, cherish, and even worship the "idols" of the entertainment industry (Elvis, for example). Such reverence may be expressed in absurd ways, but it shows that the human capacity to cherish is not yet totally eclipsed by the drive for profit and power.

Thankfully, traditions of reverence persist, even if only in limited and marginal ways. When a Native American gives a tobacco offering to the

Great Spirit before entering a sweatlodge, no artificial boundary between cult and culture exists. Even when the average suburban family offers a quick word of grace before eating, the great themes of cult (reverence) and culture (growing food) reunite, if only subconsciously.

Spiritual but not religious

We have talked about how spirituality requires a cultural context—which may or may not be religious. The person who says "I'm spiritual but not religious" possibly means that his or her spirituality is nurtured by something other than traditional religion. Persons who consider themselves "spiritual" might understand spirituality in any of these ways:

- they are religiously devout, active in a church or other religious group;
- they are active students of New Age or philosophical thought;
- they are sensitive to the nuances of complex music or the beauty of great art;
- or they are simply persons who live life with zest, enthusiasm, and a dash of faith.

A person who says "I'm spiritual but not religious" may actually be saying "My deep connectedness with life is not nurtured by the church I grew up in" or perhaps "I've never been involved in a religion, even as a child, but I still seek the Divine presence in my life." A spiritually-minded person who rejects religion has simply found another context for nurturing spirituality. These nonreligious spiritualities may be found in such places as twelve-step groups, the Rainbow Family, some businesses or nonprofit organizations, or even certain political groups. Some people may, in order to nurture spirituality, simply require some time in libraries and/or in the woods.

People outside of traditional religion may still find a cultural context for nurturing spirituality in their lives. While a fan of the Grateful Dead may have never thought he was encountering the Sacred at a Dead show, he nonetheless may have felt he was accessing some form of supernatural love in the midst of the dancing and the ecstatic music. While the language and the symbols of such a spirituality may be radically different from charismatic Christianity or Hasidic Judaism, there are enough parallels that even a phrase as specific as "I am opening my heart up to universal love" could be applied—accepted as valid—by the adherents of each form. In this context, "I'm spiritual but not religious" might be translated as "I experience Divine love just like you do, but the way I experience it is different."

Some people may object altogether to the idea of linking spirituality with religion. This is true not only of those who say "I'm spiritual but not religious" but also of some Christians and many New Age practitioners—indeed, it is true of all who resist the idea that their beliefs and practices might be a form of dogmatism. A person deeply immersed in personal spirituality might resist any kind of faith community that appears to be "organized" or "institutional." For such a person, "religion" may imply a lifeless, inflexible bureaucracy—the mission of religion being not to foster spirituality but to enforce rules—as opposed to "spirituality," which implies something much more dynamic, liberating, and open-ended. Although such attitudes are understandable, I think they may be a bit unfair to religion. Every spirituality has some kind of cultural context—if not religious, then artistic or philosophical, but still some way of providing structure and identity. New Age spirituality, for example, may involve "dogma" that arises from peer pressure, as opposed to hierarchical decree. "Since all my friends believe crystals heal, I believe it, too" is just as much a dogmatic assertion as "The Pope forbids contraception, therefore I believe it's wrong."

If spirituality (relationship with God) is like the breath, then culture (structure for fostering spirituality) is like the lung—they are different, yet both are necessary for survival. Put another way: spirituality may be like the heart—the dynamic, emotional center—while religion or some other form of culture is like the skeleton—the source of structure and stability. A breath cannot exist without a lung to expand and contract; a heart requires the skeleton in order to survive. Whether one's spirituality arises out of the tightly knit culture of Catholicism or the loose "do-it-yourself" culture of Goddess worship, the fact remains that some sort of cultural context surrounds the spiritual life.

Along these lines, I also maintain that a faith community of one kind or another is ultimately necessary for a mature spirituality—a topic we'll consider more fully in chapter 10. At the same time, I recognize that for many people the traditional religions have ceased to function as effective wombs for the gestation of spirituality. One challenge our society faces is to find creative and spirit-enhancing ways to nurture a mature spiritual life for persons who feel alienated from the church or other traditional religions.

Many people often consider religion and spirituality different in another way—in which religion is seen as a public matter, while spirituality is essentially private. As I've already suggested, this represents the triumph of the meta-culture. "I'm spiritual but not religious" would then mean that the speaker wishes to keep his or her relationship with God private, so private that for someone even to guess that it existed would not be possible! I find this position difficult to defend, because I think it is impossible to separate spirituality from all cultural contexts whatsoever, just as it is impossible to rip the breath out of the lungs. I challenge the person who thinks spirituality is wholly a private affair to consider how culture (whether religious or not) and spirituality may need each other. A public institution like a church that has members without a nurtured spiritual life runs the risk of being bureaucratic and legalistic, more concerned with external structure than inner experience—and I suspect that many people who reject religion are rejecting churches that have made precisely this mistake. However, the opposite problem is equally dangerous. A person with a rich inner life but without some form of community to support his spirituality runs the risk of being self-indulgent and narcissistic.

We have come full circle, back to the question of "inner" and "outer" spirituality with which we began this chapter. I believe that spirituality needs a cultural context, which includes material expressions (such as music, icons, and sacred scriptures) and social expressions (a community of faith to support each individual in her or his quest for the Sacred). Later on, we'll pick up some of the themes of this "outer" dimension of spirituality again. For now, the next few chapters will concentrate on some of the inner dynamics of the spiritual life. Even though cathedrals and sacred books and breathtaking vistas of nature all may reveal the Sacred presence to anyone at any time, the mind's capacity to dream and to wonder, the ability to feel reverence and awe, and the will to worship remain crucial for a spiritual life. The dynamics of wonder and belief—the subjects of the next two chapters—all arise from the vast universe within.

3

Wonder

For years after it was released, "Stairway to Heaven," Led Zeppelin's eight-minute magnum opus, remained one of radio's most requested and most played rock 'n' roll songs. The song's popularity persisted throughout the 1970s and into the 1980s and 1990s. Because rock is a style of music heavily dominated by fashion and novelty—the "new" is always preferred to the "old"—the longevity of this song is remarkable and worth considering. Musically, the song is a superb crossbreeding of British folk music (it begins with a lovely melody played on acoustic guitar and recorder) and American blues-rock (the song ends with a searing guitar solo, galloping beat, and half-screamed vocals before finding resolution in the vocalist's unaccompanied refrain). But another reason the song may have endured for years stems from the spiritual tone of the lyrics.

An oblique and impressionistic song, "Stairway to Heaven" tells about journeys—a woman's journey to heaven and the singer's journey down a road to someplace never named. The lyrics dance through a series of apparently unrelated images, including a songbird singing by a brook, a forest filled with smoke and laughter, and a piper calling people to follow him. Between this kaleidoscope of images, the song touches upon several qualities of the spiritual life—listening for a call, seeking transformation, and finding heaven through "the whispering wind." Early in the song, the singer mentions a feeling he gets as he looks "to the west" with longing in his spirit—*wonder*. "It makes me wonder" serves as the theme of the song's loveliest verses. "Stairway to Heaven" is a song about wonder—and millions have responded to its wistful call.*

Wonder is the sense of being fully present with something marvelous, fascinating, admirable, or meaningful. It's an indispensable characteristic for anyone oriented toward a relationship with the Sacred. Wonder is a doorway to higher forms of consciousness, and wonder is a key to a life fully and deeply lived. Wonder will accompany us throughout the pages to come.

In feeling wonder, we are most easily and surely taken out of our preoccupation with survival and achievement and judgment. Just as lungs expand when filled with air, so it is in wonder that we are "enlarged" by a sense of the splendor of life, a sense of mystery and unknowing, or even a sense of holiness or divinity. This "enlarging" by wonder enables us to approach life with openness—openness to joy and delight—freeing us from the too-common preoccupation in our culture with excessive criticism and analysis. Wonder is the quality of consciousness that transforms our preoccupation with survival into the capacity to cherish and to love. The joy of wonder opens the door to the possibility of compassionately caring for others—a quality central to a fully mature spirituality.

We live in a world of vast institutions, from government and business to universities and churches. Ours is a world dominated by science and technology. Our institutional, technological habitat is a "no-nonsense" realm, and *wonder* does not seem to be a widely used word in this "serious" world. Our world is affluent in many ways, but we seem to have a shortage of wonder.

We do talk of wonder in terms of uncertainty—"I wonder if it will rain today"—or in terms of hearty approval—"That's wonderful!" We remember from our childhood visiting, with Alice, a place called Wonderland—a place of marvels and mysteries, of strangeness and otherness. But wonder, in its original and purest sense—to be freely open to life and therefore filled with delightful, radiant joy—seems, alas, all too rare in our experience. Even "wonderful" carries a connotation more of *achievement*—"worthiness and excellence"—than of the deep *delight* that is "marvelous and resplendent."

Is that because our scientific world has lost all sense of wonder? Or, perhaps, is our world filled with too *many* wonders? Both may be the case.

---

* Jimmy Page and Robert Plant, "Stairway to Heaven," on Led Zeppelin, *Untitled,* Atlantic Records 7208. Used by permission.

I am typing these words on a laptop computer, a tool with which I am able to do writing and editing along with numerous other "information management" tasks. My computer uses technology that only within my short lifetime has been developed to the point of being available to millions of people at a reasonably affordable price. There is no doubt that this computer, an example of state-of-the-art technology today, will barely pass muster as a child's toy five or ten years from now. I felt some wonder at the laptop when I purchased it, but not much anymore. To some extent I still wonder at it, although my feeling is mostly of the "worthy and excellent" variety.

Similarly, I barely feel wonder now when I glance at photographs taken by astronauts on the moon, photographs that filled our entire world with wonder when I was a boy. Our habitat—our culture—has become thickly overlaid by a layer of technology that is changing so rapidly that, practically speaking, we no longer have the time to wonder. Instead of being a central part of life, wonder has become a luxury few of us can afford. To stop and wonder would be to risk losing out on the next opportunity. Wonder, so essential to the health of the spirit, has become almost a burden in our technologically driven meta-culture.

The Latin word for "to wonder at" is *mirari*—the same word from which we get *miracle* and *mirror*. Of course, a miracle is a "wonderful" thing, but it also suggests to me that wonder itself may be miraculous—a miraculous kind of consciousness, the consciousness of Divine presence (a miracle, by definition, is something that occurs by Divine intervention). When we feel wonder, we are feeling some sort of intimation of the presence of God. And like a mirror, anything that causes wonder creates a reflection—only where a mirror reflects light, that which causes wonder reflects some aspect of the beauty or power of the Sacred.

The *Oxford English Dictionary* links wonder with "the emotion excited by the perception of something novel and unexpected, or inexplicable; astonishment mingled with perplexity or bewildered curiosity" (*COED*, 3809). This definition is a feast of spiritual concepts, concepts that will surface again and again over the course of our exploration:

- newness
- otherness
- strangeness
- unknowing

- astonishment
- bewilderment
- curiosity

Wonder involves a messy, unpredictable complex of feelings.

Wonder is not something we "do" so much as something we simply are "filled with"—and therefore it cannot be engineered or created by sheer force of will. It comes unbidden and enters our life from beyond the sphere of our control. Sometimes wonder involves a feeling of "wow!"—and in that "wow," we are brought face-to-face with something other than our humdrum, daily life; something that invites us to the experience of delightful joy. Sometimes we feel wonder in conscious moments of encounter—whether encountering God or becoming mindful of the universe; encountering the mystery in a lover's eyes, or simply discovering a new way of understanding ourselves.

From the encounter with the "other" to the feeling of "wow" to the sense of delightful joy, wonder involves a state of consciousness, coursing through our nerves and veins with a power that is hearty and erotic. But not a heavy heartiness, nor a somber eros—wonder is as light and delicate as a seed borne by the wind. To be filled with wonder is, metaphorically speaking, somewhat like being filled with sunshine—being radiant with light.

If a central quality of wonder is light, then wonder is surely related to *delight*, a marvelous word that literally means "of light." For that matter, we may call wonder an "enlightening" feeling. When something strikes me full of wonder, it also fills me full of "light"—a spiritual light. Because light enables us to see, the spiritual light that comes to us through wonder enables us to "see" in a spiritual way—to see such things as the presence of the Sacred, the essential goodness of the universe, and our ability to make positive and loving choices.

Light means both "not heavy" and "not dark." But for some people, life seems to be a heavy, emotionally dark experience indeed. Yet the experience of being filled with a sense of wonder may even come, unbidden, into the life of a grieving or furious or depressed person. We must not assume too quickly that wonder and emotional burdens are mutually exclusive. I believe wonder may transform the life of anyone, even an emotionally burdened person—with profound impact.

Today, in a world more fascinated by technology than wonder, can we make the space to see with the eyes of wonder? Yes, we can, but these days we seem to have less and less of a natural capacity to wonder. Openness to wonder is something that must deliberately be nurtured and exercised. Just as the increase of sedentary work has mandated a need for aerobics and fitness centers to keep our bodies healthy, so the increase of our technologically driven, sensory-overwhelming meta-culture has mandated a need for "gymnasiums of the spirit." Living in a driven, competitive world where technological achievement and "the bottom line" dominate our attention, we need to cultivate a discipline of wonder.

A "discipline of wonder" includes several activities of the spiritual life, among which are prayer, meditation and contemplation, living in community, and offering gifts. Upcoming chapters of this book will examine each of these activities in detail, for I believe that the spiritual life is not complete without a commitment to the "discipline of wonder."

On the surface, this emphasis on discipline appears to contradict my contention that wonder cannot be engineered or artificially achieved—that it must simply be allowed to occur. But a closer look shows this is not so. Any attempt to experience wonder—whether through a spiritual discipline, spending time in the deep wilderness, or being attentive at "peak moments" such as times of giving birth or of watching someone die—must be approached not to manufacture or *engineer* a "spiritual experience," but simply out of respect for spirituality and life, with an *openness* to receive the delights of the Sacred presence, if it be God's will. ("If it be God's will" sounds like pious language—but if we believe that God is truly an autonomous Being with whom we relate, then we need to acknowledge that "the presence of God" is something God may choose to reveal or not to reveal. The experience of God's presence, like the experience of wonder, cannot be engineered or controlled. It is a matter of grace.)

Wonder, like all truly spiritual qualities, cannot be forced to occur; it can only be allowed. We cannot make ourselves experience wonder or force wonder to "happen"—we can only be willing to experience it. This is a hard lesson for our achievement-oriented society to learn, but to understand spirituality we need to accept that matters of the Spirit cannot be controlled or manipulated; they can only be encountered, allowed, and received. The spiritual life, therefore, involves openness to the possibility of being filled with heavenly wonder. Spirituality means life is lived in ways that allow for wonder to thrive—not only in our own lives but in the lives of others as well.

Wonder is lowly and universal. Wonder is not some sort of spiritual reward that a person gets for paying attention properly or for being a nature-lover or for meditating in just the right way. There's nothing elitist about wonder. As I suggested above, it can come unbidden to the heartbroken or grieving person; but the point is, it comes unbidden. Wonder is not a high achievement; it is a simple, humble experience. Anyone and everyone may be swept up into that place where eyes and hearts are open to the beauty of the universe. You don't have to be a member of the right religion or have the right amount of education or the right level of income in order to be struck with wonder. The Spirit blows where it will, and anyone, at any time, may be swept up into the Divine embrace.

I believe wonder is the central disposition of spiritual consciousness—but it is hardly the *only* important inner characteristic of a life given to cultivating a relationship with the Sacred. Several other characteristics of consciousness function alongside wonder to help nurture the spiritual life. These characteristics, including willingness, vulnerability, playfulness, serendipity, and openness—along with the more somber characteristics of awe and fear—each deserve our attention as we attempt to understand the dispositions that function in the consciousness oriented toward the Sacred. For the remainder of this chapter, we'll look at these characteristics in turn, exploring them as corollaries of wonder.

Willingness

Wonder cannot be controlled; it can only be allowed to manifest in its own way. Out of the issue of "controlling" versus "allowing," willingness emerges as an important part of spirituality. Psychiatrist Gerald May, in his book *Will and Spirit*, draws an important distinction between "willfulness" and "willingness." Willingness, he says, "implies a surrendering of one's self-separateness, an entering-into, an immersion in the deepest processes of life itself. It is a realization that one already is a part of some ultimate cosmic process and it is a commitment to participation in that process." Willfulness, however, "is the setting of oneself apart from the fundamental essence of life in an attempt to master, direct, control, or otherwise manipulate existence" (May 1982, 6). Willingness is linked with *participation* and willfulness is linked with *control*.

Catholic theologians use the term "fundamental option" to describe the foundational decision that one must make to either ally oneself with God or to oppose God. Perhaps recognizing the fundamental option can make it easier to understand willingness and willfulness. To be willing—to participate in life's process without wishing to control it—is very much like saying "yes" to the Divine. Willfulness, on the other hand, involves the desire to control or master life, rather than simply allowing it to unfold. This is like saying "no" to the Sacred.

Our meta-culture places a very high value on mastery and control. We learn "power skills" for business. We study the leadership strategies of Attila the Hun. Even our churches encourage persons to master sexual desire and control "sinful thoughts." To approach spirituality from a position of willingness—of *surrendering* control—is subversive of some of our deepest cultural values. While the culture we live in demands that we stay in control and have a "take-charge" attitude toward life, the doorway to encountering the Sacred invites us to lay those qualities aside.

This is not to say that spirituality is an "anything goes" proposition. On the contrary, most spiritual traditions place significant demands on the behavior of their adherents. In fact, whenever we form relationships—whether with God or with people—the relationships must, in order to function, involve making and keeping promises and commitments. But making and honoring our commitments is not the same thing as behaving willfully—commitments are kept not by our *efforts* so much as by our *allowing*. For example, I've been blessed with a vibrant sexuality and a flirtatious personality—qualities that make my marriage sparkle, yet also mean I often feel attracted to someone other than my wife. I cannot willfully *force* such erotic feelings to stop. But I can willingly *allow* those feelings to gently come and go—they arise and then dissipate without my acting on them. My faithfulness to my wife is a choice—but it's something I allow, not something I force.

The demands and commitments of spirituality are not achieved through willfulness—I cannot force myself to be more loving, for example. I cannot force myself to pray every day or to tithe or to work unceasingly for justice. However, insofar as I seek to become more of a "willing" person, I am prepared to allow these virtues to flourish within me. Any meaningful path of spirituality places great demands on each person, requiring faithfulness and intentionality—yet walking the path successfully requires a willingness to be faithful, rather than a willful attempt to "force" faithfulness. Spiritual willingness means choosing to be present with the Divine and choosing an attitude of *cherishing* over our culturally ingrained emphasis on *succeeding*.

An excellent image for willingness comes from the Taoist tradition—the notion of *wu-wei*, which may be translated as "going with the flow"—in the sense of a sailor working her sails to take advantage of the flow of the wind. *Wu-wei* requires an active participation in the flow, not simply a passive acquiescence. Sometimes the sailor sets a course counter to the direction of the wind or the current—using her knowledge of sailing in partnership with the wind or the current to reach her goal. A passive sailor, far from "going with the flow," would do nothing and simply drift.

Healthy willingness does not mean avoiding unpleasant issues (like anger or conflict), nor is it an aimless "drifting" through life. Rather, it involves a co-creative strategy in life, relating to others not from a position of dominance and control (nor a position of passivity or manipulation) but rather from a position of partnership and mutuality. "Others" include not only other people but also the ultimate "other"—the Sacred. A spirituality of willingness is a spirituality of partnership with the Divine.

Vulnerability

One of the most distinguished of military honors and decorations is the Purple Heart, awarded to soldiers wounded during combat. My grandfather received the Purple Heart during World War I, and after he died the medal became one of my mother's prized possessions. As an honor for the wounded, the Purple Heart commemorates the brave vulnerability of a war hero.

Despite the honor and reverence and perhaps even mystique that surrounds the Purple Heart, most of us—inside or outside of military service—live a life geared almost exclusively toward the elimination of vulnerability. Vulnerability might be thought of as "wound-ability," for to be vulnerable is to be in a situation where a wound is possible, much more possible than we wish. Just as we attempt to avoid willingness by choosing to be willful and controlling, so we attempt to avoid vulnerability through excessive self-protection. Sometimes we take our fear of vulnerability to unnecessary extremes.

Entire stores are devoted to "personal security"—an industry of technological gadgets and high-priced whatchamacallits that are supposed to reduce our vulnerability to theft, burglary, assault, or some other form of crime. Obviously, appropriate self-protection is desirable. But perhaps the message of these stores—that invulnerability can be had through the purchase of a hi-tech tool—might be just a way of responding to a fearful desire to control life. This anxious impulse to self-protect runs counter to the spiritual wisdom that recognizes we are always fundamentally vulnerable. As much as prudence and prevention may be virtues, we need to remember that we cannot erase our vulnerability, no matter what extremes we go to in the quest for self-protection. The spiritual life is not about eliminating vulnerability. It's about accepting it and even celebrating our vulnerability before the Sacred.

Even various forms of spirituality sometimes seem to support the obsession with control and invulnerability that our society emphasizes. Certain aspects of the human potential, New Age, and psychotherapy movements seem geared toward the elimination of vulnerability— theoretically making us stronger, more self-assured, more "psychically" gifted, more in control of our lives, better managers, more competent lovers, spiritual "masters," and so forth. These techniques of "mastery" seem to be little more than strategies for escaping "the wound"—whether the wound comes emotionally from a jilting lover, financially from a job lost to downsizing, physically from cancer or other illness, or some other way. The cause of the much-feared wound is not what matters. We tend to regard any wound as bad, and any strategy for preventing or eliminating vulnerability is therefore good.

A corollary to the struggle against vulnerability is the culture of victimization. Both vulnerability and victimization involve woundedness. Vulnerability involves the possibility of sustaining a wound at some point in the future, while victimization involves an experience in the past of having actually been wounded. Just as we could conceivably sustain serious wounds in the future, so some, perhaps many, or even most of us have already suffered serious wounds in the past. Traumatic social and interpersonal evils victimize people. Racism, sexism, and heterosexism; crime and economic injustice; violence; and sexual or verbal abuse—all result in untold numbers of wounded, suffering people. A victim could be someone who was mugged an hour ago or an adult who has hidden the experience of childhood abuse like a "dirty secret" for decades.

Obviously, it is essential for the well-being of society that such evils as crime and abuse be named, exposed, and fought against. Victims, especially of abuse and injustice, who are courageous enough to come forward and devote their lives to fighting future injustices deserve our support and gratitude. At the same time, we as a society need to be careful about the implications that our fascination with victimization and unrestrained self-protection has for ourselves as well as for our society. Excessive self-protection and over-emphasis on victimization are essentially narcissistic—rather than trying to find meaning in our suffering by struggling to ease the suffering of others, the dynamics of self-protection and victimization encourage us to focus primarily on our own selves—on the drama of our own past or potential woundedness.

Self-protection and victimization can lead to an emphasis on blame and vengeance, which prevents the victim from investing time and energy into strategies for bringing about deep healing—working for justice and striving to forgive. In this "poor me" culture of victimization, we encourage victims to prefer self-obsession over solidarity with other sufferers. All of this effort to flee from woundedness, whether future or past, results in a culture increasingly given over to lawsuits, mistrust among family members, alienation from others, and loneliness arising out of sense of having "no one to turn to."

If we all retreat into the shells of our own private victimization and fears of the future, we give up on community and our world becomes increasingly devoid of social values—a "moral vacuum," where even greater injustices may occur without restraint. Even today, we see some political leaders seeking to increase the power of the wealthy few, meanwhile blaming the poor (welfare recipients and immigrants) for the woes of the middle class! We are so busy blaming each other for our wounds that we are in danger of losing the ability to truly come together as a community. This is tragic, for only as a community can we really do something about easing suffering—really comforting the victims, rehabilitating the perpetrators, and finding enough safety in our relationships (as opposed to finding safety in technology or in our increasingly fortress-like buildings) to face the future with a minimum of fear.

There's a tremendous pathos in our society, obsessed as we are with protecting ourselves (justifiably or not) from possible wounds in the future and blaming others (justifiably or not) for the wounds of our past. To the extent we are driven by either avoiding vulnerability in the future or being caught up in the drama of the past, our obsession with woundedness *separates us from the present*. This is the saddest irony, for the present is all we have anyway—since the past is only memories and the future is only speculation. To the extent that we allow memories and speculation to run our lives, we are living life reactively. We are dominated by anger and bitterness (over the past) and fear (of the future), rather than by wonder (in the present).

Instead of such a passive, blaming/fearful way of living, to live spiritually is to hold memories and speculation in equilibrium—while staying attentive to being in the present. This allows us to find a kind of "spaciousness" in ourselves as we relate to past and future. In this spaciousness we may find hope, a hope that can lessen our fear as we envision the future. In the spaciousness we allow memories other than those of our victimization to assume importance—we allow our good memories to balance the painful ones in our understanding of how we've become who we are. When we see the past as a rich mixture of both happy and sad memories, we can hope for a future that we do not need to fear (or protect ourselves from). Hope not only makes us happier, but it also lays the groundwork for a deeper relationship with God.

By choosing to be vulnerably hopeful, we may more easily face life optimistically. Out of this optimism, we are empowered to make thoughtful, caring choices in the present. Naturally, the choices we make in life are informed by our realistic understanding of the past and our balanced assessment of the future. But to the extent that we nurse our fear of woundedness-to-come and our anger or bitterness about woundedness-past, our unchecked passions can prevent the kind of open, spacious response to the present that is the essence of wonder—the essence of the spiritual life.

The greatest irony surrounding all of this comes from the history of the word "wound" itself. An early spelling of "wonder" is "wounder," and an early spelling of "wound" is "wonde"—which points to the likelihood that the origin of "wound" is linked with the origin of "wonder"! It certainly makes sense, for a wound is an opening up—of the skin, of the emotions, or perhaps even of consciousness itself. Similarly, wonder "opens us up" mentally and emotionally to the astonishing glory of the Divine. Both wound and wonder are interruptions of our tightly controlled, safely constructed world—the world of willfulness and self-protection. So the question is begging to be asked—when we strive so hard to protect ourselves from woundedness, are we likewise shutting down all possibility of wonder?

I don't want to be misunderstood. I am not advocating the disregard of potential dangers, nor am I suggesting that we ignore the real ways in which people are victimized. Indeed, I think we all too often *do* live in denial of the real possibility of future suffering—a denial matched and even exceeded by the way we deny and ignore the victimization in our midst. This denial of suffering is, in itself, a way of attempting to manage vulnerability. If I pretend it isn't there, then I don't have to be present to it—I don't have to share in your wounds. To live in wonder means willingly to encounter suffering, in ourselves as well as others. Suffering may be linked to the future or the past, but it always yearns for healing in the present.

We open ourselves up—to wounds and to wonder—knowing that this opening up is the only path toward the fulfillment of our longings. Acknowledging our wounds, comforting others who are wounded, and celebrating the present moment are doors to that spiritual place where healing and transformation are possible.

Playfulness

In one of his *Songs of Innocence,* William Blake wrote,

> *And we are put on earth a little space*
> *That we may learn to bear the beams of love.*

In my opinion, the most important word in this quotation is "beams." Are the "beams of love" light like sunbeams or heavy like wooden beams? Is learning to bear these beams a joyful, delightful task—or is it heavy, somber, and serious? Blake doesn't say. He leaves his readers with an unexplained ambiguity. Within that ambiguity lies, however, a secret of the spirituality of playfulness—or, perhaps, the playfulness of spirituality. Like "beams" that may be heavy or light, playfulness is a wonderful state of mind that is both silly and earnest.

This state of mind, which we could call "playful-mind," functions in the spiritual life as a wonderful alternative to the demands of our mundane, ordinary "survival-mind"—although our society, both religious and secular, often seems to quell playfulness (at least in adults). We live in a world uncomfortable with the spiritual dispositions of wonder, willingness, and vulnerability. Is it any surprise that we are equally uncomfortable with the self-forgetful pleasure that playfulness entails?

While children seem to play naturally, we adults often need to be reminded just what playfulness is. Typically, we adults have no need for "make-believe," since we know all too well our roles in life—parent, spouse, employee, and so forth. But by abandoning the childishness of make-believe, we fall too easily in the trap of also leaving behind the capacity to let go and have fun, which is the heart of playfulness. We too easily lose interest in playing games, frolicking in the woods, catching fireflies, building a snowman, or any of a hundred other childhood activities when we stop nurturing our capacity for play.

Playfulness as a state of mind is both silly and earnest. Part of what makes playfulness so playful is that it's serious fun. When a child plays at being a grown-up, it's serious business. Imitating Mom or Dad prepares a youth for future responsibilities as an adult. In a game like cops and robbers, the serious part of play is even more evident. Not only is such a game an exploration of the serious world of work, but it also explores ethics and social values. Even our newest forms of playing—from video games to fantasy role-playing games—all have their serious edge as well (usually involving winning and losing, which prepares youngsters for the hyper-competitive, profit-dominated meta-culture they will soon inherit). Playfulness can only be playful insofar as it is also, in some ways, serious. Some element of seriousness or earnestness necessarily separates playfulness from mere buffoonery.

A healthy spirituality has a playful element—not an absurd playful-ness, but rather a joyful, earnest, loving playfulness. Admittedly, this concept of playful spirituality may be unusual and novel for persons who grew up in churches that emphasized the serious side of spirituality without talking much at all about the spirit of play. We may not custom-arily think of God or spirituality as playful—probably because we were taught to take God *too* seriously. If we conceive of God as a wrathful parent or a "cosmic policeman," we learned—usually as children—that God does not tolerate silliness. Taking God too seriously thrives in religious circles, which unfortunately hides the marvelous potential for a spirituality that celebrates the playfulness of the Sacred. This may be yet another reason why churches lose members and people claim to be spiritual but not religious.

The absence of playfulness results not in seriousness, but in *excessive* seriousness. Playfulness helps us (especially us adults) keep our serious side in healthy perspective. Playful-mind does not destroy survival-mind, but instead provides a joyful alternative, when appropriate, to the dutiful nature of responsible living. A healthy spirituality does not choose *either* playfulness *or* responsibility; it celebrates and nurtures *both* playfulness *and* responsibility. A common theme in the movies of Walt Disney—films like *Peter Pan* and *Mary Poppins*—is that of families with fathers who are just plain *too* serious. Naturally, these too-serious dads are the butt of jokes, and part of the happy endings to these movies is seeing Dad lighten up a bit.

If playfulness as a spiritual quality mixes seriousness with fun, what then does this mixture look like? As with the ambiguity of the word "beams" in the verse by Blake, playfulness as a characteristic of spirituality delights in the ambiguous, the uncertain, the paradoxical, the open-ended, the humorous. To be playful is, not surprisingly, to be willing—willing to laugh, willing to pretend, willing to not know, willing to act or try something new, willing to be foolish (and even to be made a fool of).

Playfulness functions as a powerful source of subversiveness. Playful-mind undermines our self-importance, our need to be in control and in power, our need to maintain appearances. Playfulness, the province of the holy fool and the childlike saint, has no patience for the "Important Things of the World." Rather, being playful means being too busy gazing into a lover's eyes, or trying to see faces in the clouds, or eating a double fudge sundae as slowly as possible in order to savor every bite to worry about all those things we normally want to take very seriously (in other words, *too* seriously).

I do not wish to suggest that playfulness is a virtue and seriousness a vice. Excessive playfulness—a playfulness that leads to irresponsibility or to disregard for danger—is buffoonery, as much a problem as excessive seriousness. And seriousness has its proper place. All of the world's major spiritual traditions make some sort of behavioral demands and require discipline and responsibility—along with other "serious" requirements, like behaving responsibly at work or at home. Playfulness is not the opposite of seriousness; it is the healthy corrective to overdone seriousness. Being prudent with our money is important, but playfulness reminds us that "prudence" sometimes may just mean blowing that extra bit on the concert we want to go to. Even prudence, when healthy, has a playful side that keeps the serious side of life in proper perspective.

I have suggested that while playfulness is something many or most children embody well, many adults seem to embody it poorly, if at all. In light of this idea, let's consider the commonly quoted but rarely practiced teaching of Jesus, "Whoever does not receive the kingdom of God like a little child will never enter it" (Mark 10:15). Since we are advised to relate to the Sacred as children, wouldn't that include being like a girl who enjoys singing silly songs with her mom or like a boy who loves horsing around with his dad? In these examples, the serious part of playfulness is spending time with a loved one—while the fun part might appear to be nothing more than "wasting" time! These examples show how playfulness can involve simply wasting time with someone we love, without having to prove or achieve anything. To be playful is simply to delight in the moment, to celebrate the being-together, without any focus on having to measure up. When Jesus asked his followers to be like little children, might not this have been at least part of what he had in mind?

The child frolicking with a beloved parent is a valuable model for spirituality. When we pray or meditate, too often we become so worried about measuring up that we lose sight of the possibility of simply being *playful* in the Divine presence. Too often many of us relate to God not like children, but as if we were teenagers, testing boundaries and resenting authority. We therefore limit the Divine to a model of "angry parent"—an almost useless model for developing a loving, intimate relationship with the Sacred. Playful-mind dares to wonder this: "Perhaps God offers us a relationship based less on turbulent self-consciousness and more on just plain self-forgetful fun."

Serendipity

The *American Heritage Dictionary* defines "serendipity" as "the faculty of making fortunate discoveries by accident." The word "accident" seems out of place in this context, for it conjures up such notions as automobile wrecks or spilled beverages. Perhaps a better phrase than "by accident" would be "unintentionally" or "outside of planning or control." Serendipity signifies a wonderful thing happening beyond our expectations or hopes. A serendipitous something causes a surprising change in a person's life that fills her with unplanned delight. Moreover, the very word itself is fun! Compare "serendipity" to other (much more common) words in our language, like "abuse" or "corruption" or "stress." Unlike the harsh, almost grating feel of many of the sobering words we regularly use, the sound of the word "serendipity" playfully tickles our tongue and can make a child laugh. The delight in the word itself implies the delight that the word characterizes.

Serendipity plays an important role in spirituality. Look at the words I've used to define it: "wonder," "grace," "playful," "surprise," and "delight"—all, in fact, topics that have been (or will be) considered at length in this book. Serendipity undermines the gloominess of the self-protectors and pessimists, who think that things are awful now and are sure just to get worse. Well, in many ways things really *are* pretty bad—perhaps not least because we creatures try too hard to make them better. We try so hard that we get in the way of serendipity—we get in the way of the force-bigger-than-us that really *can* make things better, if we'd only allow it.

"Grace," "the Tao," "*wu-wei*," "Zen," and "magic" are all concepts from various spiritual traditions that have at least some overlapping with serendipity. Many of these concepts imply not only the possibility of good things happening, but also the necessity of allowing, rather than forcing, serendipity. It's simply there when it's there, unbidden and outside of our control. Serendipity belongs to the realm of wonder and surprise—it's not likely to turn up on business plans or financial statements.

As spirituality involves being open to a relationship with God—a relationship nurtured by our openness to wonder—in a similar way, spirituality is nurtured by our openness to serendipity, to the possibility that good things can and will happen outside of our control. This is not a matter of denying the bad things of life. The variety of bad things that happen surprise no one. Buildings are bombed, children are killed by psychopathic gunmen, planes drop out of the sky, tornadoes and hurricanes leave swaths of destruction. To be open to serendipity is not to live in denial of such tragedies, nor is it to ignore them; rather it is to refuse to let such horrors control life. A mind open to serendipity trusts and believes, as much as possible, that the grace of the Divine is ultimately bigger than the forces of destruction and despair that cause death, sorrow, and pain. A person open to serendipity not only believes in the grace of the Sacred but also seeks to make choices based on the possibilities of love and hope rather than the fear of death and tragedy.

To believe in serendipity means to believe in happy endings. But a hope for such grace-filled surprises must be balanced by a corresponding willingness—a willingness to make choices based on hope rather than despair. This is not an easy task, for when we despair, often we feel immobilized. But serendipity asks us not to be successful, but simply to be faithful—and in that faith, to hope for a brighter future.

Dualism revisited

Earlier in this chapter I said that "when something strikes me full of wonder, it also fills me full of 'light'—a spiritual light." From there, I've gone on to explore willingness, vulnerability, playfulness, and serendipity, arguing that these characteristics are essential for a deeply "spiritual" way of living. So far, this chapter seems to be slanted toward happy, light-hearted feelings—but is that the entire story of spirituality? If the "light" characteristics of consciousness nurture a loving relationship with the Divine, what do the "dark" characteristics signify? Isn't there any room in the spiritual life for "darker" feelings or experiences, such as doubt, anger, dread, fear, or awe? If our light dispositions help us to encounter the Sacred, does that mean our dark dispositions—our rage and jealousy and temptation to violence—separate us from the Holy?

A grave risk arises out of seeing spirituality purely in terms of what can be called "sweetness and light." When we experience wonder, playfulness, and other such happy states associated with spirituality, we may be tempted to think that spirituality is concerned only with upbeat feelings. Therefore, any "dark" feelings, like rage and fear, are somehow "not spiritual." It's the equivalent of thinking that rich people are industrious and poor people are lazy. The danger here is *dualism*. We first encountered dualism when considering the idea that the soul is sometimes believed to be "higher" than the body. Dualism divides the world into two parts; it quickly becomes problematic because dualistic thinking typically views one part as better than the other: one good and one evil, one spiritual and the other *un*spiritual, one happy and joyful, the other angry and frightened. Dualism is dangerous because it claims that God's grace is confined only to certain areas of life. Just as dualism suggests that God is more present in the soul than in the body, so also it tempts us to think that happy feelings are more "spiritual" than disturbing feelings.

Alas, dualism is rampant in our world, for our everyday survival-mind needs to evaluate things, and the most fundamental evaluation is whether something is "good" or "bad." Some common examples of dualistic thinking include:

- democracy is good and communism is bad;
- environmentalism is good and consumerism is bad;
- Christians are good and humanists are bad;
- New Agers are good and fundamentalists are bad.

Regardless of our beliefs or background—liberal or conservative, religious or nonreligious, rich or poor—we tend to divide almost any part of our culture, including spirituality, into "good" and "bad" segments. Yet no matter how much we may think dualistically, the spiritual life typically undermines our efforts to categorize things that way.

We want to think "good" people are holy and "bad" people are sinful —but then we are confronted by someone like Jesus Christ, who, despite his status as a "good" spiritual leader, sought out the company of prostitutes and swindlers and other people regarded as "bad." In a similar way, we want to think that happy feelings are "spiritual" and disturbing feelings are "unspiritual," but in any sustained exploration of spirituality, we unavoidably encounter awe and fear as much as we encounter wonder. Wonder fills us with delight at the sight of a starlit sky—but then if we ponder how small and insignificant we really are in the grand design of the universe, our wonder may take on the "darker" hue of awe. Instances of serendipity may fill us with delight, but fear or doubt may arise from considering how a world filled with happy surprises is also home to child abusers, serial killers, and genocidal despots. We may like to think about wonder as a "spiritual" characteristic, but we cannot avoid the deep ways in which fear and awe likewise invite us to explore the spiritual life— through feelings such as insignificance, danger, and insecurity. These deep parts of life are the places where we most need to be loved and to feel safe. They are also the places where an encounter with the Sacred may unexpectedly occur.

Awe and fear

To be in awe of something is, in the words of the *Oxford English Dictionary*, to experience "dread mingled with veneration, reverential or respectful fear." Awe characterizes "a mind subdued to profound reverence" when "in the presence of supreme authority, moral greatness or sublimity, or mysterious sacredness" (*COED*, I, 149).

Awe arises when we engage something (or someone) so much larger and more vast and more powerful than ourselves that we feel a sense of our own *smallness*. Thunderstorms, tornadoes, earthquakes, and hurricanes fill us with awe; likewise, we respond to the Sacred with awe. Awe results from considering the difference between the limitation of the self and the vastness of God.

A few years ago I stumbled across a group of Christians on the Internet discussing the concept of "the fear of the Lord." The more conservative persons in the discussion seemed suspicious of those who did not like or use that phrase. "I love it when liberals run from the fear of the Lord!" one person gloated, suggesting that he viewed liberals as people who didn't respect God—and therefore did not respect God's capacity to inspire feelings of dread or terror. More liberal voices in this discussion insisted that accepting God's love was more important than fearing God's wrath, trusting God was more important than fearing God, and so forth.

I got the sense that the participants were all talking past one another. The more I reflected on it, the more I considered that both parties were right. Yes, it *is* suspicious when spiritual persons have no fear in their spirituality; and yes, trusting *is* far more important than fearing the Divine.

The Bible passage in question is, "The fear of the Lord is the beginning of wisdom" (Psalm 111:10), and it raises difficult questions. Is being scared of the Divine necessary? Is fear equally as important to spirituality as wonder or playfulness? Thanks to horror movies and violence that is readily accessible through the media, we have a distorted notion of fear. Perhaps awe is a more useful spiritual term. Since "awe" is defined as "reverential fear," we could reasonably rewrite the verse as "*Awe* of the Sacred is the beginning of wisdom." Awe is a significant jumping-off point for a maturing life lived in relationship with the Divine.

How do we experience awe before God? The kinds of awe that are mentioned above—at the might and power of the natural world—are as good a place as any to start. Like wonder, awe cannot be engineered or manufactured. Both culture and nature may trigger it. A person who remains unmoved by sacred forms of culture (such as Stonehenge or a cathedral or a Bach fugue) still may feel awe when confronted with 200-mph hurricane winds. Awe arises from the insight that whoever or whatever created the vastness of the heavens and the galaxies is so much *bigger* than we are that, by comparison, we are reduced to utter insignificance.

The sense of profound awe is not a comfortable feeling, nor is it something we can live with day in and day out. It is a peak emotional experience, reserved for those rare times when we stand in the transept of a great cathedral or gaze at the dark splendor of a solar eclipse. Here is the reason that awe remains only the *beginning* of wisdom. Eventually, we leave the cathedral or the eclipse is over. What holds us in relationship to the Divine then? That is when more ordinary feelings—wonder, trust, and love—take root in our soul. Those feelings are what bring wisdom—and spirituality—to fruition.

A spirituality without some sense of awe strikes me as either a spirituality in denial or a spirituality that is shallow. If there is no awe, there is probably no real engagement with just how big and powerful and almighty the forces of the Divine truly are. Such an awe-less spirituality might make a certain kind of sense in our psychologically driven, feel-good, stay-in-control culture, but it stops short of the real possibilities of the spiritual life. Likewise, the situation opposite from not enough awe— too much fear—is equally problematic. A spirituality that is stuck in fear is truly an awful (awe-full) mess: where fear dominates, other important responses to the Divine (such as trust and love) are crowded out.

The consciousness of wonder makes it possible to believe that the heart of a loving God beats at the center of all things. Awe is the uncomfortable reminder of just how big that God is and just how little we are in comparison. Wonder is the intuitive recognition that the Spirit of the Divine lives in every human heart—that we are created in God's image. Awe is the equally intuitive understanding that the Sacred is *different* from us. God is "other." God is God—and we are not.

Openness

A clever bumper sticker proclaims, "Minds are like parachutes. They only function when open." Having looked at a number of dispositions central to the spiritual life—wonder, willingness, vulnerability, playfulness, serendipity, and awe—we now come to *openness*, which is not only the final topic of this chapter, but is in some way a foundation to all the other dispositions as well. We cannot be playful or vulnerable or awestruck without being fundamentally *open* to those kinds of full-blooded, passionate experiences. Lungs must be open in order to breathe. We creatures, likewise, must be spiritually open in order to receive the presence of the Divine. Being open means, whether we are talking about spirituality or business or some other realm of life, being available to grow and change in harmony with the dynamics of life.

Openness, like playfulness, seems to be a characteristic of youth. For example, movies like *E.T. The Extra-Terrestrial, Angels in the Outfield,* and *Free Willy* all explore the idea that young people are more open than adults—whether that means being open to encountering aliens from outer space, seeing angels from heaven, or simply feeling the pain of a whale in captivity. The younger a person is, the more open she will be to experiences ranging from mastering computer technology to enjoying the latest trends in fashion. Someone once noted wryly that youth is wasted on the young, and indeed, youthful openness has qualities that adults may well envy, such as flexibility, adaptability, and, most especially, the ability to respond rapidly to change. We could even define openness as a quality involving being responsive and receptive to change.

The opposite of openness, therefore, may be thought of as *resistance* to change. Such resistance means closing oneself in order to protect against the unknown. This is a certain path to disaster, for the person who refuses to change avoids not only unknown dangers, but unknown blessings as well, leaving only the most familiar and deadly curse of all: stagnation.

As the years go by and life batters us around, we may become less open to change, less adventurous, more conservative. Granted, age has its own gifts, such as stability and wisdom. Even so, as we mature and we recall wistfully the innocence and zest of youth, perhaps what we really long for is the openness that we—and all young persons—seem innately to have had, an openness that too many older people have all too frequently lost.

Openness may be a virtue of youth, but wisdom is a quality that comes with age—though I wonder if the most truly wise person is the one who, having reached old age, has managed to retain a sense of openness, adventure, and playfulness, despite the many burdens of a long life. Perhaps openness, coupled with experience, is what constitutes the realistic optimism of true wisdom. Openness without experience is naiveté, a common and dangerous quality of youth; but experience without openness is cynicism—a grotesque parody of wisdom.

To be open is to allow one's spirit to be large and flexible, a largeness and flexibility that allow each of us to embrace the "other"—whether that other is a new person, a new idea, a new thing, or a new situation. Openness is related to hospitality. An open person offers hospitality to whatever person, group, idea, belief, or thing may be new to him. Openness allows us new ways of seeing things and doing things—ways that may seem incorrect or, at the very least, unconventional to those who do not share our openness. Such openness may seem perfectly natural to a ten- or fifteen-year-old; but for a thirty- or fifty-year-old, maintaining a fresh and supple outlook of openness may require a conscious choice. I didn't have to watch my diet when I was twenty, but ten years later things changed—what had come naturally before (staying slim) became a matter requiring intentionality. So it is with the quality of openness. The older we get, the more conscious and intentional we must be about our spiritual receptivity.

Just as we need to cultivate wonder, perhaps we need to cultivate openness. By doing so, we learn that the world is indeed full of surprises and joys. Yes, dangers and tragedies exist, too; but an open life confidently lived, even with its share of pain and heartbreak, is far richer than a life lived in retreat and fearful self-protection.

The dispositions of spirituality—willingness and vulnerability, openness and playfulness, serendipity and awe—liberate us from excessive control and usher us into a place where it is possible to live consciously in wonder. A mind opened to wonder—and to its related dispositions—is a mind open to encountering God.

4

Belief

So far, we've looked at spirituality as involving a relationship with the Sacred. We've considered spirituality's connections with the soil and culture, viewing it in terms of cultivating or cherishing this Divine relationship. We've looked at how wonder, openness, serendipity, and other similar feelings are characteristics of spirituality. Now, how do we bring these rather disparate ideas together? What is the link among culture, wonder, and the Sacred? The answer, I think, involves *belief*.

Belief and believing play a significant role in life. For example, consider how middle-class American children learn at an early age to believe in figures like Santa Claus, the Easter Bunny, and the Tooth Fairy. Parents, schools, the media, and retailers all encourage children to believe in these nocturnal beings who provide goodies while the youngsters sleep. Even though Santa and the Easter Bunny are linked with Christian holidays, many families who do not consider themselves religious or who do not go to church or otherwise practice Christianity nevertheless celebrate the coming of these mythical beings. I know that my childhood sparkled with anticipation and excitement whenever Christmas or Easter rolled around or whenever I happened to lose a tooth. My belief in these mythic figures was one of the most precious joys of my childhood.

I think Santa, the Easter Bunny, and the Tooth Fairy are useful to children in the same way that playing cops and robbers is useful. Santa and company provide children with an opportunity for learning how to believe. I feel sad when I encounter parents who refuse to let their children believe in Santa Claus because they "don't want to lie" to their kids. These adults, it seems, don't acknowledge that learning how to believe is important for

59

children and that the crisis of discovering "the truth" about Santa and his gift-giving peers is a helpful step in that learning process.

Belief in Santa and company culminates in such a crisis, usually near the end of childhood, when a youngster learns that such figures "aren't real." At that point, the child has to rethink what it means to believe. When I was a child, I resolved this crisis by learning how to think in abstract and metaphorical ways, rather than only in literal ways. Sure, there is no literal jolly man up at the North Pole, but Santa as a *metaphor* remains a powerful, real figure to me. I surmounted the crisis of learning Santa wasn't "real" by accepting a new way to view Santa—as a metaphor for generosity and gift-giving.

The "literal Santa" may not have survived my transition from childhood to adolescence, though my ability to believe did survive, and it remains a central part of who I am. But in order to learn to believe like an adult, I had to let go of my childish way of believing. Just as baby teeth must fall out before adult teeth can develop, so a literalistic way of believing must give way to a more adult approach.

Belief versus certainty

What does it mean to believe? What is belief?

Perhaps one of the reasons we have difficulty with Santa—both as children learning "the truth" and as parents struggling to be "honest"—is that we sometimes misunderstand belief, confusing it with literal *certainty*. We think of belief in a way that makes saying "I believe in" synonymous with "I'm certain about." If belief is only a matter of certainty, a child discovering that Santa isn't "real" must think her family, friends, and even the television have all been making a fool of her. With this way of viewing belief, no wonder many adults don't want to "lie" to their children.

Having been fooled once about the chubby guy up north, we may, as adults, approach questions of God, angels, or miracles with considerable skepticism. "No, I am not spiritual, because I don't believe in God." When someone says this, perhaps all she really means is, "I'm not certain about God—I have my doubts and my questions."

Equating belief with a literal certainty that is beyond doubt seems to be a characteristic of the widespread skepticism of our age—the age, remember, of the profit- and technology-driven meta-culture. But when we understand clearly what belief means, we see that "believing in something" is different from "certainty about something's existence." According to the *Oxford English Dictionary*, belief involves "trusting to or confiding in a person or thing." Only its secondary definition involves the "acceptance of a proposition, statement, or fact, as true."

Even more interesting is the etymology of "belief." It stems from an Indo-European word, *lubh-*, which means "to hold dear" or "to like" (*COED*, 196). *Lubh-*, incidentally, is the same ancient root from which *love* originates. This connection between belief and love suggests that belief has something to do with being in relationship. To believe means to trust and to love. To believe in the Sacred means to love the Sacred—and to be the Sacred's beloved. To believe in God means to trust, depend on, and rely on God.

Belief is not a matter of certainty or lack of doubt. Belief is a matter of emotional openness. Belief grows out of such characteristics of spirituality as willingness and vulnerability. Here we see culture, cherishing, wonder, and Divine relationship linked together. To believe in the Sacred means to cultivate and cherish—out of the basic human capacity for wonder and openness—a loving relationship with God.

So the little girl who believes in Santa is a child who has been encouraged to love and trust in him. Sooner or later, her love and trust will undergo a crisis, as she is faced with making a transition from thinking about Santa literally to thinking about him metaphorically. When this happens, if her family can encourage her to see Santa as "the spirit of giving," then she may be able to integrate the experience of literalistic childhood believing into an adult capability to love and to trust. But if her family merely teases her about her gullibility, such an integration may not happen. If she thinks she's been fooled, her understanding of belief and her capacity to believe may be seriously damaged.

This integrating process can also occur in regard to the Sacred. As a child, I learned that "God" was an old man with a beard who lived above the clouds. Just as I had to shed the image of Santa as the jolly man up north, so I also had to shed my childhood notions of God. As I moved from childlike to adult models of belief, my understanding of God changed, going from that gendered, humanlike figure to the imageless way I now perceive the Sacred—as a vast, dynamic ground of being, powerful and loving, merciful and just, peaceful and passionate.

Belief and openness
People often understand "spirituality" in terms of openness and such related characteristics as willingness, vulnerability, and playfulness. When someone says, "I feel spiritual up in the mountains," perhaps he is trying

to say something like, "Being in the mountains causes me to feel open to deep wonder." In this sense, spirituality seems to mean little more than a special feeling or characteristic of consciousness. I like special feelings as much as the next person, but I believe spirituality involves much more than that. To understand spirituality in a larger way, we need to recognize the difference between belief and feelings like openness. We need to see how both belief and openness play important, if complementary, parts in the spiritual life.

Openness is a subjective characteristic of consciousness—an inner psychological quality. Openness by itself is an inner experience. A person can be "open-minded," for example, even without having anything to be open-minded about.

Belief, however, is a relational action. Belief involves the experience of being open *to something.* To say that a person is a "believer" implies that the person places his or her belief *in* something. Belief and feelings like openness are different because belief is more than just a feeling or a characteristic of consciousness. To believe means to offer our feelings of love and trust and wonder and openness to someone or something.

While some persons may narcissistically choose to believe in themselves and nothing other than themselves, for most people—especially those committed to the spiritual life—belief involves something or someone "other" than the self. Most traditions of spirituality encourage belief in the ultimate "other"—the Divine creator, the Sacred whom I call God.

Openness and belief complement each other the same way that "a gift" and "the act of giving" complement each other. Choosing to believe is choosing to invite the Sacred into our lives, to actually give all the facets of our lives to the Divine, just as earthly lovers give of their lives to each other. Our capacity for love, trust, openness, wonder, delight, awe, fear, and many other feelings and facets of life—these are all potential gifts we may give to our Divine lover.

Relating to the Sacred

The experience of otherness and of relationship is central to making sense of spirituality. As much as spirituality involves inner experiences of consciousness, it's primarily a matter of relationship with the Divine. Just as air is "other" than lungs but unites with the lungs to create breath, so the Sacred is "other" than a finite, mortal human being—but when God encounters me, we unite to create the experience of spirituality.

Relationships can be sources of deep anxiety. Because of our human tendency to want to control every aspect of life, we want to control relationships—we want them to be reliable and certain. We often try, consciously or subconsciously, to control a relationship by controlling our partner. Marriages typically go through power struggles in which each person tries to exercise control, even while resisting being controlled by the other. At worst, this takes the form of domestic violence or verbal abuse; even at its best, it can feel manipulative and constricting. Yet it is such a universal experience that even the healthiest of relationships will face it at one point or another.

What occurs with such universality in human relationships is also present in spirituality. Often, a person seeking a relationship with God may subconsciously want to control that relationship. Perhaps this is why we want "belief" to equal "certainty." At the very least, we insist that our certainty outweigh our doubt. We want God to be reliable—almost like a puppet.

But God is not a puppet. God is the ultimate Source of life and love. To believe in God does not entail controlling God. To believe means being open to the Sacred and trusting the Sacred—even though the fullness of the Divine is a mystery beyond the ability of our minds to imagine.

Even for a devout lover of the Sacred, doubt and uncertainty sometimes overwhelm faith. What sets the believer apart is that she sees her doubts and uncertainties not as obstacles but as opportunities for spiritual adventure. Just as my marriage is strengthened by all the many ways in which my wife and I remain mysterious to each other, so is a spiritual relationship, paradoxically, strengthened by the unknowability of the Sacred. To one who believes, Divine mysteriousness is not a problem, but indeed is part of the Sacred beauty. Part of what makes God so alluring is the very elusive mystery that may cause doubt or uncertainty.

Teachings

The secondary meaning of belief involves accepting something as true. This is still a matter of openness and trust. Saying "I believe you" to someone who offers a rather far-fetched reason for being late to a meeting is, in effect, synonymous with saying, "I'm trusting you to be telling the truth." In terms of spirituality, when we believe, we accept as true—we trust—teachings meant to foster or support our relationship with the Sacred.

Teachings are ideas and statements about the Sacred and about the spiritual life that a community affirms as true. Spiritual communities are defined, in part, by the teachings they espouse. Such teachings help people share with each other their experiences of the Sacred, their understanding of mystical truth, and their recognition of how God affects their lives. Teachings transmit spiritual knowledge from person to person and from generation to generation, just as education in any other field transmits knowledge and understanding from experts to beginners.

In terms of religion, teachings are often referred to as "doctrines" or "dogmas"—words that may sound harsh to some, thanks to the fact that various religious groups have been heavy-handed in the way they teach. Naturally, for a teaching to be worth anything, there must be some consensus in a community that it is true. However, the normal learning process includes questioning, doubting, and skepticism. Unfortunately, some religious communities resist normal questioning and doubting directed at their teachings. Again and again, when I am in dialogue with persons who have rejected religion, I hear stories of people who, as children, were not allowed to doubt or ask questions about teachings or doctrines. That seems to me to be a sure way to usher people out the door. Normal questioning and doubting are healthy, and any doctrine that is truly of the Sacred will stand up to rigorous scrutiny.

My insistence that belief is not about certainty is very important at this point. I think teachings are important in any spiritual tradition, yet I also believe that accepting any body of teachings is impossible without some reservations or doubts. Belief is not the suppression of doubt so much as it is a willingness to engage the teachings of a tradition, accepting what rings true and wrestling with doubts and questions.

External support

To believe means to expand our awareness of "spirituality" beyond the limitations of inner experience. To believe means to trust in the Sacred, to engage teachings about the Sacred, and to make choices, decisions, and actions aimed at linking the inner universe of our minds with the far larger outer universe that is the artwork of the Sacred. To believe means seeking a relationship with the Sacred both within the internal universe and throughout the external universe, since the Sacred exists not only within the internal realm of our souls but is also external to us—throughout the entire universe of planets, stars, and galaxies . . . and beyond. Within the wonders of our conscious minds we experience the inner aspects of spirituality, yet the Divine may be found in both internal *and* external ways. Belief is the link between the inner experience of spirituality and the internal-external reality of the Divine.

To believe means to offer the gifts of our inner self—our love, our openness, our capacity for wonder—to the Sacred. But to blossom, spirituality needs to be grounded in something more than just the dynamics of internal consciousness. Persons who believe are persons whose spirituality is larger than just an inner experience.

To nurture this larger spirituality requires more than just an experience of wonder or delight or serendipity. It requires support from outside of ourselves. This support can come in two primary ways—through *community* and, as we saw in chapter 2, through *culture*. Community involves other people who support us in our relationship with the Sacred. Culture includes the teachings of our community—but also tradition, practices, art, architecture, and any "thing" that helps us believe. We even rely on our cultural traditions and ideas to help us recognize the presence of the Sacred in the mountains or among the stars.

Culture and community support belief—they help a believer, a lover of the Sacred, remain open and trusting toward God over the course of time. Culture and community provide a structure and a shape to the abstract nature of belief.

Consider these examples:

- Believing in a teaching as simple as "There is no god but Allah, and Mohammed is his prophet" may help a Muslim remain conscious of the existence of the Sacred.
- Another teaching—that the Divine is immanent, present in all things—may help a Neopagan discern the presence of the Goddess in an ancient oak tree.
- The invigorating experience of a sweatlodge ceremony may help the follower of Lakota religion believe in the presence of the Great Spirit.
- As a member of "the Body of Christ," a Christian may find that the love and support of others reveals the presence of God.

Teachings, ceremonies, and church buildings are all forms of culture. The "body of Christ" is an example of community. Culture and community help a person develop beyond an ephemeral inner spirituality to a sustained internal/external relationship with the Divine. To make belief "matter," we need teachings, stories, images, rituals, and values to inspire us, and we need one another for sharing and support. Culture and community support belief. Culture and community support being open to and trusting in the Sacred.

These external aspects of spirituality function like doorways, portals we may go through with the likelihood of encountering God, even though we feel this encounter internally. Standing silently within a majestic cathedral, listening to a Bach fugue, communing with an ancient oak, or simply reading a book and letting our imagination soar—such experiences, as we have seen, can fill us with wonder and joy and a spacious sense of Divine radiance. As much as we may "locate" the spiritual experience internally (when I am filled with wonder, I experience the wonder *inside* me), we need to remember that the external doorways are also important parts of spirituality. The cathedral and the fugue and the oak tree and the book all invited me to the place of wonder and openness, and they all helped me find that place by somehow showing the way. These things all functioned as doorways, and in moving through them, I suddenly encountered the splendor of the Sacred.

At other times, the cathedral or the oak tree (or whatever) may *not* trigger the "spiritual feeling" of wonder or awe or a sense of God's presence. But this lack of spiritual feeling does not mean external objects are unreliable as doorways to the Sacred—instead, it means the Sacred cannot be controlled by human culture or nature. During those times when we cannot seem to find or feel God's presence, these externals function not as doorways, but as *symbols* of the Sacred. Instead of ushering us into the Sacred presence, they remind us of that presence—and so continue to play an important role in the support of belief. I may not feel God's immanence every time I see an oak tree or visit a cathedral, but every time I am *reminded* of my belief (my trust and love) in That-Which-Is-Beyond-All-Feeling. Regardless of how I feel, the symbols remind me of my relationship to the Sacred.

Taking the risk

Believing that air exists and that it keeps us alive is a very fine thing, but such a belief is worthless unless we put it in action by inhaling! Inhaling, however, is not possible unless first we exhale—a scary prospect, really, for exhaling means giving up the oxygen that keeps us alive. We cannot trust exhaling unless we trust that we will be able to keep inhaling. Similarly, we cannot fill ourselves with God's presence without emptying ourselves of our desire to be in control and to be self-protected. In other words, to encounter the Sacred, we must risk being vulnerable.

But we cannot take that risk without trusting—believing—that doing so is ultimately safe. The sacred teachings and stories of our culture can, by their meaningfulness and comforting familiarity, help us to feel safe. Likewise, the companionship and sharing of others can help us to feel safe when we consider the awe-inspiring reality of the Divine, larger and more powerful than the universe itself.

To believe means to take a risk on God. It is not something we do from "the sidelines." Like a nervous teenager asking someone out on a first date, we recognize that believing means we are being vulnerable before the Sacred, trusting that love and abundant life await us in return.

Belief is a choice

Since belief means being open to and trusting the Sacred, it also means making choices—choosing the teachings and ideas and practices and communities that lead us closer to God. Belief means choosing to love the Sacred, just as "going steady" means choosing to love one's high school sweetheart.

Spirituality is not about staying put; it's about moving toward the Sacred. I believe that God is everywhere—but even when all directions lead Home, a person can only walk in one direction at a time! Not only does belief involve the initial choice to move toward the Sacred, it also involves choosing which direction to take—which teachings to affirm, which community to join.

But this is a tricky matter. What's tricky is that the process of making choices can actually take us away from openness. Part of going steady is agreeing not to date anyone else. Similarly, when I say "yes" to believing in the Sacred, I am also saying "no" to other things. Maybe I'm saying "no" to drug abuse, or to depression, or to materialism. The problem is that my "yes's" and "no's" can create a dualistic way of viewing the world, leading me to be a *less open* person overall, since I'm no longer open to the parts of life I have said "no" to. If I'm not careful, eventually my saying "no" may dominate my life, and my openness toward the Sacred can be replaced by rigid, inflexible ways of seeing God and the world.

The basic characteristics of spiritual consciousness (wonder, playfulness, vulnerability, and so forth) are all open-ended, unstructured, unlimited ways of thinking and feeling and experiencing life. Belief, which involves applying these characteristics toward a specific end—

toward the Sacred—establishes a structure around the open-endedness of spiritual consciousness. Just as surely as openness involves letting go of limitations and embracing possibilities, belief involves making choices, setting boundaries, and choosing one particular path. Both are essential to spirituality—yet structured belief and open-ended consciousness exist in a *polarity*. They tug against each other and threaten to undo each other.

When I say "I find God in church," I am affirming a cultural object (a church) as a doorway to the Sacred. But I am also drawing a distinction, suggesting either that I *don't* find the Sacred at all in other places or at least I don't find God as well or as easily. The walls of the church can become a barrier in my spirituality, separating what is *holy* (close to God) from what is *profane* (far from God). This is not just a matter of "my way's the only way," either. Even a person who studies the teachings of many different religions may still have created inner boundaries that prohibit her from seeing the resplendent presence of the Divine in, say, a homeless shelter or a political rally.

Whenever we say "God is here," we run the risk of believing that "here" is the *only* place where God may be found. Even a casual glance at history will reveal the horrible implications of this tendency, as army after army has fought and killed on behalf of its particular way of believing.

I do not mean to suggest that it is wrong to have specific beliefs, nor am I suggesting that spirituality is somehow better than religion. Although I believe in spiritual truth that lies deeper than religious teachings, I also believe that the surest route to that truth involves believing in and practicing a specific path. A Buddhist needs to practice Buddhism with devotion, and a Christian needs to practice Christianity in a similar way. Believe in your own path! However, remain mindful of the subtle ways that believing can undermine openness. Don't let belief become such a big deal that it gets in the way of playfulness and wonder and vulnerability.

One way to balance belief and openness is by balancing the devotion to your specific spiritual tradition with respect and goodwill toward other paths. Learn about other paths—other systems of belief—and not just to prove to yourself that your path is the best. If you're a Christian, take a class on Islam. If your spirituality is New Age-oriented, read a book on Catholic liberation theology. If you practice Wicca, find out what feminist Jewish leaders are saying. Approach other traditions with humility and seek to learn humbly. In that humility, you may encounter the Sacred in a new and meaningful way, a way that will make your "home" path that much more rewarding.

The context of belief

No matter what path we choose in our journey toward the Source, we do not walk the path alone. Others go before us, others will follow us, and still others walk beside us. This is true whether we experience spirituality as part of a religious tradition or whether we are more inclined to "go it alone." Even loners occasionally share their path with other loners.

Community is important to spirituality because communities shape beliefs. This is true whether the community is highly organized and structured (like the Roman Catholic Church) or very loose and informal (like, say, the Rainbow Family). Whenever we are part of a community, we interact with that community's culture—its traditions, its teachings, its ceremonies and practices, its history and folklore, and its beliefs.

If I were born into Catholic family, I might grow up learning how to recite the Rosary while always attending Mass on Sundays. I'd learn to pray to St. Jude for all of my lost causes and I'd believe that sins ought to be confessed before I received Holy Communion. I'd be fond of St. Francis of Assisi and secretly scared of the Jesuits at my big brother's university. I'd be a great altar boy. I'd be a Catholic child, through and through.

But let's say that, after eighteen years of a Catholic childhood, I went off to college and started hanging out with the Rainbow Family. Suddenly I'd let my hair grow long and I'd start listening to music by performers like the Grateful Dead or Phish. I'd begin meditating and I'd move in with my girlfriend. I'd spend my summers on the road, traveling from one Rainbow gathering to another, where I'd eat vegetarian food, dance in ecstatic drum circles all night long, and start practicing a healing technique called Reiki. After two years, I'd drop out of college and move to an intentional community in Tennessee. By now, my family would think I'd lost my mind.

In this scenario, I really haven't lost my mind, but I *have* made a significant life change, shifting from one community to a radically different new one and experiencing simultaneously a major shift in culture and beliefs. Though the Catholic church is centralized and highly structured, with a strong core set of teachings, and the Rainbow Family is loosely knit, decentralized, and almost chaotic, both communities are alike in that each has its distinct culture, its distinct style of spirituality, and its distinct teachings. Our communities shape our beliefs.

Even a loner who wouldn't be caught dead in a church *or* at a Rainbow gathering will have her beliefs shaped by her "community"—the books she reads, the radio shows she listens to, the people she admires. Unless a person is an absolute hermit who never reads or listens to the radio or watches TV, he will have some form of communal interaction with others—and therefore will experience his beliefs getting shaped and supported in some way.

Culture, community, belief

I began this chapter by suggesting that belief—lovingly trusting in the Sacred—is the link that holds the disparate elements of the spiritual life together. It's the structure that spirituality requires in order to be something more than just a collection of neat feelings. The inner experiences of wonder and openness, and the outer experience of a mysterious and beautiful and awe-inspiring world, come together in a meaningful way when we believe.

Yet just as belief is essential to a sustained, meaningful spirituality, so are culture and community essential to belief. To make this choice for God, we rely on the symbolism of sacred culture and the support of a faith community. In the next chapter, we'll take a closer look at what I call "icons"—aspects of culture that directly support belief. I'm going to save an in-depth discussion of community until later, even though community's role in spirituality will appear again and again. Just as spirituality means relating with God, so community means relating with other people. These two kinds of relationship are not easily separated—nor should they be.

5

Icons

I love Eastern Orthodox churches. I live just a few blocks from the Greek Orthodox Cathedral of the Annunciation in Atlanta, one of the most beautiful places of worship I've ever seen. The nave of this cathedral consists of a large and spacious room beneath a huge dome supported by thick concrete pillars. In the dome itself and on all the walls are huge mosaics depicting events in the life of Christ and the Virgin Mary. The images are colorful, bold, and striking. They conform to the ancient symbolism associated with sacred paintings in the Orthodox tradition, and yet they are fresh and contemporary in their design. For me, these arresting images are luminous portals to the presence of the Sacred, as spiritually significant as any awe-inspiring place in nature. These mosaics, of course, are *icons*—sacred images venerated by the Orthodox tradition as windows onto the sacred truths and mysteries of the Christian faith.

"Click here"

Ask the average person to define an icon and the answer you will most likely receive is "a symbol on a computer screen." Like "mouse" and "memory," the word "icon" has taken on a new meaning thanks to the personal computer. But while the original meanings of those other words are well-known, the original meaning of "icon" is less likely to be known —unless a person happens to be familiar with Eastern Orthodoxy. In our meta-culture, the idea of the holy icon has become eclipsed by the icon-as-computer-symbol, just as belief in God has become eclipsed by reliance on profit and technology.

71

Computer icons, however, serve remarkably well as a starting point for discussing the role of icons in spirituality. When a person selects (or "clicks on") an icon on her computer, it usually initiates something—it starts a program, opens a file, launches a series of commands, or brings up a document. The icon is merely a symbol of something larger. The computer user moves "through" the icon to reach the place or process the icon represents.

Such also is the case with sacred icons. Icons, as signs and symbols of spirituality, represent the Divine to us, in the same way a computer icon represents something on the hard drive. Any symbol or image that invites us into the Divine presence functions as an icon of spirituality.

We've looked at how belief is supported by community (people) and culture (sacred places, teachings, and things). Icons, understood in a broad and general way, contribute to the spiritual life as much as believing does. To believe is to open ourselves up to the Sacred. Icons are the means by which the Sacred is revealed to us.

The word *icon*, or *ikon*, comes from the Greek *eikos*, which means "a likeness" or "an image." In its original meaning, an icon was an image of Jesus, Mary, the saints, or angels venerated by Orthodox Christians as a "window unto heaven"—a way for a person to glimpse a reality beyond all the limits of the physical universe. Icons are central to Eastern Orthodox spirituality. Found not only in churches but also in the homes of the faithful, icons are venerated as supremely valuable tools for prayer. Candles are lit and incense is burned before them, and faithful persons gaze upon them to enter into a meditative state of communion with the Sacred. Despite all this devotion, however, icons are not in themselves worshiped. The painting is merely a painting and the materials used are but earthly materials, though the faithful person who prays before icons understands that her devotion is being offered to the One whom the icon represents.

Obviously, in the Orthodox tradition the word "icon" refers to a specific kind of cultural object. For our purposes, we may use the word in a broader sense. In this sense, an icon is *any* object, any work of culture, or even any person or aspect of nature through which a spiritual seeker may be able to find the Sacred—or through which God manages to find us. Not only paintings, but also architecture, music, and other forms of art; language, literature, and teachings; and ceremonies, rituals, and other practices—these are among the many potential icons that can support the spiritual life. Anything can be an icon, because anything can represent the

Sacred. God is present in the universe, so anything in our world may reveal the Divine presence. Yet God is also transcendent, far larger and greater than the limits of space and time. Therefore, any icon that truly reveals the Sacred to us will do so by pointing beyond itself to the Great Mystery.

Locating the One without location

Spirituality involves longing for the Sacred, longing for an encounter with the presence of God. This Sacred presence, the One who is both everywhere and beyond the universe, simply cannot be physically seen, touched, or heard. This is why the cultural aspect of spirituality, from the teachings that inspire belief to the icons that inspire prayer, are so important. The relationship between human and Divine usually requires some form of cultural context, like teachings or images or acts of worship, that enable the spiritual seeker to orient her mind and heart toward God. Icons are such forms of culture and thus play an important, if fallible, role in revealing the Sacred presence.

Where is God? God is beyond the farthest limits of the universe and deep within the uncharted wilderness of inner space, within the soul. The Sacred is everywhere—and, being everywhere, therefore has no location. How can we locate the One beyond location?

Some of the great religious leaders, like Abraham, Mohammed, and Buddha, found the Divine only by going on long journeys or spending time in the wilderness. Finding the Sacred, for them, meant leaving behind the safety and security of home and striking out into unknown territory. The mythic stories of these great spiritual leaders remind us of our need to abandon the safety of our survival-mind and plumb the depths of the Holy. To find the Sacred, perhaps we too must journey through unfamiliar territory, even if it is only the "wilderness within."

To travel safely in unknown places, we need a map to help us find our way. A good map will inform us of landmarks along the path we are following—landmarks that assure us we are on the correct path. The teachings and doctrines we believe are like a "map," and icons—sacred objects—are like the "landmarks" we find along our way.

Types of icons

Among different spiritual traditions, a variety of objects serve as windows into Divine reality. Tribal or pagan religions find the Sacred through fetishes and totems, and Neopagan religions today look to the earth as an icon for the Divine. The Abrahamic religions of Judaism, Christianity, and Islam share a basic orientation toward the use of a sacred text—the Hebrew Scriptures, the New Testament, the Qu'ran—to reveal God. Both Hinduism and Buddhism rely on the mandala as an image for meditation and the revelation of spiritual truth. Depending on her tradition, a person may find access to the Sacred through a yarmulke, the Bhagavad-Gita, or the sacred pipe. Incense at a Catholic mass or a resounding gong in a Buddhist zendo may serve as an icon. Icons figure prominently throughout the spiritual traditions of the world.

I can identify at least seven types or categories of icons. I'm sure there are other kinds, as well.

1. *Paintings or images.* Icons in their strictest sense are images used in the Orthodox tradition. But sacred art is a universal form of culture. From the earliest cave paintings to today's computer-generated fractal designs, images have a universal capacity to fill us with wonder—and to speak, implicitly or explicitly, to the nature and love of the Divine. I find particular beauty in the illustrated manuscripts of ancient Celtic monks. Manuscripts like *The Book of Kells* or *The Lindisfarne Gospels* combine Biblical texts with ornate and striking illustrations. Lavishly illustrated pages filled with charming (and sometimes scary) drawings of wild beasts, along with flowing lines and circles and intricate knot-work patterns, present the sacred words of the Christian tradition with images that point to the Divine in ways that are every bit as powerful as the text. Works of art become icons for us when we see in them evidence of God's presence, as well as evidence of Sacred truth, beauty, goodness, and mystery.

2. *Architecture, music, and other forms of art.* We've already talked about how a cathedral or a Bach fugue is designed to foster awe. Truly, any product of human creativity testifies to the reality of the ultimate creative Source. Works of art may not, however, be intended as icons. Many people find the music of the Grateful Dead to be spiritually luminous, although the band itself never claimed to be transmitting spiritual truth in their work. By contrast, the British composer John Tavener creates works of stunning beauty explicitly meant to testify to the divine presence. One of his finest compositions is called *Ikon of Light*, in which the shimmering voices of the performing chorus combine to create an aural window onto the Sacred. This is a broad category, for culture that ranges from the stone circles of pre-Celtic Britain to the technical mysticism of spiritually centered World Wide Web sites can serve as icons.

3. *Language, words, texts, teachings.* Obviously, the sacred texts of the world's religions—the Bible, the Qu'ran, the Vedas, the Sutras—function as icons. But oral tradition, storytelling, sermons and speeches, scholarly works of theology, and the writings of the great mystics throughout history can also reveal luminous evidence of the Holy. More than just "religious" words may qualify as icons, for even secular works like novels or poetry can testify to the Sacred. The lyrics of songs, a letter from a loved one, or a provocative newspaper article revealing injustice and calling for its redress all may function as icons—and as much so as the most powerful of "spiritual" words. In this category, words themselves weave together to beckon the reader or listener to a place where the encounter with God may occur.

4. *Ceremonies, rituals, practices.* Given its teachings about the real presence of Christ, the Catholic practice of Holy Communion may be the most obvious example of this kind of icon—in receiving the bread and wine, a faithful person opens himself up to the sudden inrushing of a spiritual presence that invades the ordinary rhythms of life. Going to church or synagogue, meditating, attending a workshop on learning how to pray, distributing sandwiches to the homeless, taking paper and glass to the recycling center—these practices, whether explicitly "spiritual" or not, are examples of kinetic activities that can, in themselves, suddenly surprise us by revealing the Divine presence.

5. *Nature.* The serenity of an oak grove or the majesty of the mountains, the fury of a tornado or the vastness of the heavens, the wonder of watching puppies being born or the dread of watching a snake kill and devour its prey—these are only a few of the limitless ways that nature can reveal to the perceptive eye a reality of love and power and mystery that is actually *beyond* nature.

6. *People.* Once again, here are obvious and not-so-obvious icons. The obvious ones are the saints and spiritual "celebrities"—from Jesus and Buddha and Mohammed to Martin Luther King, Jr., Mother Teresa, and Gandhi. Such persons are celebrities precisely because their lives—or the stories told about their lives—sparkle with evidence of the Divine presence. But less celebrated persons can also reveal the Sacred to us—our family members, our closest friends, and even (or perhaps especially) the homeless person we talk to on our way home from the office. And the ancient Celts believed in the importance of an *anamchara*, or "soul friend" —a person with whom one shared prayer and the deepest stirrings of one's

spiritual journey. In such an intimate friendship, the relationship itself can become an icon for the ultimate friendship, the friendship with God.

7. *Your very own self.* Yes, you yourself can function as an icon, not only to others, but even to yourself as well. I once heard a story about an Orthodox tradition that angels go before every human being, announcing to the universe, "Make way for the Image of God!" Then there's the Quaker doctrine of the Inner Light. Each one of us in body and soul is the manifestation—or at least the potential manifestation—of the image and likeness of the Divine. Each and every one of us is a child of the Sacred and a potential lover of the Sacred. We are called to be united with the Sacred and, in that mystical union, to reveal the love and truth and beauty and goodness of the Holy One, not only to ourselves but also to a world that desperately needs such love. You, yourself, are (or can be) an icon of the Most High.

Undoubtedly, even more kinds of icons exist. Just as there are no limits to the nature and the presence of the Sacred, so are there no limits to what may be chosen to reveal the Sacred's love and care and presence in our lives. Indeed, the only limitation may be our unwillingness to see the splendor of the Sacred when it is revealed to us.

No perfect icons

With all these many different kinds of icons in the world, how come we are not every one of us simply glowing with the radiant presence of the Divine?

The answer to that question is, unfortunately, that no icon is perfect or infallible. No icon is guaranteed to open us up to the Divine presence; nor can any icon help out all people at all times. Different people who follow the same spiritual tradition may not encounter the Sacred in the same icon or in the same way. For that matter, a person may find that something is an icon at one point in her journey, but later on discover that it no longer reveals the Divine to her. As she grows and changes, her relationship with the Sacred grows and changes—which means that she needs different "landmarks" to find her way. Icons carry no guarantee. In fact, to the extent that we try to make an icon a "guaranteed" window to God, we risk turning the icon into an idol.

All this may be worrisome to those who yearn for infallibility and certitude in their quest for a relationship with the Divine. Throughout history, many icons have been treated as absolute bridges to God. For example, the Bible, the Pope, and "Mother Nature" have all been regarded by various people in various times as perfect, foolproof manifestations of the Sacred presence. Looking for a perfectly reliable window to God, however, may be an attempt to replace belief with certainty. Who needs a map when we have a landmark that will magically transport us to our destination? Unfortunately, this is an attempt to replace the consciousness of wonder with the consciousness of control.

God cannot be perfectly contained in any object or created thing. To me, considering that no artifact, no text, and no person can contain the fullness of the Divine is actually comforting. God is simply too big to be reduced to words in a book or to an image. Rather than seeking the Divine presence in a certain (and therefore controllable) manner, we have the possibility of allowing God to touch us anywhere, at any time, in any way —as God wills.

Icons support the spiritual quest but no icon can guarantee the coming of the Divine presence. Still, icons are important to the spiritual life in two ways: they remind us of how the Sacred has been encountered in the past, and they offer the hope of a glimpse of God now or in the future. Such glimpses are not something we can engineer by the force of our own will, though. Encountering God directly is something that may happen only by grace—not something we can force, but something we can long for and allow.

Idols, the shadow side of icons

In the previous section, I commented about the danger of turning icons into idols—a danger that is present whenever we decide that an icon is a perfect, unquestionable portal onto the Sacred. Thus, it seems appropriate to take a closer look at what constitutes an idol. Just as I'm using the word "icon" in a broader sense than that of an Eastern Orthodox holy painting, so also do I think that idols are far more than just lifeless statues of gods and goddesses. Just as anything that ushers us into the presence of the Divine is an icon, so also is anything that diverts us from loving the Sacred an idol. Idols are truly the "shadow side" of icons, and just as almost anything can be an icon, so also just about anything can be an idol.

Idolatry is simply belief gone awry—belief misplaced, offered to someone or something that does not deserve to be believed in. An item does not need to be explicitly religious or "spiritual" in order to be an idol; indeed, probably the most notorious idol of all is money. People of all income levels, of all cultural and religious backgrounds, are susceptible to idolizing money—trusting in financial security or in "owning things" as a source for meaning and happiness in life. Naturally, an income and a lifestyle commensurate with one's perceived needs are usually regarded as good things (although much disagreement would exist over what really are "needs"). Nevertheless, excessive reliance on money as a provider of happiness and meaning is a dead end. No matter how much we "believe in" money, our finances alone cannot protect us from—or provide meaning in the face of—disease, tragedy, and death. Putting faith in money is idolatry; that is, belief placed in something not worthy of being believed in. Tragically, many people never put their faith in anything else —even people who purport to be "spiritual" or religious.

All sorts of things can function as idols—not only money and material things like houses and cars, but also intangibles like power, fame, beauty, the approval of others, and sex. We can idolize certain persons (especially celebrities or family members), countries ("my country, right or wrong"), public offices (like the presidency), and institutions (the government, the corporation, or the church).

Perhaps the most insidious idols are religious objects, since such objects are intended to function as icons. The Bible and Holy Communion are prime examples of religious objects that are too easily and too often venerated in an idolatrous way—in other words, people place their trust in the Bible or in Communion, looking for certainty in a controllable object rather than for relationship with God, who is beyond our control. Whenever we place excessive belief or hope in something, especially to the point of its coming between us and the love of the Divine, we have succumbed to idolatry.

Most of us are idolatrous on some level, placing inordinate belief in technology, government, business, entertainment, the media, science, pleasure-seeking, or religion. This tendency toward idolatry may sound like bad news, but I think it is actually a hidden form of good news. The prevalence of idolatry shows just how spiritual we human beings are. We are idolatrous because we are, by nature, creatures who believe. Idolatry reveals that our most pressing spiritual issue is not *whether* we believe, but rather *what* we choose to place our belief in.

The cure for idolatry is not so much to stop believing in a particular idol as it is to start (or resume) believing in the Divine. The problem, of course, is that belief in a mysterious, transcendent God seems so outside of our control, while belief in an "idol"—whatever it may be—has at least the illusion of certainty about it. Loving the Sacred means, on some levels, loving the unknown. Settling for a tangible idol feels safer, at least at first.

Eventually, however, idolatry lets us down—the object of our worship fails us sooner or later. Still, making the leap into the unknown that spirituality requires is difficult, so the ersatz security of idolatry will continue to appeal.

Idols, like icons, are culturally relative. Often, one religious tradition will even claim that the icons of another tradition are idols. Eastern Orthodox Christians venerate Holy Icons, but many Protestant Christians may consider the veneration of those same paintings to be idolatrous. Neopagans revere the oak tree as an icon manifesting the Divine, while others (such as Christians) would consider such nature worship idolatrous. The Neopagan, however, might think the Christian has a problem with idolizing a mere book—the Bible. While thinking that idolatry is always "the other guy's problem" may be tempting, each of us—and each tradition—is susceptible to worshiping something that distracts us from encountering the Sacred. Rather than worry about other people's idols, we better serve our devotion to the Sacred by trying to identify and let go of our own.

Finally, we need to consider the spiritual implication of "smashing idols"—destroying anything that is falsely worshiped. To smash an idol is a way of returning to belief in the Sacred, a way of demonstrating one's preference for God over the idol or idols. Destroying an idol need not be a dramatic event. It's as momentous as an alcoholic's becoming sober or as simple as a person who needs to lose a few pounds passing over a lunchtime candy bar. Smashing an idol is an act of love, an act of "giving up" that is also a "giving to." It's a form of sacrifice—a misunderstood concept that we'll consider at length in chapter 11. To smash an idol means to affirm the boundaries that are part of believing. When I affirm that my belief in the Divine takes priority over excessive reliance on something like material goods or control, I am not only giving up my idol, but I am also choosing faithfulness—faithfulness to the God in whom I believe.

From idols to icons

To let go of our idols, we need to choose to believe in the Sacred. Our best hope for letting go of our idols involves seeking the Divine presence through whatever icons speak to us. If I am a materialistic person addicted to money, I may find that by volunteering for an agency that provides social services to persons with AIDS, I discover the Sacred in the eyes of some of the most feared members of society. In that discovery I may learn to rely less on my own resources and more on the generous love of the Divine for meaning in my life. Of course, once again there is no guarantee —I could be so scared by the pain and fear I encounter that I would just retreat farther into my self-protective shell than I was before. The liberating grace of the Sacred cannot be second-guessed; the dynamics of spirituality involve an intricate dance between the will of the Divine and the vagaries of human nature.

We cannot force a sacred painting or the Bible or any other thing to magically reveal God to us on cue. We can, however, approach the icons through which we hope to encounter God in a spirit of openness, willingness, and trust. Then, when we open ourselves to the Sacred, we are most likely to let go of the idols that control our lives.

Icons and community

How does something become an icon? How do we know that something may reveal the presence of the Sacred to us? The answer to these questions is found in community. Just as community shapes the nature of our beliefs, so also a community will determine what is or is not an icon, at least for members of that community.

Just because something is an icon in one community does not make it so for others. For Muslims, the icons of the Eastern Orthodox tradition have no spiritual significance. A Buddhist may find no significance in a yarmulke. Something becomes an icon not because of any inherent or intrinsic quality, but because of external factors, usually arising from the beliefs or culture of a given community or group. As we've already noted, the original icons were a cultural expression of a specific community—the Orthodox branch of Christianity.

The most powerful icons are deeply respected and venerated by a community of some sort. The Bible, the sacred book of Christianity, is arguably the single most powerful icon in the world (which is why it is also so horribly idolized). The Bible functions as an icon in the lives of scholars and theologians who study it, in the lives of ordinary Christians who read it, and even in the lives of those who *don't* read it but think they *should*. Why is the Bible such a powerful icon? Because of its place in the Christian community. For thousands of years now, the Bible has been regarded as an authoritative statement of the word of God.

When a community finds that a sacred object reveals God, the item becomes an icon *for that community*. Even widely revered windows onto the Sacred (such as the Bible or nature) function as icons only among a certain community of believers—in other words, only among those persons who have the "map" necessary to recognize those "landmarks." With the "map" of believing, I can see that particular "landmarks" (such as sacred texts or holy objects) are leading me to my goal—to the Sacred. And as we saw in the previous chapter, we all rely on community in some form or another to create that "map" of our beliefs. To encounter the Sacred, we need the support of community.

I pray the icon, the icon prays me

Whether it is as elaborate as a gorgeous painting of Christ and the saints or as simple as a single lit candle, anything that functions as an icon does so by inviting me into the presence of the Holy One. I find Orthodox icons to be especially useful in prayer and meditation because they are images—paintings of Christ and Mary, of saints and mystics, of angels and apostles. They are images of persons, and in gazing at them, I am reminded that the Sacred is more than just an abstract principle—the Source of love is the One who loves. I gaze at an icon to pray, and yet in the prayer sometimes the Sacred seems to be the one doing the gazing and I am the one being gazed at! Once again, such an encounter with an icon reminds me that spirituality is about relationship.

Icons are landmarks on the map of belief and they are also doorways onto the Sacred. To enter such a doorway involves making a conscious effort to be close to the Divine. This "conscious effort," which may take many forms, is the basis of *prayer*. Thus, prayer is the subject to which we now turn.

6

Prayer

The shelves of bookstores and libraries sag because of all the books about men, women, and relationships. Young or old, married or single, gay or straight, everyone, it seems, longs for a meaningful, enjoyable, and healthy relationship.

The wisest self-help books typically encourage people to begin their quest for a more fulfilling love life by developing basic communication skills. Listening and self-disclosure, we are told, are essential for a successful marriage—or, indeed, for any successful relationship. These same skills, not surprisingly, play a crucial role in spirituality, where the relationship in question is not among men and women but between human beings and the Divine. To relate with the Sacred means communicating— and that means praying.

Just as our beliefs encourage us to be open to God, so in prayer we nurture that openness by listening for the still, small voice of the Sacred and by disclosing our innermost selves to God. Belief is the choice to form a relationship with the Divine; prayer is the means by which such a relationship is nurtured.

When we talk about spirituality, often we refer to ourselves—human beings—as the "subjects" and God as the "object" of the relationship: "I believe in God" or "I feel awe and wonder when I sense God's presence in nature." These and other statements make me the active agent in the spiritual life and God merely the object of my experience. In prayer, however, this dynamic begins to shift, and we become open to a different way of seeing this relationship. In the life of prayer, God is just as often the subject and human beings (both individually and collectively) the objects—the objects of God's love and care. "God loves me," "God reaches out to me," "God longs for me"—these are some of the dynamics we begin to encounter in the life of prayer, where spirituality becomes less something we *do* and more something we *participate in* mutually and reciprocally with the Sacred.

Forms of prayer

In the cyberpunk movie *Tank Girl*, the world of the mid-twenty-first century is gripped by pervasive drought and civil war. Violent factions vie for the ability to control the scarce supply of water. In the midst of this nightmare world, the Australian outlaw heroines, Tank Girl and Jet Girl, team up with the "Rippers"—a rebel band of genetic mutants who are half human and half kangaroo. In one surprising scene, Tank and Jet sit down to eat dinner with the Rippers, only to be dismayed when one of the Rippers says, "Let us pray." Praying is about the last thing that a couple of punks like Tank Girl and Jet Girl want to do, but, desiring not to offend their hosts, they close their eyes and put their hands together in the best display of imitation piety they can muster. Then as they open their eyes, they discover that the Rippers pray not by bowing their heads and reciting memorized words but by dancing playfully in a circle!

Tank Girl and Jet Girl saw prayer in a very limited way. This can also be so for those of us who grew up practicing a traditional religion, for whom prayer may seem to be a dry and lifeless practice—something one does out of duty or habit, not out of joy or delight. Because prayer is a spiritual activity where form and substance can easily be confused, one can easily think that only certain methods of praying (such as bowing one's head with eyes closed and hands clasped together) represent "what prayer is." But this one-dimensional view does not recognize that, beneath the form, prayer really consists of a deep and fundamental internal experience—the experience of fostering a relationship with the Divine. While the *form* prayer takes is certainly important, the *substance* is what really matters—regardless of the form. Tank Girl and Jet Girl were surprised by the Rippers' circle dance because they did not realize that different methods and forms can all lead to the same goal—the goal of communicating with the Sacred. Consider each of these:

*   A Zen monk sits in almost utter stillness, his body erect, his breath regulated according to strict techniques of meditation, as he intention-

ally ignores not only all sensation but even all thought, until a bell rings to signify the end of the sitting time;

- A Pentecostal minister raises her hand in praise, singing and praying passionately and emotionally, tears streaming down her face as she fervently expresses her love for the Lord and her desire to submit her life totally to the will of the Holy Spirit;
- A Wiccan High Priestess sweeps a circle in the ground with a sacred broom and invokes the powers of east, south, west, and north; then she invokes the name of the God and the Goddess and announces to her companions that they are now "in a world between the worlds";
- A dozen Episcopalian and Methodist lay adults sit in a quiet room, gazing at an Orthodox icon as a candle flickers beneath it. The group begins their contemplation by chanting, "Lord Jesus Christ, Son of God, have mercy on me," until eventually silence overtakes the group;
- Seven Native Americans crawl into a tiny sweatlodge that is covered with buffalo skins and is utterly dark within. They chant *mitakuye owasin* as one red-hot stone after another is placed into a pit in the middle of the lodge; finally, the door is closed and the leader of the lodge begins chanting and pouring water over the rocks. Steam, heat, chanting, and drumming fill the darkness.

Praying or invoking, meditating or contemplating, chanting or speaking in tongues—such practices explore various ways of communicating with or seeking communication from the Sacred. Praying may involve words and thoughts, as in "saying" one's prayers; it may involve the wordless silence of a Zen monk or of a Christian gazing at an icon. Praying can also be a full-bodied experience, as it is understood by participants in a sweatlodge—or, for that matter, by the circle-dancing Rippers! Different forms of prayer makes sense only in their appropriate religious or cultural contexts: the Zen monk and the Pentecostal minister would probably not find exchanging places to be conducive to prayer—unless they were actively involved in interfaith dialogue. For most of us, praying is something that best occurs in a familiar and safe setting, one that is at least somewhat related to our own spiritual culture and experience.

In this chapter, we'll consider several general characteristics of the life of prayer, and then we'll look at two particular kinds of prayer—contemplative prayer (a prayer of silence) and conversational prayer (a prayer involving words). Many other ways of praying exist, such as speaking in tongues, chanting a sacred text, or reading a holy book slowly and thoughtfully. Looking at all the possible ways to pray would fill up many books. Although I'm limiting the present discussion to two forms of praying, I want to emphasize the importance of openness to the various different forms. If one method doesn't work for you, then please trust your instincts and pray in a way that works. You may be like a Ripper and pray best while you dance—or you may prefer bowing your head and reciting a familiar, set prayer. Whatever works for you, that's the way you need to pray. I personally find that writing down my thoughts is an excellent doorway into prayer (that's one reason I'm writing this book—it's an act of prayer for me). Being open to different ways of communicating with, or listening for, the Divine is important for a creative and healthy life of prayer.

Before going any further, I want to take a stand for making prayer a priority. To nurture a fulfilling spiritual life, I believe we need to spend some time *every day* in prayer. Spirituality is like marriage, which requires daily communication in order to be happy and healthy. The same requirement exists for the spiritual life, which calls for a daily discipline of opening the mind and heart to the Sacred in order for meaningful growth to occur. Yet even more so than regular communication in marriage, praying every day can seem daunting—or dull. To pray daily requires discipline—but even a person highly disciplined in every other way may find that a discipline of prayer eludes her grasp. It also requires a willingness to experiment, to find ways to keep prayer fresh and exciting —even, dare I say, to keep prayer fun.

Yearning for prayer, resistance to prayer

We both seek and resist the experience of prayer. We want to be close to God, and we also find that we often "don't have time to pray." We yearn to expand our openness and vulnerability to the Sacred, and frequently we are also content when God seems remote and distant. Recognizing this ambivalence, religious traditions teach us that prayer requires discipline, commitment, and intentionality.

Historically, many people interested in deeply committed, disciplined prayer lived in monasteries, communities designed to support such demanding levels of commitment. Today, however, most of us live "in the world"—that is, our lives are centered on family and/or career—meaning that we lack the stability of a monastic routine. For us, a successful life of prayer requires a firm, conscious commitment to regular practice, and it depends upon giving prayer a high priority. Yet all too often, our desire to pray is not equaled by the time and energy we give to the actual practice of prayer. We yearn for prayer, yet we resist actually doing it.

In the previous section, I said that prayer requires discipline, along with a willingness to experiment to keep it interesting and, we hope, fun. Let's take these one at a time. "Discipline" may seem to be the exact opposite of "interesting" and "fun." Indeed, the discipline of prayer is like that of doing the laundry or washing the dishes, domestic chores that are not one-time tasks but rather are daily obligations.

Many of us who would be horrified at the thought of letting the dishes go unwashed for an entire week find that we avoid praying daily for one reason or another, such as "It shouldn't feel like a meaningless obligation" or "I just don't have the time." A messy housekeeper waits until the level of dirty laundry and unwashed dishes reaches crisis proportions before cleaning up. Many of us seem content to approach prayer in a similar way, waiting until we are in some sort of crisis—an illness, a divorce, the death or impending death of a loved one—before making the effort to pray.

How do we learn to pray with the same steady discipline we bring to our laundry or dirty toilets? In the same way a teenager learns how to do chores—simply by doing them, and with the less fuss, the better. We know there's no magic trick to managing the mundane world of housecleaning. Unwashed windows or dusty furniture will wait patiently through our procrastination until we finally surrender our dislike for the job and simply *do* what needs to be done. God is infinitely more patient than our unfinished chores. The Divine will wait for our return to prayer no matter how long we procrastinate. God doesn't stop loving us if we do not pray; but when we avoid prayer, we miss out on the opportunity to know the Sacred more fully.

I suppose by now it's obvious that I'm not somebody who loves to do housework! But I find housework to be less of a chore when I make it fun. When I clean the house, I like to listen to upbeat music. My wife, who is more of a social person than I am, enjoys cleaning with company—not only with me, but also with her mother or even a good friend. Another way my wife and I link housework with fun is to plan a cleaning day so it ends with a treat—say, a nice dinner and a concert together, just the two of us. The moral of the story is that discipline does not have to be dull—a truth that bears on the life of prayer as well.

Prayer can be made interesting or even fun in similar ways. Prayer can come alive simply by your linking it with a rich cultural or sensual experience—listening to Gregorian or Tantric chanting, taking a long walk in the forest, or spending a quiet morning at a majestic cathedral. In many ways prayer is a solitary experience, and sometimes it needs to happen in solitude—but there's also a place for sharing prayer with a spiritual companion or a "soul friend" (*anamchara*). And linking prayer with a treat makes perfect sense—sharing an ice cream cone with God is a lovely way to pray—unless, of course, you're on a diet.

Prayer requires discipline in order to become a daily part of life, and creativity and playfulness to make it fun rather than dull. By remembering that there are countless ways to invite the Sacred into our lives, we are able to look for—and create—ways of praying that are fun and interesting.

As we immerse ourselves in the discipline and creativity we need to make prayer meaningful and rewarding, we can nurture prayer by cultivating two important qualities in our life—silence and solitude. These are both internal and external qualities. We can find *external* places of silence and solitude (like the forest or the cathedral) in which to pray, but even more important is the cultivation of *interior* silence and solitude, in our own hearts and minds. These inner qualities are crucial for prayer, for in silence and solitude we may more easily move through our inner resistance—and simply be present with the Divine.

Silence

Look up *silent* or *silence* in a dictionary and you will notice that they are, for the most part, defined negatively. For example, in the *Merriam-Webster's Collegiate Dictionary*, the noun "silence" is defined in terms of forbearance (from speech) or absence (of sound). As a verb, it is linked with limitation and control ("to silence" means to compel the state of silence or to restrain expression). Likewise, the adjective "silent" is understood primarily in terms of the absence of sound—"making no utterance," "making no mention," or "making no protest" all are cited as definitions.

The tradition of the Hebrew scriptures presents silence in a much more positive light, however. "For God alone my soul waits in silence; from him comes my salvation," speaks forth the voice of a seeker in Psalm 62. In Isaiah 30, the voice of the Divine declares, "In quietness and in trust shall be your strength." These powerful statements imply that silence aids the spiritual quest. Consider also these words of the Sacred from Psalm 46 about stillness, a quality not unlike silence: "Be still, and know that I am God." Silence (and stillness) opens up our hearts and souls to places where we can wait for the Sacred, trust in Divine love, and even know the presence of God.

Silence, far from being just the negative state implied by the dictionary, is actually the natural environment of persons who wish to encounter and to be encountered by the Divine. Within every mind, beneath the thinking and feeling that ordinary consciousness entails, exists the inner silence that reveals the presence of God. Cultivating this internal silence is an essential part of establishing a regular, disciplined life of prayer. Praying in the context of external silence—in a quiet cathedral or in the stillness of early morning—is helpful because the external silence can help us to seek, and find, our internal silence. (Of course, just as God is both immanent and transcendent, both outside us and inside us, the Divine may be found in the external silence, too—although the inner silence is what creates the environment in which we are most receptive to a profound sense of the Sacred.)

We've noted that prayer can take many forms, and external silence is not always necessary for prayer—as a visit to an exuberant Pentecostal revival or charismatic prayer-and-praise meeting can attest. Yet even the loudest, most fervent ways of praying have some sort of connection to the still place where God is known. From the serene quiet of a meditating monk to the raucous "alleluias!" of a spirit-filled Holy Roller, every form of prayer has some link to silence—and not only the silence within. When charismatics pray in tongues, sweatlodge participants chant to a drumbeat, or monks recite Psalms, a point eventually comes when the voices die away and, even if only for a moment, silence reigns. The spirituality of prayer involves, consciously or not, the recognition that all words, all music, indeed all noise and sound, occur against a backdrop of what monks call "the greater silence." The greater silence—the silence that is deeper than any sound that exists—is the limitless, uncreated silence of the Sacred. The silence within each individual soul—the interior silence, where we may encounter the Divine inside ourselves—exists as a microcosm of that "greater silence."

Silence and apophatic spirituality

I began the previous section by complaining about how silence is defined in negative terms. However, in all fairness to the editors of dictionaries, I must add that silence really *does* involve the "negative" quality of the absence of sound. I come back to this point because, having made a positive statement about silence, now I want to explore the importance of negativity and absence in the life of prayer.

Over the centuries, many saints, mystics, and other experts at prayer have stressed an *apophatic* spirituality—"apophatic" being a Greek word that means "without images or concepts." For example, *The Cloud of Unknowing*, which is devoted to the unknowability of God, is a masterpiece of apophatic spirituality. Also called "negative mysticism," the apophatic tradition has long insisted that God is revealed only in terms of what is knowably *not* God (hence the term "negative"). Language and, indeed, all images and representations of God are ultimately incomplete, perhaps even flawed—imperfect and imprecise ways of depicting the Divine. Language may give voice to our imagination and conceptualization regarding the Holy One, but its range is finite and therefore cannot fully represent the infinite.

Ultimately, language fails before the Great Mystery. As language fails, so also do all of our concepts, ideas, notions, and depictions of "God," "the Sacred," "the Divine." We may say that God is eternal and omnipresent and perfectly good, but words like "eternal" and "omnipresent" and "good" and "perfect" all signify something that we humans understand in terms of our own experience. Since the nature of God transcends all human experience (and indeed transcends the universe of space and time itself), our language cannot adequately describe God, since the qualities of God exist beyond the limits of a word's possible usage. If words cannot adequately describe even the *attributes* of God, how can words ever describe God's *essence*?

Recognizing the inability of language to fully represent God, we are left only with silence. This applies not just to literal silence (both internal and external), but to metaphorical "silences" as well. Just as silence is defined as the absence of sound, metaphorical silence may involve the absence of language, the absence of light, the absence of certainty or meaning. Silence and darkness, in fact, are siblings in the realm of spirituality. God is light, but sometimes the light is so dazzling that all we can perceive is a "darkness"—like turning on a light in a dark room and being blinded until our eyes adjust. According to the Gospel of John, the Divine comes to us as the *Logos*, or "the Word"—but like the light seen as a dazzling darkness, the spoken Word of God is so full of meaning that all we may bear to perceive is a "Word" of silence. The "meaning" of the Sacred is as overwhelming as the "light" of the Sacred. Perhaps this idea lies beneath the Biblical story in which Moses is not allowed to see God's face, since a mortal could not look upon the countenance of the Divine and live. God's face is not lethal, but rather is so dazzling and meaningful that a finite human being simply could not bear it.

As a natural environment for prayer, silence is supremely helpful because it creates a spaciousness where we can truly be ourselves—and, we hope, catch a glimpse of God as God truly is, not as we would like God to be. In this spacious silence, we have the freedom to become less attached to false certainties and to useless concepts of the Sacred, like "the old man with a beard" in a heaven "up there" or the "wrathful, angry judge." Instead of filling our mind with assumptions and ideas, silence frees us to be fully open to the God who cannot be contained by any assumption or idea.

Despite the incompleteness of our knowing, we use language and icons, music and art, rituals and architecture, as "media" in our attempts to report what we have found in the silence—or, perhaps more accurately, what has found us in the silence. The Sacred Word is so rich with meaning that we may only "hear" it in silence, then we who are mortal must rely on our spoken and written language to describe imperfectly what we encounter in that silence.

The language of God is the language of silence, a fundamentally different language from that of the finite words and concepts we use. To put the experiences of silent prayer into words is like translating a book from another tongue. We can only grieve all that is lost in the translation—though we can continue trying to learn that "foreign language" for ourselves by becoming regular visitors to the silence, both by finding stillness outside of ourselves and cultivating it within ourselves.

Solitude

We live in a society that is simultaneously crowded and lonely. We live in large apartment communities and sprawling subdivisions; we commute on congested highways and on crowded trains and buses; we work in large office buildings with hundreds of employees on every floor. For entertainment we go to stadiums or theaters filled with thousands or tens of thousands of people. We complain about the traffic and the crowds and the congestion—and yet, for all this, ours is a lonely society. Newspapers are filled with hundreds of "personal" ads taken out by those who wish to find romance. Bars and dance clubs are filled with people aching to make connections with one another. For too many, the television set is their only friend; for others, it's the computer. Thousands, maybe even millions, of people are devoting hours and hours to Internet "chatting"—typing conversations online with total strangers, each participant known to the other only by a clever nickname and witty (or flirtatious) typed dialogue. Sadly, these electronic forms of communication and entertainment tend toward the banal—suggesting that large segments of our society are either terribly bored or terribly lonely.

Thanks to the overcrowding and in spite of the loneliness, many of us suffer from a lack of solitude. Solitude refers to the state of intentionally being alone, usually for some purpose related to spiritual nourishment. Solitude is not the same as being lonely, for loneliness is the sense of being *imprisoned* by aloneness, while solitude involves a sense of *liberation* through aloneness. However, solitude is not necessarily just a matter of getting away from other people—true solitude may be experienced on a crowded bus or at a busy shopping mall, just as a person can feel lonely in such situations, as well. Nonetheless, physical aloneness benefits a person wishing to cultivate a sense of solitude, just as actual external silence is useful for those of us who wish to nurture our own inner silence.

How may we find a liberating solitude in our crowded world? For that matter, how may those of us who suffer from loneliness shift the oppressive quality of such feelings into the featherlight joy of solitude? We find solitude by intentionally setting aside time to be alone, if for no other purpose than to cultivate an intentional discipline of prayer. We can transform loneliness into solitude by choosing to nurture a relationship with the Divine in the very midst of our loneliness. This is not an easy task! It means embracing an approach to life that honors the pain of loneliness without trying to fix it and honors the craziness of crowded city life without having to escape it.

The spirituality of solitude means, for a lonely person, hanging in there when alone, perhaps choosing to be alone for the sake of such nurturing inner activities as prayer—even though it may hurt at first. The spirituality of solitude also means, for those who live in crowded conditions, learning how to cultivate "stolen moments" of solitude—while sitting at a red light, waiting for a train, standing in line at the post office —opportunities when, in the midst of hundreds or thousands of people, we may for a moment savor our aloneness. In such fleeting moments of solitude, we can take the time to relax, cultivate an inner sense of silence, and perhaps even experience an unbidden sense of wonder—or of God's presence—in ourselves and our surroundings.

Jesus advocated solitude as a prerequisite for prayer. He taught his followers, "Whenever you pray, go into your room and shut the door and pray . . . in secret" (Matt. 6:6). Why should solitude be good for prayer? Why should we savor aloneness? Solitude, like silence, needs to be understood not just in terms of "absence" (the absence of other people) but in terms of "presence"—the presence of the Sacred. To be alone is to be present to the mystery of spirituality, to the uncertainty and unanswered questions about a God whom we cannot see or always feel, yet whom we trust is there. To truly enter into these mysterious, unanswered questions is something each one of us must do alone. It is not something that can be dipped into once and then left behind, like a one-time pilgrimage to the waters of Lourdes. Rather, solitude is more like an ever-present ocean, constantly beckoning us to dive in. Once the mysteries of this ocean have been encountered, there is no going back. The devoted diver will long for the ocean the rest of her days. So it is for the person who enters fully into silent, solitary prayer. The inaudible whispers of the Spirit will lovingly beckon forever after.

Solitude, like most elements of spirituality, is honored in different ways in different religions and cultures. Some Native American traditions include the "vision quest," in which a seeker spends several days alone in the wild, fasting and praying and crying for a vision. We've already considered Jesus' teaching about entering a room and shutting the door to pray—significant in a religion that has understood itself primarily in terms of community. Indeed, Jesus himself entered into long periods of solitude in the desert, which can be compared to the quest of the Buddha, who sat alone for days under the Bodhi tree before he achieved full enlightenment. Zen Buddhism honors the experience of solitude—in Zen monasteries, each monk typically meditates with his back to all the others, essentially alone. To embrace solitude may not come naturally to many members of our anxious, extroverted society—a society that fears loneliness even as it struggles to cope with its own congestion. But the possibilities for spiritual discovery in solitude are too great not to be explored honestly and meaningfully.

Contemplative prayer

Contemplative prayer, which is essentially a cross between prayer and meditation, is the form of prayer that most explicitly manifests the qualities of silence and solitude. Even though contemplation may be practiced in a group setting, it is still a solitary form of prayer—since it involves listening for God, not speaking. Contemplation is a prayer of listening and waiting patiently upon God. This method of prayer involves gently letting go of the thoughts and concerns that usually dominate our consciousness and allowing our minds and our bodies to rest peacefully in silence—the silence that holds us in God's love.

Contemplation is very similar to meditation. As commonly understood, meditation refers to a practice in which mental activity (like thinking and daydreaming) is set aside in order to find spiritual truth within the spaciousness of the human mind. Technically, contemplation differs from practices like transcendental meditation or zazen only in minor ways. Silent contemplative prayer does not place demands on the body like those associated with meditation—a specific posture or a specific rhythm of breathing is not required for contemplation. Probably the main difference between meditation and contemplation involves assumptions about the presence of God. While meditation usually means a private process involving only the mind of the meditator, contemplation is a form of prayer and is therefore relational—contemplation involves nurturing a relationship with the Sacred. Meditation seeks the realization of "truth," while contemplation seeks encounter with the Divine. Just as belief means being open to God, contemplation means waiting in silence for God.

The word *contemplare*, from which "contemplation" is derived, literally means "with time," so this is the prayer of "spending time with" God. "To wait" and "to spend time" mean contemplation is not something that's done in thirty seconds. Rather, it requires a commitment more like thirty minutes—and not just thirty minutes "here and there." To make a difference in a person's spiritual life, the prayer of contemplation needs to be practiced as often as possible—if not daily, then I suggest at least five times a week. In my experience, this prayer is easiest when practiced either the first thing in the morning or just before going to bed at night.

On the surface, the prayer of contemplation may seem silly—just spending a half an hour or so in silence. Nothing to it! That is exactly the point—there is nothing, *absolutely nothing* to it—no agendas, no expectations, no anticipated rewards, and no guarantee of mystical "goodies." What initially seems so simple and so easy often proves to be almost agonizingly difficult. Silent prayer plunges us into uncertainty and longing; it's a wordless opportunity to embrace openness and willingness. Contemplative silence includes a subversive element, in that it undermines our desire for, and sense of, being in control. We ordinarily "control" our minds and our bodies through our thoughts—our thinking mind is the author (authority) of our hopes, dreams, attitudes, worries, anxieties, and all our ways of maintaining order in life. To be silent, truly silent, for more than just a momentary few seconds is to loosen that control. This is not something that our ego, our survival-mind (the "authority" or "controller" of consciousness), takes to naturally or easily.

In the context of prayer, silence assumes a radical or revolutionary role, getting to the root of our ego and causing a "spiritual revolt" against the survival-mind's authority. This "revolt" causes a "wound"—an opening of silent spaciousness within the mind, a space in which the silent whispers of Divine love may enter. To the authoritarian ego, letting go of mental activity in order to enter deep contemplative silence feels not only like a wound—it's almost like dying. At the very least, it feels "useless" and "like a waste of time." Actually, contemplation *is* a symbolic form of dying—a death that, like all spiritual deaths, leads to a resurrection. Silent prayer slays the survival-mind but leads to its resurrection as the mind of wonder. Trusting this process is not easy, however. When something feels like dying, even in a symbolic sense, our instinctive impulse is to resist and fight back.

The survival-mind fights back against the silence by filling our consciousness with scattered, chatty thoughts or "distractions." Trying to fight those distracting thoughts is a trap, though, for the more we resist the ego, the stronger it seems to become. Thinking about stopping thought is like worrying about worrying too much—it's a strategy the mind uses to exacerbate its own problem (but which allows the ego to maintain control).

In my experience, my survival-mind does not acquiesce to silence easily, and when I've tried to sit in silence without discipline and intentionality, I've quickly discovered that I was sitting in nothing more "silent" than my busy mind full of daydreams and ideas. To move beneath the incessant chatter of the authoritarian, thinking ego to the wordless silence where the Hebrew Scriptures commend us to "be still and know God" requires time—and perseverance.

To find the silence beneath our thinking mind, our best approach typically involves gently setting aside all our thoughts—and continuing to do so over and over again, lightly disregarding the many distractions that will arise as we spend time in contemplation. Fortunately, a number of mental techniques for enhancing silence in contemplation have been developed by spiritual practitioners over the years—strategic techniques to help a seeker stay focused or "centered" on the Divine silence. Such techniques often use words to help open us up to silence—reminding us that words and thoughts are not "wrong" in prayer. Even though contemplative prayer seeks to commune with God in a wordless way, language itself remains valuable—and, of course, central to conversational prayer and other ways of praying.

These centering techniques include such practices as reciting a repetitive prayer (such as the Rosary), chanting sacred verses or hymns (such as Psalms), or the use of a mantra—a short word or phrase repeated silently and in rhythm with breathing in order to keep one's mind attentive to God. Other techniques, such as drumming or gazing at an icon, can also help one maintain a wordless attentiveness to the silence. Alas, even these techniques rarely shut the thinking ego up for long. Nevertheless, they provide a helpful way at least to slow down the ongoing chitchat of the mind. They offer a gentle way to refocus in those frequent times when the mind goes its own way and wanders from the silence.

To persevere in silent prayer requires trust—a trust in which, beyond the seeming "uselessness" of waiting for the Divine in silence, the possibility of a more deeply felt sense of God's loving presence exists. Although it most certainly will feel useless, contemplation as a spiritual practice invites the praying mind to a deeper use*ful*ness—the usefulness of resting in the Divine presence, even when God doesn't "feel" present. Of course, the experience of contemplatives throughout history is that perseverance in silent prayer *will* reveal God's presence—sometimes in a "felt" way, but often in a way deeper than words or feelings.

In our busy, frenetic world, contemplative prayer not only makes good spiritual sense but it also makes good physical sense, as it is an excellent antidote to stress. Increasing numbers of heart patients and other health-conscious persons turn to meditation and contemplation, finding in the discipline an increased sense of well-being as well as measurably lowered blood pressure. Therein lies a spiritual lesson. Contemplation is beneficial even if it doesn't "feel" beneficial—just as the mystery and wonder of Divine love is really present in our lives even when we don't consciously "feel" the Sacred.

Contemplative prayer may only last half an hour a day, but that time is a training session for a transformed life. The contemplative way finally involves seeking the Divine presence, a sense of wonder, and a spacious, loving mind all the time, not only when we're "sitting." Just as physical exercise makes us stronger and slimmer twenty-four hours a day, so sitting in contemplative silence on a daily basis may, over time, help cultivate a supple consciousness and a subtle sense of Divine loving presence—hour after hour, day after day.

Conversational prayer

All of this talk of silence and solitude and contemplation may seem unusual for persons raised in traditional religious homes, where prayer generally means "talking to God." Having stated that I consider silence to be the ideal state for prayer and the most useful means for fostering intimacy with the Sacred, I now want to reaffirm my belief that words still have an appropriate and important place in prayer.

No matter how inadequate our concepts and our words may be for relating with the Divine, we still need language to support our spiritual journey. Teachings, memory, storytelling, visionary imagination, and the ability to reflect thoughtfully are all important to the spiritual life—and all depend on language and images. Also, as important as contemplation may be for some spiritual seekers, such a disciplined, silent practice is not for everyone. Therefore, rather than considering prayer only in terms of silence, we need to acknowledge the value of old-fashioned, conversational (verbal) kinds of prayer. Just as contemplation is the prayer of listening, so conversational prayer is the prayer of intimate self-disclosure —the prayer of expressing love for the Sacred.

A primary way of showing people we love them is to speak with them. Therefore, if we love the Sacred, one salutary way to express that love is by using words—whether "out loud" or in our interior thoughts—in our prayer. To adore the Divine, to talk with God, to praise the Sacred—these are all poetic ways of expressing our part in the love affair of spirituality— the love affair between a finite human being (you) and the infinite creator of the universe (God).

While the prayer of contemplation involves silent waiting, the prayer of self-disclosure involves intimate conversation with the Divine. I believe these forms of prayer complement each other to create a full and rich spirituality. Together, they foster a deeply lived and intimate relationship with the Sacred.

Conversational forms of prayer provide an opportunity to be intimate and vulnerable with God—not so much for God's sake, but for our own. When we pray honestly and vulnerably to the Sacred, we open ourselves up—open to receive the Divine love we long for.

Naturally, we do not always feel loving or adoring toward God. Many of us grew up in families that believed God is to be feared, not loved. In the ups and downs of life, even the most mystical person will go through times of feeling angry or afraid or confused or bored in relation to the Sacred. Conversational prayer, in these circumstances, can be compared to a husband and wife telling each other "I love you," even after having just had a major fight. Affirming our loving relationships is important for our own sense of security, even when such relationships may not "feel" loving. Just as this is important in human relationships, it is also important in our relationship with the Divine.

Conversational prayer takes many forms. In the Christian tradition, verbal forms of prayer include adoration (expressing feelings of love and praise for the Divine), confession (admitting to God our mistakes and wrongdoing, as well as our doubts and fears), petition (asking for God's blessings), intercession (asking God's favor on behalf of others, especially the sick, needy, or dying), and thanksgiving (expressing gratitude to God for blessings received). Although some of these categories may seem a bit stiff and obsolete, the overall notion of prayer as a conversation—in which we take our needs, desires, problems, and joys to God—has much to offer us today.

Conversational prayer can feel awkward and clumsy, sort of like "talking to yourself," since obviously the Sacred does not carry on an audible conversation. But that doesn't mean God does not communicate with us. Often, the "words" of the Divine come in simple and very ordinary ways to a person who is praying—through a random thought, an offhanded comment from a passerby, or a momentary ability to see things in a new and hitherto unthought-of way. In fact, if a conversational period of prayer, in which a person strives to be as intimately honest and vulnerable with God as possible, is followed by a period of silent, contemplative waiting, the entire experience often will seem radiantly filled with God's loving response. The silence will seem to be teeming with simple things that carry an inexplicable sense of significance—significant because these little things are imbued with God's message.

But spoken prayer is almost as difficult as silent, contemplative prayer; and a major difficulty arises from God's sheer silence. At least in contemplation, both parties share in the silence. But in conversational prayer, God's continued silence can feel awkward—or even cold. Despite the little things that appear to be resplendent with Divine meaning, the fact remains that conversational prayer can, and regularly does, feel like a spiritual monologue. God's subtle ways of communicating are easily missed or easily misinterpreted—leaving only the silence, in which the

Divine seems absent. No matter how faithful a person is and no matter how comfortable a person is with silence, sooner or later God's silence in response to conversational prayer may be unnerving. Prayer can seem meaningless; to use a common phrase, prayers will seem "to bounce off the ceiling." This experience can lead to profound doubt.

Aridity

Feelings of doubt and meaninglessness that can arise in prayer are common—and significant. *Aridity*, or spiritual dryness, starts with the sense of God's utter silence, a silence that suggests God is absent. This absence can seem all-encompassing, even in the midst of a faithful practice of prayer and contemplation.

Anyone who is serious about the spiritual life eventually will experience this "dryness." Although it can seem devastating, it is a normal and common problem of prayer, just as a head cold is a typical experience in wintertime. In fact, just as depression has been nicknamed the common cold of mental diseases, aridity could be called the common cold of spiritual problems.

To enter into spiritual aridity is simply to enter into a place where the Sacred seems finally, forever, absent. Not only do previous experiences of the Divine presence begin to seem wholly unreal, but any future hope for the felt presence of God also seems entirely beyond belief and even absurd. Aridity is a state of grief and mourning in which we grieve and mourn the loss of our prior sense of God's presence.

The sense of aridity usually doesn't just spring up overnight. The person whose spirituality has become dry has, over time, probably experienced numerous setbacks in prayer, many situations where "my prayer time seemed rather blah"—situations where silence seemed unattainable or where God seemed not to be listening and earnest requests apparently went unanswered. After a while, disappointments in prayer can add up to a perceived inability to really connect with the Sacred. In this state, prayer may even become painful (if we can manage to pray at all).

For a person whose spiritual life has seemed vibrant and lively, fully open to the Divine presence, this experience of aridity can be deeply unsettling. One might easily assume that aridity is the fault of the person experiencing it—that such a person probably is not admitting to wrongdoing or is in some other way at fault and responsible for this spiritual problem. A rather pointed bumper sticker asks, "If God seems far away, guess who moved?"—implying that if you experience any feelings of dryness during prayer, it's because of your own doing.

Great mystics such as Teresa of Avila, however, have suggested that it is more useful to understand aridity as a normal development in the life of prayer. Instead of representing a problem, aridity can actually signify a new challenge and therefore is a mark of spiritual growth and maturity.

Spiritual dryness challenges us to recognize that, while our perception of the Divine may change over the course of time and while our sense of Sacred presence may change or diminish over time, our *longing* for God does not decrease. As we persevere in prayer, it becomes more evident that, far from lessening our desire for the Sacred, prayer actually causes us to feel our longing more acutely.

This sense of longing for God is never satisfied—not during those times when God's loving presence seems most real and most vibrant in our lives and certainly not when the Sacred seems absent. Nothing can assuage this longing for God's love. This desire for Divine love is the most basic human longing, which not only helps us to understand what we are, but in a paradoxical way also shows us what we *aren't*. In longing for God, we encounter all the ways we are not the masters of life, as much as we would like to think we are. We encounter our finite incompleteness, our weakness and uncertainty, our unknowing and our neediness.

The arid time, far from being a problem, is a productive time of "stripping away"—for like a snake shedding its skin, the spiritual person in a state of aridity sheds old illusions about her relationship with the Sacred. Underneath the old, dry skin is new, supple skin. So it is with prayer. As a cocoon promises butterfly wings to a caterpillar, so do times of spiritual dryness promise new insights about God's presence and a renewed joy in the Divine relationship. Aridity is a gift, because it is an invitation to go deeper into our love for God, relying less on how the spiritual life makes us "feel good" (although there's nothing wrong with that) and relying more on our trust and openness to the Divine presence, whose reality transcends the limits of our thoughts and feelings.

Prayer changes things

God is the ultimate source of love, life, and power in the universe. Our very being springs forth from the center of love and meaning and holiness that is the Sacred. We look to the *love* of the Divine for meaning and purpose in life, and we bring our neediness to the *power* of God, seeking security and shelter in the strength of the Most High.

Primarily in this chapter, I have stressed that prayer is a way to enter into a deepening love relationship with the Sacred. But what about relating to Divine power? Certainly, prayer is more than just being God's loved one—it also involves asking for things. Whether we are asking for a good grade on a test, a place to park, a special toy for Christmas, healing for a loved one with AIDS, or the strength to work for social justice, we cannot help but bring our needs to prayer.

I grew up in a very nice, middle-class Lutheran family and as a child learned a lot of very nice, middle-class Protestant values. One core belief I learned was that *my* will should always be subordinate to "*thy* will" in prayer—in other words, whenever I asked for something in prayer I had to give God an easy out by ending my request with "thy will be done." I now understand that the purpose behind "thy will be done" is to teach a child that sometimes God *isn't* going to give him the thing he wants just because he prayed for it. But there's a shadow side to "thy will be done"— the shadow side being a subtle message that perhaps "*my* will" is not very important and perhaps even that God doesn't really care about my will to begin with.

To this day, I have difficulty expressing my neediness in prayer. That is too bad, for it blocks me from going that much further into intimacy with the Sacred. Nowadays, I am trying to be more vulnerable and more honest in expressing my needs—whether it is a little need (finding a parking spot) or a big need (discernment in my career path). We who pray need to learn greater and greater "nakedness" before God, hiding nothing —not even our most basic needs or our most self-centered wants. If I want to be honest when I pray, I must be willing to ask that *my* will be done.

Now, about "thy will be done." I still believe in the supremacy of the will of God—when I talked about willingness in chapter 3, I was simply stating that "thy will" needs to take priority over "my will." Obviously, if we're going to consider the balance of power between a finite, mortal human and the Source of all love and creativity throughout and beyond the universe, I daresay there's no contest. But prayer is not just about power; it's also about relationship. God wants to be more than just a cosmic Santa Claus, granting some wishes and withholding others according to some unknown formula. The Sacred seeks passionate, loving involvement in our lives. This means that a dance of love and power—and mutuality— pulsates throughout the life of prayer. Thus, despite the priority of "thy will be done," we also can trust God to listen, to respond, and to make changes in our lives arising out of the Sacred will relating lovingly with the human will.

I believe that prayer changes things. Perhaps prayer can change the will of God, who relates to us in part by giving us good gifts. But even when God says "no" or "not now" to our requests, prayer still changes things.

When we pray, we ourselves are always changed. We enter into new insights about ourselves and about the part we play in the process of God's creation. In prayer, we discover new ways to see ourselves and our world, new ways to understand our motivations, and new possibilities for action in life. Prayer inspires us to make changes in our own lives or to do things that impact the lives of others.

People who pray regularly take it seriously and will certainly attest to the fact that prayer has made a difference in their lives. Prayer brings about change—sometimes in dramatic ways, only rarely in "miraculous" ways, and quite often in tiny, subtle ways. But the subtlety doesn't mean the change is not important. Just as the two lines in a one-degree angle get farther apart as the distance from the vertex increases, so a small and subtle change in my life today may lead to major, significant differences in my life ten or twenty years from now. God may inspire a woman to talk to a homeless person today—a small and insignificant change in her life. But by being open to that tiny change in her normal routine, she may be setting in motion a chain of events that will lead to her starting a success- ful shelter for hundreds of homeless persons five years from now. We must not underestimate the power of prayer as an agent of change. When we pray, we are putting our openness and vulnerability on the line, and the Sacred One who loves us will enter into our vulnerability and shape us— for the purpose of greater love and peace in our lives and in the world.

7

Change

The previous chapter concluded with the assertion that prayer—our effort to nurture a relationship with God—changes things. When we pray, we often ask for change and at other times we may feel that a change is asked of us. Making changes is not always easy. To think of the spiritual life as a pleasant mix of wonder, playfulness, believing, and praying is lovely enough—but the thought of real changes in life, especially unexpected or unasked-for changes, can be deeply unsettling.

More than just a characteristic of spirituality, change is an essential quality of life. Changes are sometimes thrust upon us (just think of the technological changes that have swept across the world in the past fifty years); at other times, we initiate change ourselves. Even when we choose to make a change, we cannot control the outcome—will the change be for the better or will there be unforeseen negative consequences?

Change is not a private matter, either. Regardless of how changes in our life come about, they almost always impact others as well. Sometimes others applaud the changes we make, and sometimes others present us with conflict and resistance when we make changes. The alcoholic who decides to join Alcoholics Anonymous will probably find loved ones applauding the action as a constructive step, while conflict awaits the promising young student when she announces to her family that she is going to pursue a music career instead of finishing law school.

How does change—whether it's small or large, applauded or conflicted, an internal change in consciousness or an external change in the world—fit in with spirituality? Where does change belong in the Sacred realm of willingness and openness, of wonder and belief?

103

Change and religion

Many people view spirituality as being inimical to change, and religious people seem particularly to resist change. Whether it's the "family values" rhetoric of the Christian right that opposes any change in the social standing of gay and lesbian persons; or the orthodox Jewish insistence on observing the minutiae of kosher laws, along with resistance to any change in the way the tradition is practiced; or an anti-American statement from a Shiite Muslim leader implying that accepting Western values will change the Islamic world for the worse—again and again, religion seems typically to function as an obstacle to change.

This is true of religious leaders and also of rank-and-file believers. For example, one way many Christians resist change is by avoiding contemporary translations of the Bible. The best-selling Bible in English continues to be the King James Version, a translation first published in 1611. This means that most ordinary Christians have not changed their sense of the "best" Bible translation for many generations.

It's a marketing truism that consumers demand the newest, the improved, the latest and greatest, this year's model, and/or the current version. Not so with religion, it seems. Despite dozens of newer translations of the Hebrew and Christian scriptures, many reflecting the "latest" and "greatest" scholarship, people still prefer the hoary old King James Version. Different persons will suggest different reasons why. "The language is so majestic." "I don't feel as spiritual when I read or hear the modern translations." "The King James is more accurate" (utterly untrue, but people still think it). Perhaps another reason, which often remains unspoken, is the most important—that people tend to have a deep-seated resistance to change, and religion is often the one place where they ardently seek refuge from change.

Of course, the resistance doesn't stop with Bible translations. Many Christian denominations have suffered wrenching internal debate in recent years over the ordination of women, changes to hymnals and prayer books, and whether noncelibate lesbians and gay men should be admitted to the ordained ministry. As Christians struggle with these and other issues, most seem simply to resist change, though a few press for it. While a few do strive for change in their religion, many others give up and leave. One reason why young people stop practicing Christianity may be that they get impatient with what appears to be an irrational resistance to change—even while others lament that Christian churches are changing *too* rapidly.

Given the evidence from religion, should we assume that to be *spiritual* means to resist change? Perhaps this is true for many practitioners of conventional religion, but it does not hold in every circumstance. The spectrum of New Age spiritualities, for example, reflects an entire subculture of persons who experience spirituality as being virtually synonymous with embracing change. Even the label "new" carries an implication of change. Some of the ways the New Age might inspire change include changes in diet (from meat-eating to vegetarianism), changes in theology (from worshiping God to worshiping the Goddess), and changes in spiritual practices (discarding Sunday morning church services in favor of Native American sweatlodges or Wiccan circle-casting). Truly, the followers of alternative paths seem to find change in spirituality and spirituality in change.

Biology and change

What conclusion may we draw? Does involvement with religion—or spirituality—entail resistance to change or the embracing of it? When Christians resist change and New Agers embrace it, does that shed light on the nature of spirituality—or on other cultural or communal factors that distinguish the two paths?

Perhaps natural science provides an answer to these questions. The survival of a species over time depends on its having two capabilities: the ability to adapt to change and the ability to resist it. Resisting change is important so organisms can continue to do whatever has previously ensured survival. If robins suddenly changed their migratory patterns and didn't fly south for the winter, they would all freeze and face certain extinction. By resisting change in the rhythm of migration, the robins ensure their survival.

On the other hand, adaptation to change is equally necessary, for change is an inevitable fact of life—somewhere, somehow, things are all the time becoming different. Now that the tropical rainforests are being decimated, North American songbirds are flying to Central America only to find their old winter homes destroyed. If humans continue to destroy the rainforest, the birds will have to adapt (in other words, find new destinations) if they hope to survive.

Resisting change and adapting to change are both necessary for biological survival, and both also seem to play a role in human spirituality as well. Neither one nor the other is more spiritual; rather, spirituality involves both resistance and adaptation, with each held in an appropriate balance relative to the other.

Religions resist change for the simple reason that any given change might prove to be spiritually harmful. The attitude in such resistance is, "If it isn't broken, don't fix it." If a sacred text like the Bible serves as an icon for people, they will resist any attempt to tamper with it. Even so mild a change as a new translation will be resisted. In the Episcopal *Book of Common Prayer*, a prayer for the end of the day includes this request to God: "Protect us through the hours of this night, so that we who are wearied by the changes and chances of this life may rest in your eternal changelessness" (*BCP*, 133)—stating in a lovely way how stability and reliability are seen as Sacred virtues. Religions resist change because indiscriminate change is viewed as unsafe. Stability nurtures the spiritual life.

Yet the spiritual life involves embracing change as surely as it involves resistance to change. People engaged in the spiritual life often will work to make changes within themselves—for example, Christians practice repentance, the act of changing beliefs or behaviors for the sake of God; and New Age adherents often believe that one's thoughts shape one's life circumstances ("change your mind, change your life")—and thus will strive to change mental processes as a means of creating material change. Alongside such efforts to change the self are spiritually motivated attempts to change the world, such as the Christian effort to combat racism in the 1960s or the efforts of many New Age persons to protect the dwindling Native American autonomy in regard to mining and fishing rights. Resistance to change, adaptation to change—both belong in the spiritual life.

Adaptation and resistance in spirituality and religion

Although they are not quick to admit it, even strongly conservative Christians go through vibrant, dynamic religious change. In the past, some fundamentalist Christians used the Bible to justify slavery, but now even conservative Christians find inspiration in the Bible for a nonracist understanding of both church and society. While patriotic fundamentalists historically have advocated a Biblically justified obedience to civil authority, in recent years many fundamentalists see in the Bible a call to civil disobedience in connection with their opposition to abortion. Once known for condemning the perceived wickedness of rock 'n' roll, evangelical Christianity today has its own thriving entertainment industry, with Christian rock stars like Stryper enjoying widespread popularity.

As we consider all the ways that religious conservatives embrace change, we might notice as well the ways in which alternative spiritual practitioners resist it. Many followers of Native American traditions, especially among European-Americans who have adopted native ceremonies, are careful to perform a ceremony such as the sweatlodge "correctly"—in other words, without any changes. This tendency to resist change in rituals is also evident among the practitioners of Eastern religions, such as Buddhism, in which a great emphasis is often placed on practicing meditation in the one proper (unchanging) way. And in the historically rationalistic and humanistic Unitarian-Universalist church, older members resist the encroaching of Neopagan influences among younger UU's—an influence that represents a possibility of significant change in the UU culture. Resistance to change among spiritual seekers can take political or cultural forms, as well. For example, some Neopagans engage in political action to resist the destruction of natural resources, such as the logging of old-growth forests.

Some spiritual paths, like conservative Christianity, seem proud of their resistance to change, while others seem proud of the ways in which they embody change. Meanwhile, I believe that the healthiest forms of spirituality seek a creative equilibrium between resistance and adaptation. Of course, which changes are embraced and which ones are resisted vary from path to path. But that fact sheds light not on the nature of spirituality so much as on the fact that spirituality is shaped by political, social, and other communal/cultural values.

Spirituality seeks an equilibrium—a dance—between embracing change and embracing constancy. But what does *that* mean in light of the idea that prayer changes things? How do we know when a given change is in the best interests of our relationship with the Sacred—or when not changing is healthier? How can we tell the difference between change inspired by the leadings of God and change that may ultimately be nothing more than a "mistake"?

These questions take us to the heart of the spirituality of change. They are questions of *discernment*—that is, of trying to discern the leadings of the Sacred in our lives and in the lives of our communities for the purpose of accepting (or initiating) change that conforms to the Divine will. In this book we can only begin to explore the depths of the spirituality of change, and rather than attempt to make dogmatic statements about what is and what is not the will of God, I'm simply going to look at several examples of change and attempt to understand more about the spirituality of change in the process. In the rest of this chapter, we'll consider change as falling under two broad categories—change that comes upon us in ways that are outside of our control and change that we initiate ourselves. Both kinds of change have spiritual implications.

To consider change that comes from outside of ourselves, change that seems to be thrust upon us, we'll look at the spirituality of *interruption* and *surprise*. For change that we ourselves initiate, we'll consider change that breaks us out of limitations (*transgression*) and change that fosters healing and harmony (*peacemaking*). These are only a few models for the varieties of change that course through life. Some changes we experience may be inner and personal and some may affect others besides ourselves. Some seem to come from God, while others appear to have no apparent spiritual meaning. Yet, while not all of them are obviously "spiritual" in nature, every change may nonetheless have a spiritual impact. The spirituality of change invites us to consider how change affects us spiritually and how our spiritual life affects the changes we make and accept.

Interruption

In 1992, my life underwent a significant, life-transforming change—I was in a serious accident. The accident, including the lessons I learned about myself in its aftermath, proved to be one of the most spiritually significant experiences in my life.

On that fateful night, I was coming home from a business trip, which involved flying into Nashville, arriving about nine p.m. I had a ninety-mile drive to my home (I lived in rural Tennessee at the time), but I never made it there. I dozed at the wheel and drove under the rear of a semi. My car was totaled and I spent the night in a hospital with my jaw broken in three places, a few teeth missing, and various lacerations on my right arm and forehead.

The following day I was in surgery for five hours having my jaw put back together. My mouth remained in traction for six weeks. I missed several weeks of work and, for years after my convalescence, have had chronic problems with my neck and my jaws. I was fortunate because my life was never in danger—but of course I didn't know that at the moment I stood, dazed and in shock, by the side of the Interstate with blood flowing out of my mouth. At that moment and over the six weeks that followed, I felt intensely how fragile and contingent life is. I became conscious of the grace by which we live and the ever-present possibility of death or injury.

I did not have a near-death experience. I had a "brush-with-death" experience. I could easily have felt a harrowing sense of panic, but interestingly enough, I didn't. As the ambulance sped me to the hospital, what little panic I felt was overwhelmed by my profound sense of gratitude—gratitude that my life hadn't ended; gratitude for the EMT personnel who had left home late on a Thursday evening to come and care for me; and gratitude simply because I believed in a loving, Divine being. This belief helped me to feel remarkably safe, even in the midst of sudden, unexpected trauma. I entered the emergency room strapped into a stretcher, scared, and in shock—but also feeling myself glow with a sense of God's presence and loving mercy.

The accident and the strange way it catapulted me into gratitude instead of panic became a powerful icon for me—an icon not only of Divine grace, but also of God calling me to change. I had the accident because I was exhausted—I was the manager of two stores and had numerous social and spiritual obligations—so I heard in it a clear signal to slow down. But I took that even deeper. One evening, not long after the accident, I had a powerful and moving conversation with my soul friend, Mary, in which I realized that my "busy-ness" was a strategy designed to keep myself from writing—which was what I really wanted to do, but I feared that I lacked the competence to do so. Tears streaming down my face, I prayed to God, admitting my fears and apologizing for making too many external commitments and not attending to my soul's deepest desire. In the months that followed, I began to cultivate a discipline of prayerful writing that is now, five years later, a central part of who I am.

Life is filled with interruptions. Some are dramatic, like my accident —like losing a job or the sudden death of a loved one. Less dramatic interruptions may range from significant life changes, such as the ending of a relationship or a change in one's health to interruptions that are merely annoying, such as a flat tire or an unexpected visit from the in-laws.

Interruptions are not usually something we choose, and we may generally even regard them as negative. We don't have to see them that way, though. (There are *happy* interruptions, but I'm including them next, in the section on surprise.) When we experience a "negative" interruption, we can regard it as a gift from the Divine—as an opportunity that creates the possibility for a new or different encounter with the Sacred, such as how I spontaneously recognized God's grace in the aftermath of a traumatic accident. In fact, every time life hands us an interruption, it just *might* be an invitation into the presence of the Sacred—into the presence of a God whose constant love and compassion are both higher and deeper than any trauma or any irritation. Without our planning it or engineering it, an interruption can catapult us into the presence of the God whose dynamic creativity and energy literally empowers the atoms and the stars.

Interruptions can open the door to an unexpected encounter with the Sacred, no matter how traumatic—or boring—they may be. Nevertheless, given the mundane reality of most events in our day-to-day life, prayer and spirituality are still likely to be the last things on our mind when we're interrupted. What, after all, could be the least bit spiritual about having to deal with yet another call from a telemarketer or an unplanned visit from a talkative neighbor at the worst possible time—say, when we're trying to get the house cleaned before having the boss over? I suspect that for most of us most of the time, the many interruptions of life are not like sudden visions of angels, but rather are just plain annoying—about as pleasant as filing your tax return. We don't feel any sense of wonder or gratitude or serendipity when we are interrupted; we're more likely to feel cross and irritable and sometimes downright furious.

If interruptions make us feel "cross," perhaps, before we go any farther, we might profitably explore the pun and think about Jesus on the cross. That was an interruption of the first degree. A free man twenty-four hours before he died, Jesus was arrested and sentenced for political reasons to death by crucifixion—a brutal and agonizing method of execution. Yet it became the defining moment for an emerging tradition of spirituality, the beginning of what would develop into one of the world's largest religions. Christians believe the crucifixion opened the door to Jesus' resurrection from the dead, which means that what began as a traumatic interruption has become, for millions of people, an icon of the Sacred potential to redeem suffering and bring life out of death.

Jesus is not the only spiritual leader to have experienced profound interruption. Gautama was a prince in India who lived five centuries before Christ. Gautama's parents sheltered the boy—he was not allowed to see any evidence of disease, old age, suffering, or death. For years the young prince, surrounded only by beauty and luxury, lived a life of carefree leisure. But one day that carefree life was interrupted. On an excursion from the palace, the prince noticed an elderly man; Gautama was so surprised by the old man's wizened appearance that the charioteer had to explain to the prince what he had seen. On subsequent trips, Gautama, for the first time, encountered persons suffering from disease, others who were mourning in a funeral procession, and, finally, a holy monk whose appearance was marked by peacefulness. The combined effect of these four chance encounters interrupted the young prince's carefree perception of life and so moved him that he resolved to abandon the life of privilege. He took to the road as a spiritual seeker—a seeker whose journey, almost a decade later, brought him to a place where, sitting beneath a bodhi tree, he finally achieved pure, total enlightenment and became the Buddha.

Perhaps these heroic interruptions in the lives of great spiritual leaders can help us keep our everyday interruptions in perspective. We can respond to interruptions gracefully if we remember that Divine good may happen in our lives, even our interrupted lives, in ways that may be beyond our wildest imaginings.

Interruptions may not fill us with rapt wonder, but they can usher us into the present moment. They snap us out of the future-oriented plans we are busy making or the past-oriented thoughts we are busy thinking and force us *to be*—in the present, right here, right now. In that sense, interruptions are related to vulnerability. Interruptions serve as keys to unlock the present moment—the here-and-now we often ignore in our attempt to keep life under well-managed control. Since we cannot control our interruptions, they can serve as metaphors for the actions of the Sacred, which also lie beyond our control.

The meta-culture encourages us to live according to the fiction that we can be in control of everything if we only put forth enough effort. Thus, we may feel angry when interruptions rudely remind us that, no, we are *not* in total control, whether we'd like to be or not. Interruptions remind us who we are. Underneath our carefully constructed images of appearing to be in control, we really *aren't*—and we think interruptions are lousy because they remind us of that fact.

But in that annoyance, bubbling up in the present moment, we are faced with a choice. We can just keep on being angry until some other distraction calms us down, or we can choose to notice our feelings, be aware in the present moment, and remind ourselves that we are in the presence of the Sacred, who really *is* in control. Sometimes in having that recognition, we may be rewarded with a real sense of God's presence, like I encountered in the hospital. At other times, there may not be anything so dramatic—just a choice we make allowing an interruption simply to be, rather than railing against it. The choice is not easy and the rewards for choosing well are not always apparent. But like the choice to live in wonder or the choice to believe and to pray, the choice to allow interruptions "simply to be" takes us close to the heart of the Divine.

Surprise

If an interruption is a change that's outside our control, a *surprise* is a change from totally "out of the blue." A call from a telemarketer is an interruption, but a call from a long-lost college friend is a surprise.

At their best, surprises are sources of deep delight. Think, for example, about a surprise party. An exciting event in the life of a family or a group of friends, a surprise party involves secret planning, with instructions that are whispered, passed in notes, and explained in surreptitious letters (or faxes or e-mail messages). On the appointed day, everyone gathers, hurriedly cooperating with the people who planned the event. In the days leading up to a surprise party, no *faux pas* is greater than that of revealing the secret to the person for whom the surprise is planned. And once "SURPRISE!" has been yelled and the party is underway, the chief topic of interest is invariably, "Was the person really surprised?"

Why do we love to surprise others? I believe it's because deep down, we want so much to be surprised ourselves. Unlike annoying interruptions, a hoped-for surprise is a fun change, a happy change, a graced change. Surprises are usually unexpected, unasked for, or unearned. Whether it's a gift, an experience, or merely an unanticipated change of plans, a surprise represents a shift from what we expect to what we actually get. If the guest of honor at a surprise birthday party were actually involved in the plans, the event would, of course, no longer be a "surprise" party—it might still be a very nice event, but with no surprise. For something to be a surprise, it must be from "out of the blue," from beyond our control.

Spirituality is full of surprises. The most fundamental surprise, so obvious that we do not even think of it, is the surprise of our birth. Before a person is born, his or her universe consists entirely of the womb, set to the soundtrack of the mother's beating heart. And then—surprise!—this universe gives way under the powerful forces of the labor contractions, and suddenly we are born into a strange, cold, huge world. Our very lives are a "surprise" gift to us, courtesy of our parents—and of God.

More and more surprises follow that most basic surprise: the surprises of learning to talk and to walk; the surprise of making friends; the surprise of discovering the beauty of nature and the goodness of food and shelter and comfort. With adolescence and young adulthood come the surprises of blossoming sexuality and of falling in love; soon comes the surprise of children and of discovering our capacity to be productive and creative.

All of these core life-events are changes, surprising changes—surprising because they are not matters within our control but, rather, are presented to us by others, by society, by God. Even those changes we plan for, like marriage or retirement, still have an element of surprise to them. No matter how extensive our planning may be, the actual experience will always differ somehow from our prior envisioning of the experience. The difference between what we envision and what we actually experience is the element of surprise.

Of course, not all surprises are happy surprises. There are also the terrifying and painful and deadly surprises. Pearl Harbor was the site of a surprise attack at the outset of World War II. The Kennedy assassinations took us by surprise, as did the Kent State shootings, the *Challenger* explosion, and the Oklahoma City bombing. In our personal lives, accidents, illness, death, or other tragedies only too often take us by surprise. But like "happy" surprises, these awful (awe-full?) surprises usher us into a sudden, unimagined change.

Regardless of whether it is welcome or not, any surprise can be unsettling—and perhaps this is one reason why many (perhaps most) of us trade a vulnerable approach to life for a protected way of living. Instead of being vulnerable, we often choose this course: "I will plan my life and work hard to stay in control of my plans. I won't allow anything unusual or risky to affect me." Such an attitude may effectively create an illusion of safety, but at what spiritual cost? In other words, how does it affect the quality of our openness to God? Excessive self-protection does not buy any real security—and living in ways that are too protected and guarded is to risk living without wonder, adventure, and growth. Trying to prevent surprises may seem sensible, but it also may lead to our rejecting a full-blooded, adventurous life.

To live spiritually means accepting the idea that the Sacred has as much—or more—influence and "say-so" over our lives as we ourselves have. Spirituality involves accepting the idea that God will surprise us with changes in our lives—changes we did not plan, we did not control, we did not expect. To be in relationship with the Divine means to live a life that is, at least on some level, risky, unpredictable, and hospitable to surprise.

This is not to say that common sense should be thrown out the window. Risk-taking is not the same as foolhardiness, but it is clearly different from being excessively guarded, protected, or controlled. The spiritual life involves finding equilibrium between the craziness of foolhardiness and the equal craziness of over-protectedness. I can't tell you where that balance lies for you and your life—only you can make that call. But I believe finding that balance begins with trust—trust in the love of God, trust in the basic goodness and friendliness of our universe, trust that the dangers we face will, in the end, not overcome us. By trusting God and trusting life, we embark on an adventure that is sure to leave us with a few scars. Yet it also leaves us with a life not half-lived, but fully lived. Trusting the Sacred means living a life in which we meet surprises (and interruptions) with gratitude and hope, rather than with resentment and pessimism.

Transgression

Interruptions and surprises are changes that are thrust upon us—changes we do not initiate, but must respond to. We hope we can respond to such changes soulfully (with the spirit of openness and wonder and trust). But the spiritual life is not just about changes that *happen* to us. Praying not only changes circumstances, but it changes *us* as well, and it inspires us to make changes. In prayer, we can be inspired to ask for change, to seek change, to initiate change—both internally (like a change in attitude) and externally (like a change in behavior). These changes can, and usually do, affect not only ourselves, but others as well.

If a change in my life is my idea, then making it happen will feel "right." Such self-initiated change, in whatever part of life I make it, would almost certainly feel empowering and liberating—though it also might feel subversive or radical, particularly if it's a change that others may not welcome.

Why do we make changes? Presumably any change, big or small, is made for the purpose of choosing something better—a better way of doing things, a better job, a better car, a better diet, a better self-image, and so on. Changing involves crossing a line that separates one place from another, when the other place is believed to be *better*. What I find interesting about change, and where I think we can discover the spirituality of change, is in considering the "crossing the line" aspect. This is why I think *transgression* is an important quality of the spirituality of change. To transgress means to cross the line. In order to explore this concept, I'd like to tell a story about my childhood.

I think I was probably a boring little kid. I remember myself as a "goody two-shoes." Both at home and at school I was obedient and compliant. I always did what my teachers told me to do—or almost always. My most vivid memory of the first grade is of a time when, shortly after checking out a book on dinosaurs from the school library, I ignored the teacher's instructions for an assignment and spent a significant period of time (it seemed like an eternity to me then, but it was probably only ten or fifteen minutes) drawing a picture of a brontosaurus instead of doing what I was supposed to do. As I remember it, I thought it was a great picture, too. I was quite the budding artist! Then suddenly the teacher realized that I was doing something other than what I was supposed to be doing. She confiscated the "illegal" art and proceeded to humiliate me in front of the class, telling the other students that Carl didn't have his work completed because he was busy drawing pictures instead of following instructions.

How ironic that decades later, this is the event from my first-grade class that most vividly sticks in my mind. On that day, for some reason I was so caught up in the wonder of drawing a picture out of the dinosaur book that without even intending to be naughty and despite my inclination to be compliant, I broke the rules. I had committed my very first transgression (and it wouldn't be my last!). My infraction was not even particularly "wicked"—since I wasn't being disruptive or willfully disobedient. I was merely caught up in cultivating my own education, pursuing science (paleontology) and art (drawing) simultaneously. But that did not matter, for I wasn't following the teacher's rules. I was "out of control," even if only until the teacher realized what I was up to and reined me back in.

Even though I could not have articulated it at the time, I was exploring dimensions of spirituality—not only the spirituality of art and science, but also the spirituality of transgression. I had chosen to follow my wonder and playfulness. But in doing that spiritual exploring, I crossed the boundary of what was acceptable. I was following a call, but it took me to a place where I wasn't "supposed" to go. Now that I'm a grown-up and I worry about how my stepdaughter is behaving in school, I'm not entirely convinced that such transgressions are always the will of God. On the other hand, maybe it *was* a Sacred call I heard that day. It was only a small and short-lived change, a change within me—allowing my self-directed interests to overshadow the need to obey. But it's an example of how changes have both spiritual and social implications. My little infraction taught me that wonder can illuminate the choice to follow one's guidance. It also taught me that following such an inner call may not always please others.

Spiritually speaking, transgression is an important form of change, because sometimes God calls us to break the rules—not because the Sacred is chaotic but because God knows that sometimes "the rules" need to be broken in order for something wonderful to happen, according to the dictates of a "higher" set of rules—the rules of the Sacred.

If the spiritual life calls us to make changes in our soul and in our behavior, such changes involves crossing a line somewhere. Sometimes these changes are easy or welcome—for example, I loved the changes that accompanied my "crossing the line" between being a student and being a professional. Everyone involved in my life supported that change as well. At other times, however, "crossing the line" means "breaking the rules," and that can be difficult and controversial. When I decided to become a vegetarian, I had to adapt to an entirely new diet, and my family and friends also had to adjust to my limitations—not only about what I'd eat but also about where I'd eat. My vegetarianism "broke the rules" of our habits involving food, and we all had to adjust. While I think it was a spiritually beneficial change, others in my life may have found it to be an annoying interruption.

In an abstract sense, transgression may mean breaking many kinds of rules. It could mean crossing the boundary between what is acceptable and unacceptable or between rational and irrational, practical and impractical, familiar and strange, profane and holy, what is sanctified and what is sinful, what is God and what is not-God.

The rules we transgress may include a "rule" we've set for ourselves or a rule handed to us by our parents, teachers, or employers. It could be a civil law or a religious commandment. The boundary may be nothing more than a social code or a personal habit. Crossing the line can be as simple as deciding to skip that habitual daily cup of coffee—or as significant as choosing to leave an abusive spouse. In either case, it means breaking a rule, whether it's the "rule" established by the comfortable routine of a habit or the much more terrifying rules of "proper" behavior we may have internalized as children. My body tells me it wants its cup of coffee. My mind tells me getting a divorce is wrong. If I choose to make a change, I am breaking a rule.

Breaking the rules may involve an action as minor as skipping church on Sunday or as major as refusing to pay taxes as a means of political protest. Transgression beckons us out of the safety of "following the rules" into the scary freedom of a choice intentionally made—a choice to break a rule for the sake of a higher ethical imperative.

What is the spirituality of transgression? Basically, transgressions are spiritual whenever a boundary is crossed for the sake of something higher. Leaving an abusive spouse may "break the rules" regarding the sanctity of marriage, but it is a way of obeying the higher imperative of self-preservation. Refusing to pay taxes used for unnecessary military spending may be illegal, but it is a way of obeying the higher law of peacemaking. Transgressions are changes made in order to be faithful to the Sacred, even if they mean we are disobeying "the rules." This is not to say that all transgressions are above criticism; when rules are broken for the wrong reasons, chaos ensues.

Not all forms of spirituality are open to this idea of Sacred transgression. Resistance to the acceptability of transgression will be found particularly in religious or political cultures that place a high priority on obedience. Obedience has an appropriate place in spiritual life, as we will see in chapter 11, but a culture that over-emphasizes obedience will resist even a healthy understanding of transgression. According to such more rigid ways of thinking, transgression means disobedience and is probably "sinful." This view of transgression is typical of a culture where power is organized in hierarchical lines and goodness simply means being obedient to those with more power than oneself. I personally am very uncomfortable with such a model of power. All communities need legitimate forms of authority, but I believe individuals have a moral imperative to disobey and fight against those whose authority is unjust or abusive. This "moral imperative" is rooted in the spirituality of transgression.

When we are expected to "follow the rules" of someone more powerful than we are but we choose disobedience, we transgress. While I think transgression is a good and necessary spiritual value, I don't want to make a stand for sheer anarchy. When the authority is just and reasonable, accepting the rules is likely to be more spiritually appropriate —but at other times, transgressive, rule-breaking behavior may be the only spiritually sound choice.

I think one of the finest exemplars of the spirituality of transgression is Jesus Christ. The New Testament portrays Jesus and his followers as hell-raising, rule-breaking radicals in a politically repressive culture.

Although it was illegal to work on the Sabbath, Jesus and his followers gathered food and healed the sick on that day. Jesus disregarded the popular legal customs by forgiving a woman caught in adultery. He broke social codes by dining with tax collectors and prostitutes (as an analogy, imagine a religious leader in our time who publicly socialized with investors who finance pornographic movies). Rather than expressing meekness toward the religious leaders of his day, Jesus reacted aggressively to the criticism leveled against him by the priestly establishment. When the Pharisees (the "establishment" leaders) criticized Jesus, he responded by calling them a den of vipers and accusing them of being spiritually harmful to the common people! Part of Jesus' identity as a spiritual leader was associated with his disregarding or breaking boundaries—not for the sake of anarchy but for the sake of the Sacred.

Some of the persons respected as great spiritual leaders—who also have been notorious for transgressive behavior—include Martin Luther King, Jr., a central figure in the American Civil Rights movement; Dorothy Day, who founded the "Catholic Worker" movement, supporting the poorest members of society while loudly condemning the culture of the wealthy; Gandhi, whose commitment to the spirituality of nonviolence combined with his political agenda for ending British rule in India to make him the twentieth century's leading spokesperson for nonviolent political resistance; and, of course, Moses and Jesus and Buddha, each of whom created a new religious tradition by daring to break out of the limitations of the culture they grew up in.

Earlier we considered how religion often is a conservative force that resists change. Transgression, however, is the element that makes spirituality—even the spirituality of conservative religion—a vehicle for Divine change to manifest in the world. The radical nature of spirituality can be breathtaking, transforming us at the roots of who we are and opening us to the possibilities for personal and communal transformation.

Peacemaking

With all this talk of transgression, spirituality is beginning to look like it involves Molotov cocktails more than prayer and meditation! But acknowledging the spirituality of transgression is important, if for no other reason than that we do not typically think of breaking the rules or disobedience as "spiritual" qualities. Spirituality suffers from an unfortunate stereotype as something *nice people* pursue—with "nice people" a code word meaning middle-class, educated, law-abiding people. The idea that Sacred wonder would inspire radical behavior seems too big a pill for many people to swallow—even though Jesus, who remains the best-known spiritual leader in the Western Hemisphere, regularly hung out with disreputable and radical persons and was actually pretty impatient with the "nice people" of his day.

I have intentionally focused on transgression to emphasize that the love of the Divine is available to everyone, even people who are rule-breakers and subversives, even people like radicals and punkers, or prostitutes and pornographers. I'll step down from that soapbox now. At this point, however, I would be deeply remiss if I didn't put transgression in a larger context. Therefore, the last topic in this chapter on change comes from Jesus' comment, "Blessed are the peacemakers, for they will be called children of God" (Matt. 5:9). Note that Jesus did not bless pacifists or draft dodgers or isolationists. He blessed peace*makers*. People who make peace, who actively work for reconciliation and conflict resolution, have the honor of being included among God's playful, open, wonder-filled children.

To make peace is a beautiful ideal for the spirituality of bringing about change. In my opinion, peacemaking is really the most important kind of change, the one by which all the other kinds of change must finally be evaluated. Any changes that serve the spiritual life and nurture a relation-ship with the Divine are changes that ultimately serve the Sacred call for peace. The opposite of peacemaking is not conflict, but aggression. Whereas aggression arises from an excessive desire to control life and others, peacemaking is a logical extension of a life dedicated to wonder and vulnerability.

Even a troublemaker like Jesus was motivated by the longing for peace. His teachings reveal that he clearly longed for a world where oppression no longer exists and where the weakest and humblest members of society have the same access to the joy and wonder of God's blessings that affluent, educated persons enjoy. The example of Jesus also reminds us that peace is not the same as appeasement—that avoiding conflict is not the way to resolve conflict. In fact, one of the biggest mistakes a person dedicated to the Sacred can make is to equate spirituality with the absence of conflict—a mistake no doubt fueled by the idea that spiritual living equals peaceful living. Peace certainly is a central goal of the spiritual life, but it comes about through *active* peacemaking, not through passive avoidance. Since peacemaking is dynamic, it also will inevitably and ironically produce conflict—conflict with persons and institutions that do not particularly want peace, those who do not serve the wonder of the Sacred, but rather serve the forces of excessive power, self-protection, and control.

Does all this sound too political, too public, and therefore like a shift away from true spirituality? Our common ideas of spirituality encourage us to think of spiritual peacemaking as more of an inner quality ("making peace with God") than an external, political quality of hard-nosed conflict resolution—whether that means the "politics" of public life or even the "politics" of a family. This perception of spirituality as an exclusively inner, private experience is yet another symptom of how the meta-culture we live in assumes that spirituality is little more than a subjective preference, irrelevant to the public world of government, business, and education. Common as that idea is, it is a modernist assumption about spirituality and culture. Jesus, Buddha, and Mohammed were all public figures who advocated a spirituality that made a difference (i.e., made changes) in people's inner lives and also in the public realm. What those leaders understood was that spirituality must nurture peace not only on the inside but on the outside as well, in order truly to be faithful to the love—and peace—that originates in the Divine Source.

A world where spirituality and peacemaking and prayer are seen exclusively as "inner" pursuits is a world where crime, injustice, and oppression are allowed to thrive, because it is a world where spiritual values have no real power in the community. In many ways, we live in such a world today. Crackhouses rot away the soul of urban neighborhoods while drug lords get rich. Corporate downsizings throw thousands of people out of work and indirectly contribute to wage stagnation for those lucky enough to keep their jobs, all in an economy where the wealthiest few are rapidly increasing their riches. Our overly private spirituality is incapable of leading us to see how our actions affect others. This makes it possible for a teenage boy to insist that his girlfriend have sex with him, only to disappear when the girl gets pregnant, leaving her the awful choice of getting an abortion or having an unwanted child (and facing the rage of her family). Private spirituality means that our culture has no public values other than profit and consumption—values that combine to create, among other problems, environmental devastation, the reducing of human sexuality to a commodity, and increasing difficulty in forming meaningful relationships with others. If we retreat into private spirituality, we retreat into a kind of spiritual narcissism. A healthy, full-blooded spirituality is a spirituality that challenges the hostility of the world we live in, seeking to replace it with love and trust, wonder and vulnerability, prayer and peacemaking.

Spirituality changes communities as much as it changes individuals. Further, the community issues I have mentioned transcend the conventional political divisions of left and right, liberal and conservative. If I want a relationship with the Divine, I cannot nurture it in a vacuum. My spiritual well-being affects and is affected by the spiritual well-being of all my neighbors and, in the words of the Lakota, "all my relations" (*mitakuye owasin*), not only humans but animals and plants as well. If we wish to be more spiritual, we need to help communities change in prayerful ways.

A time for prayerful change

We live in an era of change, of dramatic and, at times, wrenching change. Many philosophers and critics call the period of history that began roughly with World War II the "postmodern" era, suggesting that the culture and worldview of the modern era (the era of rationalism and scientific empiricism that began with the "Age of Enlightenment" in the eighteenth century) have become obsolete. Many different and conflicting theories exist to explain what "postmodernity" is and how it differs from the obsolete modern worldview. However, several common themes of our age seem to be widely embraced:

- *Postmodernity is an age of skepticism.* We have lost faith in science and progress, we've lost faith in the benevolence of government and business, and increasingly we're losing faith in religion and spirituality. Cynicism reigns throughout our culture.
- *Postmodernity is an age of pluralism and diversity.* In chapter 1, we considered how pluralism has changed the shape of Western spirituality. The rise of religious pluralism is a postmodern trend. Parallel to that trend is the growing recognition that we live in a "global village," where persons of differing racial, ethnic, social, political, and religious backgrounds are suddenly living in the same shrinking community. Isolationism is obsolete, and a crucial task facing all people is learning how to accept diversity and still create shared values.
- *The postmodern age marks the triumph of technology.* The last fifty years have brought sweeping technological change, from orbiting satellites to nuclear power to the Internet. Like so many changes, these advances involve both promise and peril. Splendid abilities to communicate and to work efficiently are balanced by the troubling speed with

which technology is replacing jobs and contributing to the devastation of the environment. When Gutenberg invented movable type, that fifteenth-century technological advance had a direct impact on the Reformation in Christianity the following century—which showed that technology has a real effect on spirituality and suggests that the massive technological changes of our day could bring about unforeseen, significant changes in religious and spiritual practices.

- *Postmodernity is an age of crisis and promise.* The twin threats of nuclear and ecological devastation have created a sense of urgency— and of impending doom—that previous generations never knew. How these crises will affect the unfolding of our culture is a question we can answer only by living into the future. But alongside the crises are the promises of a world where racial, gender, and other forms of oppression may at last be transcended. Thanks to the media, we live in a world where more people have a chance to speak and be heard than ever before. As our stories are heard, we have the opportunity to create a world that is more humane and just than ever before.

On a vast and foundational level, our worldview has changed. That the current era is *"post*modern" suggests we are in a transition time—not only after modernity but also *before* something else. But what? Our society is not sure where we're going next. Events such as the Jewish Holocaust, the Stalinist purges, and "ethnic cleansing" in Bosnia have shaken our faith in human nature. What, then, will reestablish the faith that humanity so desperately needs?

Despite these wrenching events, spirituality is not dead, although it has tended to be marginalized and private in the post-modern world. As this has occurred, many alternative forms of spirituality have developed, collectively and informally adopting a label for themselves more optimistic than "postmodern"—"New Age." Pointing to the idea that epochal changes are taking place, "New Age" culture suggests that our society is undergoing a shift as major as that of the transitions between earlier "ages," such as from the Stone Age to the Bronze Age. Various pundits have labeled our postmodern culture the "Space Age," the "Information Age," and (with true postmodern cynicism) the "Plastic Age." "New Age," however, seems to suggest that maybe what we are attempting to create is the "Spiritual Age."

Religious fundamentalists tend to perceive current social changes in terms of decadence and dissolution. Fundamentalist Christians worry about the rise of "secular humanism," while fundamentalist Muslims denounce Western values in general. To the average fundamentalist, modernity was bad, postmodernity is even worse, and probably only a miraculous intervention from God will be able to set things right. Religious liberals respond to social change in a more pragmatic way. For example, the former Roman Catholic (now Episcopal) priest Matthew Fox brought to America a style of Christian liturgy first popularized in Sheffield, England, called a "Rave Mass"—a worship service involving the use of music and video in the style of the underground music/dance/party culture popular in cities like London and San Francisco. Fox and other religious leaders recognize that a postmodern spirituality must adapt to cultural changes in order to play a meaningful role in people's lives.

In this postmodern world, we are living in a swirl of constant, colorful, dangerous change. All of these epochal changes will continue to take place whether or not we are committed to spiritual values. But what the life of wonder, belief, and prayer offers us is the chance to engage this world of dizzying change from a centered perspective—the perspective of being lovers of God. We who choose to relate to the Sacred are choosing to open ourselves up to change and to be agents of divine change as well.

We will experience unasked-for changes—surprises and interruptions —whether or not we are spiritually-minded, though living spiritually means approaching surprises and interruptions with trust. Such trust can also inspire us as agents of change—to make intentional changes according to God's call, which I believe is a call to peacemaking, healing, and community. The changes that are inspired by the spiritual life are all possibilities, large or small, to re-create the world we live in—to re-create it according to the life-affirming wonder and trust that links us with God. Opening ourselves to the Sacred is to open ourselves to changes—changes that make our lives and the lives of others better.

8

Matter

In chapter 1, we considered the diversity of views associated with the relationship between the spirit and the body. We considered how the physical universe—the world of matter and energy—could be seen as the "body" of the Sacred. My belief that prayer changes things brings us to the question of spirit's relationship to matter again. What is the connection between prayer and the "things" that prayer changes? Put another way, what is the relationship between spirit and matter?

Let me begin by clarifying what I mean by matter. Since modern physics has demonstrated the subatomic unity between matter and energy, when I refer to "matter," I mean the entire scope of the physical universe, including both matter *and* energy. Matter, as modern physics shows, is simply energy "at rest." So my question about the relationship between spirit and matter may be put this way: what is the relationship of the inner, unseen world of the spirit to the outer, visible world of space and time, matter and energy?

"Matter" is derived from the same Latin root word from which we get "mother" (consider the similarity between "material" and "maternity"). So the first and perhaps the essential quality I'd like to consider is the maternal, nurturing quality of matter. Mother Nature is the matrix—the womb—out of which we are born. Just as the Hebrew Scriptures suggest that Adam was created out of the earth, so all physical beings come from their "mother," the universe of matter.

But just as the material world is conceptualized as mother—Mother Nature—so the Sacred has often been conceptualized as father—God the Father. In this traditional Western view, the Divine breathes life into clay

125

and gives life to humanity. Our life arises out of the union of Father Spirit and Mother Matter.

Even Goddess spiritualities like Wicca tend to conform to this view. The Goddess is usually regarded as synonymous with the Earth—that is, with matter. While this gendered way of understanding spirit's relation to matter has a long history, it needs to be considered carefully. Linking matter with the feminine and spirit with the masculine can be a subtle form of sexism.

I believe this view suffers from a dualistic privilege of masculinity and spirit—in other words, this view regards masculinity as being higher or better than femininity and therefore presumes that spirit is higher or better than matter. The masculine spirit has been regarded as holy and godlike, while feminine matter has been seen as profane and sinful. This way of thinking views the soul as somehow fundamentally separate from the body and considers spirituality to be a quest for liberation from the material world. It is a sexist view that has had many consequences, including the denial of the Christian priesthood to women and the persecution of alleged witches—female sorcerers—in late medieval/early modern Europe.

The observations of feminist thinkers have encouraged us to reevaluate the ways in which we honor masculinity at the expense of femininity. Therefore, the conceptual split between matter and spirit also needs to come under scrutiny. Alternative religions like Wicca have made a point of celebrating matter as equal to spirit in sacredness. In many forms of Wicca, the Earth is a manifestation of the Goddess and is every bit as holy (if not holier) than the masculine principle of the "Sky Father." The danger here lies in affirming matter but then discounting spirit!

I am dissatisfied with any theory of matter and spirit that seeks to make one "higher" than the other. To find a nondualistic or nonhierarchical view of matter and spirit, we need to acknowledge the polarity between matter and spirit without suggesting that one is better than the other—just as the society we live in is seeking an innovative understanding of men and women that honors their differences, but does so without judgment or rank or privilege.

In the confines of this introductory book, I cannot develop a fully formed theory of the relationship between matter and spirit. However, I'd like at least to make a proposal that I believe will both honor traditional views and take into consideration contemporary concerns for gender justice.

Since masculinity and femininity are natural parts of life and represent different spheres of experience, the metaphor of masculine spirit and feminine matter continues to be useful—although I think an alternative characterization of feminine spirit and masculine matter works just as well. As men and women are different, so also is there a fundamental difference between the reality of spirit and the reality of matter. Simultaneously, however, we need to view the material realm as being as fully sacred and divine as the spiritual realm. Even though men and women differ in many ways, both share much in common as human beings. Thus, my proposal regarding the relationship between spirit and matter recognizes that the differences between the two are also undergirded by a fundamental, mystical unity of spirit and matter.

Since I believe God is ultimately bigger than the universe, this model still has the male God as ultimately "higher" than the female universe. The way out of that problem is to affirm that God is beyond all gender; therefore, feminine images of the Divine, like that of the Goddess, are equally useful representations of the Divine. A relationship between the female Goddess and the male universe works just as well (for that matter, models of a male God/male universe or female Goddess/female universe might be particularly appropriate for gay and lesbian spiritual seekers!).

My overall point is this: we need a spiritual cosmology that honors the material world as *loved* by the Sacred, not as somehow inferior or second-best. True, some spiritual traditions, like Christianity, view the universe as "fallen"—but even if we view the realm of matter as somehow flawed, our choosing to love the materiality of life is the essential first step toward healing and transformation—two forms of change that are particularly spiritual in nature.

Matter and spirit out of balance

The problem with the spirit-matter polarity arises when either pole is dualistically rejected. While the classic tendency in the West was to exalt spirit and reject matter, our postmodern meta-culture often celebrates matter but rejects spirit. Actually, in our culture today, overemphasizing either one is easy.

When we fail to hold spirit and matter in equilibrium, unbalanced forms of spirituality result. The privileging of spirit over matter tempts us to see spirituality as a wholly interior activity, consisting exclusively of internal "spiritual experiences" but unconcerned with infusing spiritual values into the messy world of politics, economics, or even family or community relationships. On the other side, the privileging of matter over spirit tempts us to become so absorbed with the external aspects of life— from making a living and amassing wealth to such practices as political activism or caring for the poor—that we forget that the external parts of living are possible only insofar as they arise from the fruitful cultivation of interior spiritual awareness.

For lack of better terms, I call the excesses of these dualistic views *materialism* and *spiritualism*. Both terms, as I'm using them, refer to excesses—by "materialism" I mean an excessive obsession with owner- ship and wealth, while by "spiritualism" I mean an excessive obsession with paranormal or preternatural experiences. Materialism is in essence a rejection of spirit; spiritualism is a similar rejection of matter.

At their worst, materialism and spiritualism are deadly. Materialism inspired the repressive regimes of communism, whose commitment to a society based strictly on materialistic principles led to the persecution of Christians and other kinds of dissidents. Spiritualism at its worst is epitomized by the Heaven's Gate sect, whose members committed suicide to free themselves of their "mammalian" physical nature.

Fortunately, most people avoid the deadly extremes of materialism or spiritualism; nevertheless, if we are out of balance in either direction, our lives can be diminished. For example, materialism diminishes the life of the successful young businessman who has no time for spirituality (or, for that matter, no time to be compassionate to those less fortunate than himself) because he is so very busy amassing a fortune and living his life by what is "reasonable" or "scientific." The bumper sticker that says "He who dies with the most toys wins" reflects the values of a materialist.

Spiritualism is evident in the life of a young woman who feels that, in order to become enlightened, she must chant or meditate compulsively for hours each day and who feels repulsed by sexuality and other bodily functions. Eventually she may come to the point of detesting her body as an obstacle to her "ascension"—her hoped-for transformation into a purely incorporeal, spiritual being.

Both of these extremes are likely to use denial as a means of maintain- ing their way of looking at things. Materialists are likely to approach life in reductionist terms, discounting any evidence for spiritual reality. They will dismiss evidence of persons with psychic powers or of miraculous healings as psychological trickery. For that matter, such persons might repress or ignore feelings of wonder or awe, and certainly wouldn't ascribe spiritual meaning to such emotions.

Spiritualists, however, tend to view everything in terms of metaphysical beliefs—even the slightest coincidence becomes evidence of magic or of the intervention of spirit guides. Such persons may uncritically accept the word of psychics who claim to channel beings from other planets or other "dimensions," believing that the world is about to end catastrophically—just because somebody in a trance said so. Where the materialist views the world in "reductionist" ways, refusing to admit the possibility of spiritual reality, the spiritualist views the world in an equal but opposite "expansionist" way, insisting on projecting esoteric meaning into every corner of life.

I'd like to affirm a middle path. I suggest that both the reductionist materialist and the expansionist spiritualist would be more open to creative and fulfilling life if they admitted that other possible explanations exist for their experiences. The problem is not that a person chooses to believe a certain way so much as it is his or her unwillingness to consider that other legitimate ways of seeing things exist.

Materiality: the spirituality of matter

We've explored the inner experiences of spirituality, such as wonder, belief, and prayer—dynamics of consciousness that play important parts in the spiritual life. However, we err if we assume spirituality only involves subjective or psychological states. We need to balance our exploration of the inner realm of spirituality with an examination of its external, material manifestations—not just theories of spirituality, but also the practice; the way spirituality makes a concrete difference in the lives of people. By doing this, I hope to show that materiality is as essential to spirituality as the body is essential to the soul.

I've suggested that spirituality has its roots in the cultic aspects of culture. We need to remember that culture is as much an external, material phenomenon as it is an "internal" phenomenon. We cultivate our art, architecture, technology, and so forth from raw *materials*. Just as culture represents the material manifestations of the splendor of human creativity, so do spiritual practices, rituals, sacraments, and icons represent the external, embodied manifestations of the inner experience of spirituality.

For example, I may have a consciousness-altering experience of the Divine presence, which is an internal spiritual experience. And if I respond to that experience by spending a half hour every morning in silent contemplation for the rest of my life, that is my spiritual practice—an observable, concrete practice that makes up part of my spirituality. To use

examples from the Christian tradition—praying, going to church, receiving
Holy Communion, reading the Bible, giving money to the church, and
helping out poor persons are all typical forms of Christian practice—
externals that constitute the material or embodied manifestations of
Christian spirituality.

Inner and outer forms of spirituality are like matter and spirit—they
are separate and they are one. To develop and practice spirituality requires
understanding and enacting some sort of external practice just as much as
it means understanding and cultivating some sort of inner consciousness.
"Internals," like wonder and playfulness, and "externals," like disciplined
prayer and working to help others, are mutually interdependent. It's a
mistake to divide spirituality into two unrelated "compartments," inner and
outer, for a healthy spirituality has both in unity.

In the pages to come we will look at concrete, material ways in which
we manifest the abstract characteristics of spirituality. Instead of just
talking about generosity, we will consider the practice of tithing; instead
of just talking about wonder and prayer, we will consider the practices of
ritual and ceremonial activity. If we think spirit and matter are separate, or
spirit and body are separate, we also will think that prayer has nothing to
do with something like political activism or that wonder has nothing to do
with activities like feeding hungry persons. But just as the air cannot be
separated from the lung in the process of breathing, so the experience of
wonder or believing cannot be separated from the concrete choices a
person makes as a result of faith.

But first, I want to celebrate matter. So, for the remainder of this
chapter, we'll look at some earthy, materialistic concepts like nature,
beauty, eroticism, and darkness, simply to celebrate the ways in which
they open us to encounter the Sacred in physical ways. In addition, we'll
consider the ideas of incarnation and sacrament as specific spiritual
concepts that enable us to encounter the Sacred here in the "real world."

Nature

"It's easier for me to find God in nature than in a church." I think
many people who do not participate in organized religion (as well as some
who do!) feel this way.

Although finding the Divine in nature is only possible if one's culture
interprets nature as "spiritual," the fact remains that, for many people,
culture provides precisely that interpretation—and has for some time now.
Beginning with the philosophers and the artists of the Romantic period in

the nineteenth century, nature has been viewed by many as an ideal bridge to God. The idea of finding the Sacred in nature instead of in church is a variation on the assertion, "I'm spiritual but not religious." We think of nature as spiritual while churches are just religious; it's not hard to figure out which one seems to be the better of the two.

Like many spiritually-minded people, I too love nature, and one of my favorite spots is an Episcopal Church camp called Camp Mikell, located about two hours north of Atlanta. As with all camps, it is full of trees, wildlife, streams, and quiet. The evidence of human habitation is simply a few cabins and other small buildings, with a couple of gravel roads and dirt paths into the woods. How different this is from my normal, day-to-day life in Atlanta! My life there, like the life of everyone else in the city, is dominated by technology and encased in culture—from cars and buses and trains to concrete and steel, asphalt, computers, telephones, and fax machines. The artifacts of humanity completely surround me in the city. My everyday life includes hours spent on concrete, but hardly any time spent walking on soil. I see hundreds of cars every day, but only a few trees. Despite all the conveniences it affords, urban life has a fatal flaw, which is that it makes me, and, I suspect, most people, feel alienated from nature.

What is nature, and why do I claim that it must be culturally interpreted in order to find God? *Nature* refers to any part of the environment that is more or less undeveloped or untouched by human culture and technology—and the more untouched the better. Thus, the pristine wilderness of the Minnesota boundary waters or the Alaskan tundra is more purely "natural" than Shenandoah National Park, which in turn is more "natural" than Central Park. A tent is closer to nature than a building, and backpacking is closer to nature than a weekend at a commercial RV campground.

The opposite of nature is culture. Consider this continuum:

Nature/Wilderness ————————— *Culture/Technology*

The continuum extends from unexplored wilderness on the "nature" end to the urban tangle of concrete and asphalt on the "culture" end.

We've already considered at length the spiritual component of culture—we attend church or other kinds of spiritual gatherings, we read sacred texts or devotional books, we listen to spiritual music, we meditate on holy icons. Going to a cathedral or seeing a beautiful stained glass window can take our breath away—and fill us with the "breath" of God. We call such experiences "inspirational," which means that they bring *in* to us a sense of the *spirit*. The Divine comes to us through the medium of culture, as it should. One of the foundational purposes of culture is to create the arena where we may encounter the Sacred.

But not always. "It's easier for me to find God in nature than in a church." The implication is that for many people, the sacred buildings and the holy books and the religious art and music have fallen mute. They no longer attest to the presence of the Divine. If the buildings and the books are silent, where then do we hear the whispers of the Spirit? In nature, at the opposite end of the continuum, away from the interfering hand of human creation.

For many persons, God cannot be found in a mere human-created object, even if that "object" is as grand as Chartres Cathedral. Instead, evidence of the Divine is found away from the work of humans—in the clarity of the forest, the river, the mountains. To these people, spirituality is not just a cultural experience, but it is a natural experience as well.

However—here's something to consider. To say "I find God more easily in nature than in church" is simply to say this: nature is, for the speaker, a *more profound icon* of God than any human-made icon. Indeed nature may be a window through which we encounter the Sacred, but if it's a window onto God, it's an icon.

How did nature get to be an icon? In the words of folksinger Arlo Guthrie, "You can't have a light without a dark to stick it in."* The "light" of nature-as-icon only became visible to humanity when we became concerned about the "dark"—the excesses of culture and technology. With the dawning of the industrial revolution, technology became increasingly pervasive; for the Romanticist writers of the nineteenth century, nature became the beacon of light that promised to liberate humanity from the "dark satanic mills," to use Blake's famous phrase. Today, as we recognize just how serious the ecological crisis is, the ideal of nature untainted by culture seems more sacred than ever before. So nature functions as an icon. But though nature herself is culture-free, our interpretation of nature—as a place where we may find liberation from the dangers of technology—is, ironically, itself an aspect of culture, in that we "cultivated" that understanding of nature over time!

---

* Arlo Guthrie, "The Neutron Bomb," on Arlo Guthrie/Pete Seeger, *Precious Friend*, Warner Bros. Records 3644. Used by permission.

Another word for farming (the basis of culture) is *husbandry*. The word *nature* is etymologically related to "natal," having to do with birth. These word associations suggest that to cultivate the ground is to be a "husband" to Mother Earth as she gives birth to crops. Thus, nature and culture, viewed as polarities, are related to the polarity of gender—bringing us back to masculine spirit and feminine matter again, back to the interplay between God the Father and Mother Nature. Our words reveal the hidden beliefs and biases of our cultural worldview.

Like the exaltation of spirit over matter, the exaltation of culture over nature is intimately bound up with the privileging of male over female. The historical position of Western monotheism has been that the Sacred is greater than nature, since all nature is God's creation. For centuries, Christianity has taught that salvation is found "in the church," not in the wilderness—therefore, culture is spiritually superior to nature. But in our time, we are seeing more searching for the Sacred away from culture, in nature rather than in church. This suggests that we are now finding God more in a "feminine" sphere of nurture and wildness and mystery than in the traditionally "masculine" sphere of cultural order, law, and reason—an idea corroborated by the explosion of interest in Native American spirituality, Goddess spirituality, Wicca, and the other Neopagan religions. Even the churches are turning to nature, with church camps like Camp Mikell. Perhaps they, too, will increasingly become more "feminine" in their future spirituality.

I want to finish this discussion of nature with two caveats. First, I think that privileging nature at the expense of culture is as big a mistake as the opposite. If we say that the Divine is found in nature but not in culture, we have limited God just as surely as we limit God if we say that the Sacred is found only in religion. I believe the most appropriate understanding of nature and culture views *both* realms as potential icons of the Sacred. A creative spirituality will stress the nonhierarchical unity of masculine and feminine, of nature and culture, of matter and spirit, all within the Holy One.

My second concern regards the notion of purity. If we think God is to be found in nature because nature is "pure," we are being naive about nature and we are idolizing purity. Something as ordinary as watching a housecat eat a mole will convince any thoughtful person that nature is messy and brutal—nothing pure about it! As for the temptation to idolize purity, that is a form of spiritualism—remember how the spiritualistic person was disgusted by the messiness of her own body? That flight from messiness also has ominous political overtones—for example, it was a dream of purity (racial purity) that spurred Hitler on to his atrocities. The power of nature as an icon stems not from its purity, but indeed from its messy earthiness. The impurities of nature do not keep nature from functioning as an icon—a fact that reveals that the love of God can be found anywhere and everywhere, not just in "pure" settings.

Beauty

In the summer of 1995, a gallery near Atlanta featured a major exhibition of sacred art from the Russian Orthodox Church spanning seven hundred years. I was thrilled to see the intricately designed icons, vestments, and liturgical objects such as chalices and censers, some centuries old, all exquisitely beautiful. The delicate, ornate craftsmanship of the sacred objects was lovely to behold—and a bit overwhelming, especially in a crowded art gallery.

A year later, Oglethorpe University sponsored an exhibition of sacred Tibetan art, including pieces from the personal collection of the Dalai Lama. In the midst of the various ornate images of Buddha and Bodhisattvas, four Tibetan monks were hunched over a table, meticulously creating a mandala out of sand. Dozens of people gathered around the monks, watching intently, some taking photographs. Once again, I felt overwhelmed as I marveled at beautiful works of art created for the purpose of prayer and spiritual growth, now presented in a secular exhibition.

Like cut flowers in a vase, these works of sacred art seemed beautiful, but also removed from the "soil" in which they were given life. All the imagery spoke of sacred consciousness, but the atmosphere of these busy galleries felt nothing like a Buddhist monastery or an Orthodox church. I usually find churches and monasteries to be sources of awe and wonder, but these exhibitions of sacred art left me feeling exhausted rather than inspired.

The items on display were originally created for a spiritual purpose, that is, to be used in religious worship. I was distressed at how such items, which were never meant to be viewed as mere "art," had been reduced to objects on display in a gallery. People seemed to come to these shows not for spiritual sustenance but for mere entertainment—seeing the sacred art was almost like going to a baseball game. Like the great cathedrals of Europe, which in recent years have become little more than museum-like tourist attractions, the Russian Orthodox and Tibetan Buddhist displays struck me as evidence of how our meta-culture has become secularized, to the point where spiritual culture is something only worth being displayed in a museum.

I shared these concerns with a Jesuit priest I know. He smiled and said, "Yes, our culture reduces icons to mere objects of art. But remember that it works the other way, too, and ordinary art can easily transport us to the presence of God." Humbled, I remembered that spirituality is not limited to something that goes on inside churches. Art galleries and studios can be resplendent homes for the Sacred presence, just as monasteries or forests can be. Remembering how I have redefined the word "icon" to mean anything that serves as a window onto God's presence, I knew my Jesuit friend was suggesting that literally *anything* can reveal the Divine to us, if God wants to be revealed and we are open to see.

As I reflected on my experience with the sacred art in the secular galleries, I realized that the deeper issue here involved the role of beauty in the spiritual life. The sacred art was truly beautiful, which is why it deserved to be shown in galleries. But my sense of dislocation suggested to me that a deeper beauty in these sacred objects pointed beyond the objects themselves, to the Divine—the origin and source of all beauty.

Beauty is a spiritual quality reflected in the material world. In the experience of something beautiful—whether a majestic natural vista, an exquisite work of art, or a person radiant with life and joy and compassion—we can be ushered into the higher presence of the Sacred. Beauty is an iconic quality—a quality through which God may be encountered.

"Beauty" is derived from the Latin *bellus*, which is a diminutive form of *bonus*, the Latin word for "good." So, at least in terms of language, beauty has its roots in goodness. When we see something we consider beautiful, it pleases us and we consider it good. God, as the "first principle" of life and love, is the source of goodness—and also of beauty. Beauty originates in the existence of the Sacred.

I believe that "beauty" as a category of human experience only makes sense in terms of spirituality. When the song of a bird or the majesty of a mountain fill us with wonder and awe, we are responding to their beauty—but that wondrous response only makes sense if we have some inner sense of God's beauty, from which all other beauty is derived. When I think, "That tree is beautiful" or "The sky is lovely," I can make such an evaluation because the tree and the sky remind me of the ultimate origin of beauty—the Sacred. This is a bold statement for me to make, and yet it is a traditional, spiritual understanding of the origin of beauty. Appreciating earthly beauty comes from an intuitive awareness of Divine beauty.

Furthermore, the Divine source of all beauty radiates through and illuminates every corner of the universe, meaning that God's beauty resides even in places where our finite minds cannot (or will not) apprehend it. Once about ten years ago I was at a congested airport waiting in a grimy parking area for a taxi—hardly a scenario I would deem "beautiful"! As I waited, thinking about nothing special, suddenly the entire parking lot seemed aglow with the unexpected radiance of the Holy. Only for a moment and then it passed—yet in that moment, I learned that God's beauty is knit into the structure of the universe at a level deeper than our normal awareness of things allows us to see.

Beauty's splendor resides both in nature and in culture. The majesty of Mount Everest, the delicacy of a monarch butterfly, and fearsome strength of a grizzly bear each manifest a different nuance of the beautiful. That Beethoven's Ninth Symphony or the Taj Mahal or *Hamlet* should evoke within us a sense of sublime beauty is a mystery far deeper than can be plumbed here. We find beauty in the disciplined performance of an Olympic athlete or in the dancing words of a poem by Keats. For all this, however, part of the mystery of beauty lies in the fact that it is not revealed to everyone the same way—I find beauty in the Grateful Dead's modal jamming, while my wife finds such music boring and prefers listening to Mozart. Beauty is subjective (for not all persons are moved by any one work of art) and paradoxically it has an objective quality (for many great works of art retain the power to move persons across time and cultures).

Beauty is not simply known by its presence. It is also known by its absence, as revealed by the brutally realistic writing in Alice Walker's *The Color Purple* or Sapphire's poem *Wild Thing* (both of which explore the terrible, violent horrors of racism, sexism, and abuse). The music of punk rock bands like The Clash and the Sex Pistols was ugly, but the ugliness fit the music's stance of social protest. Artists like Sapphire and The Clash create an "inverse" beauty, in that the uncensored honesty of rage, anger, and alienation in their work testifies to the beauty of truth—even truth that may be painfully difficult to face. What makes such art so provocative is that the beauty of the truth-telling is overshadowed by the absence of apparent beauty in the rage and alienation that the art dares to explore.

Since I believe spirit and matter interpenetrate and are embedded in each other, I also believe that the beauty of the Sacred is embedded in the world of matter. This is not to say that all things are equally beautiful, nor do I wish to deny the reality of death, pain, and other aspects of reality we may find repulsive rather than beautiful. But simply because God's beautiful presence is not immediately apparent does not mean the Sacred is absent. As my Jesuit friend reminded me, anything—no matter how beautiful or "ugly" it appears on the surface—may function as a vehicle through which divine beauty is revealed. God's beauty is everywhere, and part of the task of the spiritual life is learning to recognize the evidence of that omnipresent splendor.

This omnipresent splendor is an abundant gift to us from God, a gift not limited by the vagaries of human taste. The Divine may be revealed through the most glorious masterpiece—or through the tackiest painting of "sweet Jesus." I believe it's a mistake to assume that the "more beautiful" a work of art is, the better God is revealed through it. Excessive aesthetic judgmentalism can thwart the experience of wondrous beauty; it's an attempt to reduce beauty to something manageable and controllable. To the extent that we are devoted to the rightness of our taste, we neglect the possibilities of the divine presence in all culture, lowly as well as grand. In the words of Evelyn Underhill: "The sick man gazing hour after hour at *and through* a badly modelled Crucifix, and thus entering ever more deeply into the mystery of love and pain, has an experience of Spirit denied to the exquisite taste which rejects all images except the very best" (Underhill 1933, 42. Italics added).

Does this mean the spiritual life ultimately is just a lighthearted claim that "everything is beautiful" and therefore perfect just as it is, meaning that nothing needs ever to be changed or improved upon? Hardly! The pervasive presence of Sacred beauty is part of a paradox—the other part being that change is a reality of life and choice is a part of the human condition. We are free to make choices on behalf of nurturing and celebrating beauty, but we can also make choices that serve to obscure or hide the radiance of the Divine. Every time an artist strives to create a beautiful work of art, he is striving to make choices and changes in the world in the service of beauty. Every time a spiritual seeker prayerfully attempts to live her life according to her understanding of God's call, she likewise is striving to create beauty, as a gift to the Sacred.

Eroticism

Part of having a material nature—in other words, of having a body—is the undeniable fact that we human beings are fleshly, erotic beings. Eroticism is the embodiment of human longing. The erotic impulse is the impulse for the fulfillment of the body's desire, the appreciation and enjoyment of the body's beauty. Our body naturally longs for the touch of another body, which is why the foundational (and most notorious!) erotic impulse is the impulse to mate. However, eroticism is much more than just sexual desire. Eroticism covers the entire spectrum of bodily desires, which includes the desire to be physically fit, the desire for pleasurable touch, the desire to become a parent, and the desire for family or marriage or any safe, long-lasting relationship.

Since spirituality is as much a matter of the body as it is a matter of the mind, our eroticism is a spiritual longing, just like the longing for wonder or peace or beauty is a spiritual longing. We are, most of us, not culturally accustomed to thinking along these lines, though. Indeed, in most spiritual traditions, we encounter varying degrees of anxiety over eroticism and sexuality. Nothing seems to sum it up better than Paul's dour proclamation, "It is well for a man not to touch a woman" (I Cor. 7:1). Of course, not only has Paul been the traditional Christian voice opposed to male-female sexuality, but he is also seen as a source of the condemnation of gay and lesbian sexuality.

Unfortunately, Christianity is not the only major religion that is anxious about human sexuality. Whether your spiritual home is Christianity, Judaism, Islam, or one of the Eastern traditions, you can easily find yourself confronted by various anti-sexual attitudes: that celibacy is holier than sexuality, that marriage is the only acceptable arena for sexual expression, that homosexuality or indeed any sexual expression for purposes other than procreation is forbidden.

With the advent of technologies such as the contraceptive pill, widespread questioning of religious sexual codes ensued. Today, many individuals, especially in the West, who consider themselves religiously devout have sexual norms far more liberal than those of even a mere thirty or forty years ago. And yet, the idea that religion is the great protector of virginity and abstinence still looms large in the public consciousness.

The irony of all this is embodied in the spiritual quality of erotic longing. This is evident in how much of the imagery in the Judeo-Christian tradition, beginning with the Hebrew and Christian scriptures, expresses the longing for God in erotic terms. The most obvious example of this is the Song of Solomon, a collection of love poems in the Hebrew Scriptures that are frankly sexual in character. For centuries, Christians have tried to explain away this poetry as an analogy illustrating the love of God for creation or the love of Christ for the church!

But the Christian tradition continues to employ erotic imagery to express spiritual longing. Christians describe the church as the "Bride of

Christ." Doesn't this imply that the church—the community of believers—is Christ's *lover*? At least in the West, religion seems to have generated conflicting messages about the relationship between eroticism and spirituality. Perhaps the anxiety expressed by Paul has its root in the recognition that eros truly *is* a powerful element of spiritual longing. Regardless, today we surely may benefit from considering the eroticism of spirituality, acknowledging an aspect of spirituality that has historically been underemphasized.

I believe that one reason religions have tended to take cautious positions toward sexuality is that sex is one area of life where the risk is great for exploitation and abuse. Truly, while I believe spirituality needs to include a positive, celebratory understanding of eroticism, such an understanding must include a commitment to ethical standards that respect the dignity and worth of all people. But a positive sexual ethic does not require the repression of sexuality. On the contrary, I believe that honoring the spirituality of eroticism is a necessary step toward ensuring that the sexual values of a community are compassionate and just for all people.

In his book *Will and Spirit*, psychiatrist Gerald May acknowledges that erotic feelings can be a normal part of the spiritual life. May writes: "I am convinced that once human passion for the divine is allowed into awareness it is bound to have sexual effects" (May 1982, 150). If prayer or meditation or any other "spiritual" activity arouses feelings of erotic longing in us, rather than being embarrassed or upset, our best response is to smile and recognize that such feelings of arousal are often part of the territory. Erotic feelings in a spiritual context, far from being something to be ashamed of, serve as gentle reminders that spirituality is a material, fleshly experience as well as an inner journey. Our relationship with the Sacred is "embodied" in experiences such as longing and desire. To be spiritual is to be erotic, and to be prayerful is to long for the Divine with all the passion of our body.

Some of the newer religions in our culture—the Goddess spiritualities, Wicca, and other forms of Neopaganism—have made creative attempts to celebrate eroticism and spirituality as the twin flames of one sacred impulse. These earth-centered religions often use imagery of "Mother Earth" and "Sky Father," with their sacred marriage being central to life, to fertility, to human creativity and generativity. The Wiccan path uses two images for the Divine: the Goddess and the Green Man. The Goddess symbolizes the divinity inherent in all creation while the Green Man is a sort of God of the forest, a divine manifestation of the spirituality inherent in all life. Here, the roles of Mother Earth and Father Sky are inverted, as the Goddess embodies the transcendence of the heavens and the Green Man embodies the fertility of the earth. Yet the point remains the same. Their coming together in a sacred sexual union is what symbolizes the fulfillment of all our Divine longings.

Too sexy for some? Perhaps. Yet alternative religions are growing rapidly, which implies that a spirituality attempting openly and positively to celebrate eroticism speaks to the needs of many people. Moreover, the erotic imagery in the ancient sacred texts of Judaism and Christianity—as well as erotic scriptures from other traditions, such as the Kama Sutra—suggests that this is not really such a radical idea after all. Perhaps, if our religious traditions lightened up in their understanding and treatment of sexuality, then eroticism in all its glory—the *full* range of the physical longings and abilities of the body, not just sexuality—could be fully celebrated as part of a rich spirituality. To be spiritual means not only to nurture the consciousness of prayer and wonder, but also to maintain high standards in regard to exercise, diet, grooming, and hygiene. Our erotic nature reminds us that our bodies are beautiful, that is, good. Our erotic nature reminds us that our bodies are gifts from God.

Darkness

In the previous section, I suggested that religious traditions might "lighten up" a little about sex. That was also an intentional pun, for spirituality is often linked with light.

In Christianity, for example, a major theme of spirituality involves understanding Divinity in terms of light. The Gospel of John, in describing Jesus as "the word of God," says "in him was life, and the life was the light of all people" (John 1:4). So as a foundation of Christian spirituality, God, light, and life are knit together in Christ. Nor is this only a Christian concept. In Buddhism, the goal of the spiritual life is enlightenment—a splendid word that means "to be filled with the light of knowledge."

Darkness is the absence of light. Traditionally, as light has been linked with spirituality, so darkness has been linked with matter and materiality. This reinforces the notion that matter is the antithesis of spirit, just as darkness is the antithesis of light. But in fact, darkness and light are not so much antithetical as they are complementary parts of the material (physical) world. The dark of night follows the light of day, just as surely as winter follows summer. Light and dark are not enemies so much as they are the opposite aspects of a polarity.

Just as both light and darkness are complementary parts of the material world, so also in some spiritual traditions a concept of "divine darkness" exists, providing a balance to the traditional equation of spirit with light. It is a darkness that is light's "partner," just as matter and spirit are partners in the fullness of the Sacred. To the extent that spirituality seeks only to honor the light and to repress or deny or otherwise avoid the reality of darkness, spirituality falls into the old trap of dualism again—a dualism that says God is limited by "light," whether such light is understood in a physical or spiritual sense. Just as the beauty of the Sacred transcends the limitations of our human conceptions of beauty, so the presence of the Divine illuminates every corner of the universe, whether "light" or "dark"—including the "darkest" parts of the human soul!

Spiritual traditions abound in literature that points to "light" as good and spiritual, and "darkness" as fearsome and unspiritual. One example comes from the Gospel of John again, where not only is Jesus described as the "light," but his enemies—whether evil spirits or human opponents—are described as the "dark" that could not comprehend or overcome the light.

But not all spiritual traditions view darkness so dualistically. One excellent, nondualistic model for the spirituality of darkness is the "yin-yang" symbol of Taoism. This symbol is a circle divided into paisley-shaped halves of black and white, with a white dot in the middle of the black half, and vice versa. The Tao suggests that light and dark interpenetrate each other and, indeed, join together to make one unified whole. The message of the Tao and of its yin-yang symbol is that unity and duality coexist—the elements of duality function as parts of a greater unity. This, of course, echoes what we have been saying about the polarity between spirit and matter. The statements "spirit and matter are one" and "spirit and matter are distinct" may be paradoxical in terms of the limitations of human language, but both are true nonetheless.

Several times, I've mentioned *The Cloud of Unknowing*, the fourteenth-century treatise on contemplative prayer. This medieval mystical book gives an excellent overview of the spirituality of darkness. Using the metaphor of a cloud, the anonymous author discusses the life of contemplation as one dedicated to searching for a God who is hidden behind a thick cloud of "unknowing." Hidden behind that cloud, beyond the limits of our reason or even our imagination, the Divine appears to us as darkness.

Our control-based society feverishly attempts to deny "the dark"—whether this means denying death, denying limitations and unknowing, or denying the "dark side" of the human personality, including rage, sloth, avarice, and other "not nice" passions. One consequence of our cultural denial of the dark is the tendency of some religious and spiritual leaders to promote spirituality exclusively in terms of mastery, triumph, and good feelings. This, however, is just another way of trying to limit God. We may not wish to admit it, but in darkness, uncertainty, and death, we have powerful opportunities to encounter the Sacred and to find transformation, a transformation that can fill the darkest parts of ourselves with the radiance of uncreated light. But this transformation arises not from denying the dark, but from accepting it.

The spirituality of darkness reminds us that the Sacred is not always about "sweetness and light." Just as being spiritual means exchanging mastery and control for vulnerability and awe, it also means being willing to remain faithful and to continue believing even in the dark times of life. To seek the sacred means to walk into this darkness of unknowing, uncertainty, and doubt—to maintain our tiny faith when we are confronted by the vast reaches of doubt we encounter at every step along life's way.

The greater our struggle to protect ourselves from the dark, the greater our pain will be when the dark finds us. The more we choose to live a life of believing and vulnerability, the greater is the likelihood that even in the dark, we will hear the still small voice of the One who loves us. Once again, we come back to this fundamental choice—do we try to protect ourselves from the dark and thereby risk missing the call of God altogether? Or do we make loving the Divine our first priority, regardless of the darkness that may await us in life?

Incarnation

The "middle path" of a creative understanding of matter and spirit is exemplified by the Christian notion of incarnation, as well as the Hindu notion of the avatar. According to this way of thinking, God—the transcendent Divine mystery who is beyond all names—took on human nature and became immanent and embodied, having a physical body just like all people. This incarnation (literally, "en-fleshing") of the divine is believed by Christians to have occurred in Jesus and by Hindus to have occurred in Krishna. Incarnation suggests that the Divine spirit is not incompatible with matter or the body; that the Sacred considered matter good enough and worthy enough that it would live within the constraints of matter; and that for God's Spirit to live and move in space and time, God requires (or at least chooses) to have a body just like the rest of us.

Joan Osborne's song "One of Us"[*] created a bit of controversy when it came out in 1995. The song dared to ask questions like "What if God were one of us?" and "If God had a face, what would it look like, and would you want to see, if seeing meant that you would have to believe?" Because the song linked God with images of humans as slobs and strangers on a bus, it offended persons who want to keep their image of God pure and unsullied, in an antiseptic heaven far away from the dirt and grime "down here" on Earth. The beauty of the song is that it dares to ask questions about incarnation—about how the Divine and the messy imperfections of the world of matter, space, and time interpenetrate. I believe, however, that not only should we be asking, "What if God were one of us?" but we should also be asking, "Why are people offended by the thought that God *might be* one of us?"

The teaching of the incarnation carries numerous implications for spirituality—it says that matter is good, that spirit relies on matter in order to function in the world, and that matter relies on spirit for ultimate meaning and purpose. It suggests that spirit bestows a blessing on matter just as the Divine bestowed a blessing on the fleshly body of the incarnation. These are important ideas, ideas that help us maintain a healthy equilibrium in our understanding of matter and spirit. If the Sacred became flesh, then flesh has the potential of being sacred. If spirit lives within matter, then spirit vitalizes the material. To be in relationship with one requires being in relationship with the other.

The sacramental way

A sacrament is a material manifestation of spiritual truth or experience. The concept of sacraments originated in the Christian tradition, so the most obvious examples can be found in Christian spirituality. According to the Episcopal *Book of Common Prayer*, sacraments are "outward and visible signs of inward and spiritual grace" (*BCP*, 857). The "inward and spiritual" element is the manifestation of the Sacred in and through the "outward and visible" material element.

In the Christian tradition, the two primary sacraments are Baptism and Communion. Baptism, an initiation ritual for new members of the

[*] Eric Bazilian, "One of Us," on Joan Osborne, *Relish*, Blue Gorilla/Mercury 314 526 699. Used by permission.

Christian faith, consists of using water to symbolically wash the person being baptized—a representation of Divine cleansing love, used as a parent would lovingly use water to wash a child. Communion consists of bread and wine that represent the ongoing presence of Divine love in the spiritual life—as symbolized through a ceremony of feeding, suggesting that God nurtures and cares for us, as a parent would feed a child.

Sacraments are important for the same reason that icons are important. A sacrament involves a *particular* material object or objects (like water or bread and wine) that point to the truth that *all* things in space and time can, in some way, manifest divine love and the divine presence. A sacramental spirituality is a path that seeks to celebrate the presence of God in nature, in matter, in the physical world. This is the spirituality of icons and incarnation. This is the spirituality that says we need not flee the world we live in to find God; on the contrary, God loves us passionately here and now, in the universe of matter and energy.

Christianity is not the only sacramental tradition. The sacramental encounter with the Divine may come through the ritual of a Lakota sweat-lodge, where the Great Spirit is encountered through steam and hissing stones. The food consumed in a Passover Seder, where the exodus of the Hebrews from Egypt is commemorated, celebrates the love and care God shows for the Jewish people. The resounding gong of a Buddhist temple or the steady drumbeat at a Neopagan circle can lead the listener into a place where the physical vibrations of the sound testify to the immanent presence of the Most High.

Why do we need sacraments if God is present in all things? Why must we look to a religious ritual or ceremony to inform us that *this particular* water is holy while *that* water is just ordinary? The distinction between a sacramental act or object and an ordinary act or object is helpful to remind us that the distinction between matter and spirit exists, even while matter and spirit are one. All matter is filled with God's love, yet matter is not the same as God. I carry the spark of the Divine within me, yet I am not the creator of the universe. The point behind honoring a *particular* visible sign as an indication of God's universal presence is not to "put down" all other things, but rather is a simple recognition that by honoring the holiness of one thing, we may more easily remember that *all* things are potential vehicles for the Sacred. The president of the United States is no better than anyone else, but he (or she) has been chosen to lead. In a similar way, sacraments are not holier than anything else, but they have been chosen to "lead" us into a place where we may encounter the Sacred.

Who does the choosing? Who determines what things become sacramental? Sacraments, like icons, derive their power from a community. Baptism and Communion are powerful signs of divine presence because the Christian community has practiced them from the day Jesus first encouraged his followers to perform such rituals two thousand years ago. This tradition was created in a community and has been preserved by community over the years. Just as a fully developed spirituality includes a celebration of the material world, so the spiritual life reaches its full potential when we join with others in a community devoted to the Sacred. In such a community, we can celebrate the spirituality of the physical world by celebrating the sacramental presence of God in matter.

The sacramental way is optimistic. It undermines the dualistic idea that spirit is higher or better than matter. It sees our bodies and our nature as gifts from the Divine, and instead of trying to escape an awareness of these gifts, the sacramental way says, "Thank you." When there are problems with our bodies or the natural world—problems such as disease, death, the darkness of doubt and fear, the pain of crime and injustice—the sacramental way does not avoid such problems, but embraces them in the belief that the Sacred will lead us to transform the world into a better, more loving and just place for all people.

The spirituality of matter involves a paradox—that matter and spirit are separate, yet matter and spirit are one. Both parts of the paradox seem necessary and true. If we separate spirit totally from matter, spirit becomes a mere abstraction, irrelevant to the realities of the physical world. If we identify spirit totally with matter, then we have no distinction between the universe as it is and a transcendent, loving God. Without that distinction, we have no reason to believe that our world could be better than it is— thus, spirituality loses its incentive to seek and work for a better tomorrow. The sacramental way holds both parts of this paradox in a creative tension. A sacramental spirituality celebrates the presence of spirit in matter, but also bows down before the mystery of Divine transcendence.

Celebrating matter

Nature, beauty, eros, darkness—these are just a few qualities of the infinite splendor of the physical universe. I've focused on these specific qualities because I believe they are each a doorway into a spiritually healthy relationship with matter. Incarnation and sacraments are specific doorways, arising out of spiritual traditions, that help us encounter the Sacred here and now.

Prayer changes things. The "things" that prayer changes can include aspects of our inner life, such as our attitudes, emotions, and thoughts. Painful memories, brought to God in prayer, can be healed. The wonder of prayer is like the wonder of love, for it ushers us into a place where, through a relationship (with the Sacred), we have the opportunity to discover who we are—and in that discovery to find healing and transformation.

Of course, prayer is more than just an inner exercise. The spiritual life has the potential to move mountains. I believe prayer changes not only the inner worlds of our mind and spirit, but also the outer world of our body and our environment. Perhaps such outer changes come as a result of inner changes. If, in prayer, I'm inspired to work for economic justice, ten years from now an entire neighborhood may be lifted out of poverty, thanks to programs I've helped to start or administer. Is that miraculous? Maybe. Maybe not. Is it a real, embodied, material change? Absolutely—and it all began in prayer.

I don't want to suggest that genuine miracles can't happen, either. I personally believe that God chooses to work within the divinely ordained natural laws of the universe—*most of the time*. So a "miracle" will almost always have a perfectly ordinary and reasonable explanation behind it. But the possibility always remains for something beyond the ordinary. The Sacred can surprise us. Miracles happen.

If we want our relationship with the Sacred to matter, then we need to practice a spirituality that is embedded in matter. More than just a pun, this is a central truth in the life of wonder. To be mature and fully developed, a spiritual path must be as material as it is spiritual; it must be as practical as it is theoretical; as social as it is psychological; as physical as it is metaphysical.

9

Equipoise

In the previous chapter we examined some of the polarities that feature prominently in the spiritual life, such as spirit and matter, light and dark, and male and female. According to the *Oxford English Dictionary*, a *polarity* involves the "possession or exhibition of two opposite or contrasted aspects, principles, or tendencies" (*COED*, 2225). Polarities are any sets of two categories that function as opposites of each other, alternatives to each other, or opposite ends of a continuum. The spiritual life includes a number of polarities (and their accompanying tensions).

The tensions and oppositions of polarities frequently tempt us to think in dualistic ways. In the strictest sense, dualism simply means dividing a category into two parts. However, such a division often carries with it an assumption that one part is better than the other. In this way, dualistic thinking involves an "either/or" choice—that either "male" or "female" is the better gender or that either "spirit" or "matter" is closer to God, and so forth. Such dualistic views are limiting. By contrast, a mature spirituality, recognizing the unlimited nature of the Sacred, approaches most polarities not with an "either/or" way of thinking but rather with a "both/and" way, one that seeks to honor both of the polar opposites as aspects of a creative equilibrium.

Equilibrium, or balance, is a necessary characteristic of healthy spirituality, for balance is necessary if we are to accept polarities without the temptation to view one part as better and the other part as worse. As we nurture a sense of God's presence in our lives, we encounter conflicting demands—for example, the need for solitude conflicts with the need for community, and the need to feel in control conflicts with the need to

147

be vulnerable before the Sacred. These and other conflicts in the spiritual life cannot be dualistically resolved by claiming one need is "more spiritual" than the other. Spirituality asks us to develop *equipoise*, to seek balance and equilibrium in life.

This chapter explores a variety of topics in which balance and equipoise bear on our relationship with the Sacred. First, we'll abandon the dualistic split between survival-mind and spiritual-mind, seeking instead an optimum balance between wonder and control, between discipline and openness. We'll look at the spirituality of equipoise by considering how inner spirituality needs to be balanced by outer practicality, as well as how the encounter with the Sacred can involve both strangeness and familiarity. Finally, we'll explore the place of ceremony and ritual in the spiritual life, in terms of a polarity involving meditation and dance.

Redeeming control

Up to now, a major theme of this book has been to consider spirituality in terms of a particular conflict in consciousness—between the need to remain in control and the need to surrender to wonder. I repeatedly advocate approaching life from a posture of open-minded, open-hearted wonder and vulnerability, suggesting that such an approach is far superior (and more spiritual) than the more familiar, "common-sense" approach to life of "being in control" and "managing" and "being in charge." I've even suggested that we have two fundamentally different dispositions of mind —"survival-mind" and "spiritual-mind." My treatment of these fundamental ways of approaching life has, in essence, claimed that wonder is good and control is bad.

Honoring wonder at the expense of control has been temporarily useful, if for no other reason than this: our society is so oriented toward control that we need to affirm wonder in order to redress the way it's been slighted. The truth of the matter, however, is that the polarity between control and wonder needs to held in equilibrium, just like the other polarities I mentioned in the preceding several paragraphs. Control and management and self-protection are not inimical to the spiritual life, and a life without those qualities would probably not last very long. Think of it—a person with no active survival-mind would not bother to wear seatbelts or keep the doors locked at home and would be careless about being out alone at night, irresponsible at work, and indiscriminate in choosing friends and associates—in short, such a person's life would quickly be filled with daunting, insurmountable, and *preventable* problems.

To live a life of wonder, vulnerability, and prayerful openness, we need to have the appropriate amount of self-care, control, and management in our life simply to maintain our health, our sanity, and our well-being at a level that's required for the open-ended, "spiritual" values to flourish. For this simple reason, control, caution, and discipline are just as important to the spiritual life as are wonder and playfulness. In fact, we could say that control and discipline are earthy, grounded, "material" values that are needed in conjunction with the open-ended "spiritual" values of wonder and vulnerability. Control and wonder are just as much a polarity of the spiritual life as are matter and spirit.

A healthy spiritual life seeks to keep these polarities in balance—in equilibrium, or equipoise. To live in equipoise is to live in a dynamic, "poised" balance between the two aspects of a polarity. Spiritual equipoise is the quality of taking care of two needs that may seem to be at odds with each other, recognizing that these needs may make different demands on us at different times and that both are important. Equipoise may mean emphasizing one need at one point and then another need at another point —as has been my approach in this book in terms of wonder and discipline.

I think that when we begin our study and practice of spirituality, we need to give wonder precedence over discipline. This is because, though we were born with a sense of openness and wonder, we probably obscured it with an overlay of discipline as we grew up. So our spiritual progress must begin with our regaining a sense of wonder. However, as we mature, wonder and discipline need to become twin aspects of life, two complementary spheres of consciousness that work together for survival and enjoyment. Spiritually speaking, discipline enables us to make and keep agreements with God, while wonder opens us up to the mysteries and marvels of the divine radiance.

Once again, I am reminded of the phrase "I'm spiritual but not religious." I believe "religion" and "spirituality" can each represent a loss of equipoise, as being "religious" can mean a life that overemphasizes control, while being "spiritual" can mean a life where control is underemphasized. To illustrate my point, consider a hypothetical "Joe," who grows up in a strict, fundamentalist church, where God is regarded as a remote, angry parent and every person's job is to live a rigidly disciplined, overly controlled life so this wrathful God will not be displeased. In such a setting, wonder is all but absent. This God is not a source of love and life, but is simply a raging authority figure. Many young persons who grow up

in this environment quickly leave the church when they reach adulthood—
and why shouldn't they, since they've experienced God as angry and
jealous rather than loving and merciful.

Suppose our friend Joe one day has a profound mystical experience,
a deep sense of God's presence, and decides as a consequence to jettison
his overly structured religion, having determined that he now wants to be
spiritual but not religious. However, he essentially adopts a way of living
that manifests the shadow side of his fundamentalist upbringing. He
refuses to engage in any kind of spiritual discipline, for such practices as
daily prayer or meditation will, he thinks, "thwart the spontaneity" of the
spirit. Neither will he give any money to charitable organizations nor do
volunteer work, since such practices remind him too much of the "guilt-
tripping" he received as a child.

He resists becoming involved in any kind of spiritual organization,
worrying so much about the ways he perceives religion as being hostile to
spirituality that he never considers how a creative and healthy community
may foster growth in the Spirit. The religious life makes sense only as a set
of commitments designed to foster a vibrant spirituality, both for
individuals and for the entire community. I believe one reason why many
religious groups have faced declining membership has been their
unwillingness to balance the duties of religion with a meaningful sense of
vision and interior nurture. However, just as religious communities need
to emphasize a visionary spirituality, so too do "spiritual" persons who
choose not to participate in religion need some form of discipline, the
same way a tomato plant needs a stake. Of course, a tomato plant may live
without the stake, but it is not likely to thrive, nor will it bear much fruit.
A spontaneous spirituality may feel terrific, but without the challenge of
community and discipline, the spontaneity will almost certainly wither
away and the spirituality is likely to stagnate.

Jesus taught his followers to become like little children—certainly an
affirmation of wonder and playfulness. But he also taught them to live in
community, to practice justice and peace, and to be intentional in prayer—
all characteristics of mature discipline. In fact, his followers were called
"disciples," implying that discipline was central to who they were. Jesus'
teaching encouraged a spirituality that existed in equipoise between the
joyfulness of wonder and the practice of discipline.

Practicality and spirituality

An Episcopal priest once told me, "I'm more of a practical person than a spiritual person." I challenged his implication that "practicality" and "spirituality" were incompatible or mutually exclusive. Yet as we talked further, even though I still disagreed with his viewpoint, I did understand more clearly what troubled him. Depending on how you define spirituality or practicality, the two concepts really can appear to be mutually exclusive —especially when spirituality lacks a sense of balance.

If we limit "spirituality" purely to matters of inner experience, it could imply a tendency to ignore the everyday material concerns of life, whether they are as small as balancing the checkbook or as large as combating homelessness. It could mean a tendency to avoid conflict by retreating into the safe world of the spiritual imagination. It could mean adopting an excessive concern with magic, faith-healing, and miracle-working— especially when such a concern involves rejecting down-to-earth ways to solve problems, such as medical care or psychological counseling.

At its worst, an imbalanced spirituality can mean leaving the "real world" behind, choosing instead to see life, people, and conflicts or difficulties exclusively in terms of abstract, esoteric beliefs—hiding behind misty ideas and using them to avoid conflict. For example, if I don't get along with my boss, one "spiritual" way to interpret the conflict is to believe I have "a lesson to learn" from her. But if I try to explain the conflict away in metaphysical terms—saying something like, "Oh, my boss is a Virgo and I'm a Sagittarius; no wonder we don't get along"— rather than simply buckling down and improving my conflict management or interpersonal skills, or maybe even just improving my work performance, then the conflict may remain unresolved, with the spiritual lesson unlearned.

In scenarios such as this, a reliance on spirituality might actually impede rather than nourish a mature engagement with life. Whenever "spirituality" is a code word for beliefs or ideas that claim to impart some sort of inner truth but in actuality have little or no bearing on down-to-earth issues in life, it truly is the opposite of "practicality."

For people who regard themselves as fundamentally "practical" and perhaps may actually be overly practical—those to whom even a balanced kind of spirituality doesn't make much sense—activities such as praying and meditating are distractions, means of wasting time that could (some would say "ought to") be spent volunteering at a nursing home, participating in local politics, or responding to whatever other pressing needs may be at hand. For example, knowing that global warming and acid rain are obviously serious problems that can only be stopped by direct political action, these people might regard taking time to meditate about them as indecisive at best and downright useless at worst.

Many forms of spiritual or religious behavior do seem to be impractical. For priests or nuns to voluntarily choose a life of celibacy is "impractical," denying themselves the joy of the emotional and sexual intimacy in marriage. Another "impractical" characteristic of spirituality is generosity—such as tithing, or giving away ten percent of one's income or time, with no measurable "return"—and yet many spiritual practitioners do precisely that. To devote one's life to the apparently useless practice of prayer is impractical, just as basing one's entire life on the unprovable hypothesis that God exists is impractical, or as undertaking a seemingly hopeless cause like ending homelessness is impractical. These "impractical" things, however, are exactly what many spiritual practitioners do.

So is spirituality impractical? The answer, I think, is a paradoxical "yes and no." Yes, because some of the practices common to mature spirituality simply violate common sense. Common sense may tell us that being celibate is useless, yet even in our sophisticated age men and women continue to respond to the call to celibacy. Common sense tells us that trying to solve the problem of homelessness is hopeless, yet every night thousands of prayerful volunteers minister to the lowliest persons in society. Common sense tells us that praying for a miracle when a loved one lies dying in the hospital is hopeless, and yet many faithful persons continue to pray for their loved ones' healing and seek the prayers of others when they themselves are in need. In these and other ways, many aspects of spirituality may be defined by their literal and thorough impracticality.

What about the other side of that "yes and no" answer? To see the practical side of spirituality, let's look directly at the world of practicality, effort, and achievement from the vantage point of the person who seeks a deeper relationship with God. Perhaps in the mind of the spiritual seeker, those who *resist* spirituality are the impractical ones! To the lover of the Divine, the impractical ones are those who struggle to make it through life without seeking guidance in prayer; or without nurturing the joy of generosity by giving away time and money in an open, no-strings-attached way; or without choosing to place greater faith in love and trust rather than in fear and suspicion. In this way of seeing things, spirituality is not a matter of impracticality, but rather is a matter of *greater* practicality, greater than others may even be capable of seeing.

Spiritual people do not engage in their spiritual behavior (be it celibacy or serving others or prayer or whatever) because they think it's impractical, but rather precisely because they view it as *supremely* practical. Understanding spirituality, therefore, involves a process of enlarging one's notion of what constitutes practicality. That's where the question of equipoise comes in. The Divine calls us to find a creative balance between the dreamy world of wonder and the practical world of discipline and control. Seen from the inside, spirituality is not impractical so much as it is a highly practical marriage of efficiency and curiosity, of discipline and wonder.

One example of this kind of spirituality may be found in Curious George, the chimpanzee who is the star of a series of children's books by H.A. Rey. Curious George gets himself into all sorts of trouble because he is so, well, *curious*—he happily romps through life following his instincts for wonder and playfulness and getting himself in trouble because he is so impractical. In one story, George's human friend buys him a bicycle and admonishes George to stay near the house. George's curiosity gets the better of him, and off he rides, looking for adventure. He helps a paperboy deliver newspapers—until he decides that making boats from the papers would be more fun. Eventually he wrecks the bike, only to be picked up by a traveling circus troupe. After several more adventures and misadventures, George gets to perform in the circus, delighting the crowd so much that even the people who never got their newspapers end up smiling (Rey 1952).

Now Curious George is not a very practical chimp. I'm not even sure I approve of George's irresponsible behavior, although I do think he exemplifies wonder and transgression. What George teaches us is that by taking risks, he is able to live a full and exciting life. Instead of simply playing with his bike at home (which would have been the practical thing to do), he opens himself up to a series of adventures, culminating in his chance to perform in the circus.

Spirituality invites us to be more like Curious George. Maybe not to the point of making boats out of other people's newspapers, but certainly to the point of allowing our bias toward practicality to be balanced by a willingness to take some risks, break some rules, and nurture wonder and playfulness in our life. Even celibacy and tithing and praying can be, when approached the right way, adventurous risks and playful ways of breaking the rules—risks and transgressions that turn out to be more practical than the safe, conventional forms of practicality.

We can see this "spiritual practicality" in the "impractical" behaviors we considered previously. To celibate persons, giving up marital intimacy is a matter of urgent and utmost practicality—it frees them to be wholly available both to God and to those to whom they minister. To a person who regularly prays for others, such prayer is of utmost practicality—for while she cannot show in a scientific way the "results" of her prayer, she knows her prayer changes things—and even if praying doesn't, for example, prevent a loved one from dying of cancer, it nonetheless makes a difference to the loved one's soul and, perhaps just as importantly, is good for the soul of the person doing the praying. To the persons who faithfully give away ten percent of their income, doing so is of the utmost practicality. Not only does tithing help others, but givers believe that such generosity is good for their own spiritual health as well.

In the experience of spirituality, one finds seeming contradiction, unknowable mystery, and apparent paradox. The spiritual life appears utterly impractical to persons outside its realm, yet those who choose such a life are rewarded with an enlarged sense of what actually is practical—behaviors that seem useless to others are viewed as being of central importance and urgency by the practitioner.

I choose the word *practitioner* intentionally. I still disagree with my friend the priest, with his statement implying that spirituality and practicality are mutually exclusive. Spirituality may be just a passive inner experience for some people, but it need not be only that, as a dynamic, full-blown, balanced spirituality can also be practiced actively in the real, everyday world, where it will produce tangible effects. The spiritual life can be *immensely* practical. If someone's spirituality is getting in the way of his or her balancing the checkbook or dealing responsibly with interpersonal conflict, then that person has an *im*practical spirituality, although that does not mean spirituality itself is impractical.

I believe a healthy spirituality is practical in a balanced way. It includes the "impractical practices" of prayer and contemplation and also cultivates a sense of wonder along with such down-to-earth efforts as giving money away, feeding the hungry, and working to create peace in our communities. Although the practices of my kind of spirituality may seem useless and a waste of time to some people, to me those practices are central to who I am, inside and out.

Strangeness

When I was a child, a common admonition from my parents and my teachers was, "Don't talk to strangers!" The stranger—the unknown person—was not safe for children. The Hebrew Scriptures convey a similar warning. God is portrayed as forbidding the worship of "strange gods" (see, for example, Deut. 32:16). Like the strangers who can be dangerous to children, these gods, by virtue of their strangeness, are not only unknown but unsafe.

These warnings relate to a polarity—between that which is familiar and that which is strange. The good/bad dualism here is obvious enough. What is familiar is "good" and "safe," while what is strange is to be mistrusted and feared, for it is probably "bad" and "dangerous."

Given the way that strangeness is linked with false gods in the Hebrew tradition, we might assume that spirituality does not involve things that are strange. Yet on closer inspection, that is precisely what spirituality does involve. Why are increasing numbers of Westerners fascinated by the exotic aspects of alternative spiritual cultures, such as Neopagans chanting at Stonehenge on the summer solstice at sunrise; Buddhist monks sitting in a zendo, backs to one another, seemingly immobile as they are lost in their contemplation; or the hissing sounds of water poured in a sweatlodge, with the only thing visible in the lodge's darkness being steam rising from red-hot rocks? Perhaps the allure of strangeness also explains why Christianity has had such an appeal when it has been preached in non-Western cultures—where people may likewise have been won over by the religion's newness and strangeness.

But as the warning against "strange gods" suggests, for many people strangeness is not a doorway into spirituality at all. For some, spirituality is something that happens only in safe and familiar and predictable ways. Instead of incorporating an appreciation of chanting Neopagans or meditating Buddhists, spirituality for many people can be summed up by the line from the old gospel tune, "Give me that old-time religion, it's good enough for me."

The reason old-time religion is "good enough" is not that it is old so much as that it's familiar. Like Christians who won't read any Bible translation other than the King James Version, many spiritual seekers prefer to find the Divine in well-known ways. In this sense, spirituality is their haven from a chaotic and unpredictable world. Such a preference involves seeing spirituality not as embracing strangeness, but indeed as a refuge from it. The Christian who insists on interpreting the Bible in only one, approved way or the Orthodox Jew who walks to synagogue week after week since driving on the Sabbath would break Torah are typical practitioners of the spirituality of familiarity.

Where does the most authentic spirituality occur? In the novelty that attracts persons who find spiritual sustenance in the "strange" or in the safety that attracts persons who find spiritual sustenance in the "known"? Is God most surely to be found in what is new and exotic or in what is ordinary and consistent? Any attempt to answer these questions in an "either/or" way will fail to provide a holistic view of spirituality. The encounter with the Divine cannot be limited in terms of either novelty or familiarity. Spirituality involves both things strange and things familiar, thus functioning squarely on both ends of the polarity. God loves people who have a thirst for adventure, and God loves people who thrive in stability.

Much misery can arise when adventurers try to become stable and well-grounded, or when the stable try to become more adventurous. Only when we are true to ourselves are we really able to live a spiritual life. Asking what makes "strangeness" spiritually nourishing to one person and "familiarity" spiritually nourishing to someone else is like asking why Eastern Orthodox icons fill some people with rapt wonder but leave others unmoved. The answer is not a reflection on the nature of God so much as it is a consideration of psychological, social, and even political differences among people. Because you and I are each unique, the presence of the Divine will be revealed to us in unique ways.

I personally am the kind of spirit-lover who thrives on adventure and strangeness and the thrill of the not-yet-known, so I fall into the category of people who like to explore other traditions in addition to the practices of my "home" path. If a different person had written this book—someone who thrives on the very constancy that I find stifling—this section might have emphasized "stability" rather than "strangeness." The wildness and unpredictability I look for in the Heart of God might be deeply threatening —or at least meaningless—to others. In our fast-moving and chaotic world, contending with uncertainties in spiritual practice may simply not be useful for some.

However, even when we clearly prefer one aspect of the familiar-strange polarity, I think we are wise to nurture the other side also. For me, balancing my preference for exploring the many spiritualities of the world with a grounded commitment to my chosen path helps me have a centered sense of my relatedness to God and keeps me from being a dilettante.

Conversely, I support the efforts of persons who, while they prefer a conventional spiritual practice, nevertheless seek to learn about paths and traditions that are "strange," at least for them. If nothing else, their exploration of different forms of spirituality can prevent them from adopting intolerant attitudes and can even makes their "home" paths come alive with new insights.

If we think of this polarity in relation to the Divine, it can be stated this way—God is the source of endless mystery, yet God is also the heart of safety and familiarity. The Divine is perfectly stable and perfectly flexible. We are created by the God of strangeness and mystery, and we are created by a safe, secure God of comfort.

Ritual and ceremony

In examining the place of practicality and discipline in the spiritual life, we face the general question of spiritual behavior—of concrete actions that people take, putting their beliefs and their choices into motion in the "real world." The old proverbs "Put your money where your mouth is" and "Walk your talk" hint at this juncture of spirituality and behavior. To enter into a glorious sense of wonder and vulnerability and relatedness with God in the realm of consciousness is one thing. To follow through on this inner experience of the spirit and do specific things or make concrete changes in behavior and action in response to the inner calling is quite another thing. It is the mature consequence of spirituality. To "walk our talk" means to behave in accordance with our spiritual values.

Spiritually motivated behaviors extend well beyond the few "practical" examples I suggested earlier, such as praying for others, tithing, or feeding the homeless. They also include another activity crucially important to the spiritual life—performing ceremonies and rituals.

Ceremonies and rituals are common to many cultures, although they clearly take different forms. While the most common form of ritual in North America remains the worship service in a church or synagogue, the many other and different spiritual traditions and communities all have their own forms of ceremonial or ritual activity. For example, Native Americans of the Great Plains celebrate the Sundance or smoke the sacred pipe. Wiccans and other Neopagans perform magical ceremonies, often on the night of the full or new moon. There is the intricate ceremonialism of an Anglo-Catholic Solemn High Mass (where incense, holy water, Gregorian plainchant, and colorful vestments on the priests combine to create a dazzling display of religious culture) and the stark simplicity of a Quaker meeting (where the members of the meeting gather simply to sit in silence for an hour, waiting for those who feel inspired to speak briefly). Ritual behaviors may also extend over long periods of time, sometimes spanning several weeks—for example, Muslims and Catholics observe ritual periods of fasting, Ramadan and Lent, respectively. Ornate or plain, the feature common to all of these traditions is *ritual*—that is, any specific, repeated behavior with spiritual or religious meaning.

The words "ritual" and "ceremony" are somewhat interchangeable, but I tend to think of "ceremony" as a highly organized ritual act, with rules and rubrics (specific directions), while "ritual" refers broadly to the practice of repeated spiritual observances. Thus, a Pentecostal prayer meeting, which has a very loose structure, is not ceremonial but is nonetheless a form of ritual. The coronation of a new Pope, however, is a highly ceremonial form of ritual—not only is it a repeated event (repeated every time there's a new Pope), but it is also an elaborate one, performed according to strict Catholic protocol.

One way to understand ritual and ceremony is as a balancing of meditation and dance. Consider the definitions (from the *Oxford English Dictionary*) of these two words. *Meditation* is the "continuous application of the mind to the contemplation of some religious truth, mystery, or object of reverence, in order that the soul may increase in love of God and holiness of life." *Dance* is a "rhythmical skipping and stepping, with regular turnings and movements of the limbs and body, usually to the accompaniment of music" (*COED*, 643, 1759). Meditation is an offering of the mind, while dance is an offering of the body. Meditation is internal and personal, while dance is external and communal. Meditation is spiritual, dance is material. Ritual, consisting of specific acts performed for prayerful purposes, brings dance and meditation together in a setting that, at its best, is filled with both dynamic playfulness and quiet wonder.

Of course, different rituals do this to different degrees. A Pentecostal service, with its exultant praying, praise for God, upbeat music, and sometimes even "dancing in the spirit," is explicit in its combination of these two elements. On the other hand, a dignified Episcopal service of Holy Communion may not seem to have much "dancing" at all. But that is only a surface impression, for as the service progresses, an observant participant will notice the rhythmic movement of repeated standing and sitting (something Episcopal churches are notorious for) as well as movements such as the deacon carrying the Gospel book to the middle of the congregation before the reading or the congregation itself gathering around the altar for Communion. All of this movement, of course, is accompanied by music. It is indeed a dance, if a stately and reserved one. Even a simple Quaker meeting, with its emphasis on silence and prayer, has a "dance" element to it—persons stand to speak and sit when they're finished, and the leaders of the meeting shake hands to mark the meeting's end. These are simple, slow movements in a ritual in which the ingredients may be 98% meditation and only 2% dance—but a little bit of dance is there nonetheless.

Besides meditation and dance, another common element in ritual is drama. A ritual is a drama, in that it is an "acting out"—often of a sacred story. Sometimes this is explicit, as in the Catholic mass, which is a stylized acting out of the events of the Last Supper. The Christian sacrament of Baptism is an acting-out of the original baptism of Jesus by John the Baptist. The Wiccan ritual of Casting a Circle dramatizes, in the circular motion of the participants, the motions of the moon around the Earth and of the Earth around the sun. Rituals like these speak to the importance of memory and storytelling in the spiritual life.

Yet even when the drama—the story—is not explicit in the ritual, an implicit story is often acted out. A Pentecostal worship service, despite the freewheeling lack of structure and the emphasis on spiritual spontaneity, nonetheless is dramatic—a ritual enactment of the process of "being saved," with the climax of the drama coming when the minister invites people to come forward to be born again or to be prayed over to receive a spiritual experience called the "Baptism of the Holy Spirit." In rituals like these, rather than a narrative story being acted out, the belief of the gathered community may be dramatized. Even in the minimalist Quaker service, belief is being dramatized—in that case, the belief in the value of silent prayer, the accessibility of the Spirit to everyone, and the right of everyone to speak with Spirit-led authority.

If icons are the sacred paintings of the spiritual life and scripture is the sacred literature, then ritual is the sacred drama and dance. Like icons and texts, ritual is an embodiment—a bringing forth—of spiritual qualities into a material context.

Ceremony and ritual contribute to the equipoise of spirituality by functioning as fulcrums on which inner, solitary spirituality and outer, communal spirituality are balanced. While ritual and ceremony do not inherently require community, and while some rituals or ceremonies are even practiced in solitude, these aspects of the spiritual life are nonetheless most typically practiced in a group or community setting. Whether it's half a dozen people cramped inside a tiny sweatlodge or half a million people attending a papal mass, rituals usually involve community. Insofar as rituals and ceremonies are practiced in a community context, they create an environment where the inner and outer realms of spirituality can find an equilibrium.

10

Community

One particular element of the spiritual life, *community*, has appeared again and again over the course of this book. We saw in chapter 4 that communities shape the way we believe; it seems obvious to me that community shapes how we view the world, not only in regard to spirituality but in regard to all other aspects of life as well. For example, a typical Quaker's belief in the importance of silence and in the politics of nonviolence stands in stark contrast to, say, an average Pentecostal's belief in exuberant styles of worship and in "spiritual warfare" as a way of defeating evil. Such differences in values and beliefs are formed out of their respective faith communities.

We can see another illustration of the way community shapes experience in the lives of persons who have moved to countries other than their homeland. Even a move between two countries where the same language is spoken—such as between the United States and the United Kingdom—can involve a significant experience of "culture shock." Culture shock occurs because different communities have different cultures, and the experience of moving from one to the other is stressful as we learn to adapt. Between the U.S. and the U.K., for example, not only do idiomatic differences in speech exist (for example, an American truck that runs out of gas near the traffic circle would be, in Britain, the lorry out of petrol by the roundabout), but styles of dress, diet, and social customs differ as well. Money is different, holidays are different, popular movies and television are different—clearly, the variations between the two cultures are innumerable. In countless big and little ways, people from different backgrounds experience life in unique and culturally relative ways. We are all shaped by our culture—and our culture is a product of our communities.

Even persons who disaffiliate with a community may still carry its distinctive "mark." Sonia Johnson, a feminist activist who was excommunicated from the Mormon Church for her pro-ERA activities, comments in her book *From Housewife to Heretic* how deeply she was shaped by the Mormon ethos, a shaping she recognized as being present in her even after she and Mormonism parted ways.

Every individual's experience of spirituality is formed and shaped by communities—including the "communities" of our families, our friends, our churches or other religious groups, our ethnic or political environment, and our nation. Like the Quaker and the Pentecostal, each of us is shaped by the values and beliefs we receive from our various communities. In addition to forging beliefs, spiritual communities also create the cultural signs—icons—that help us recognize the presence of the Sacred in our lives.

Within the context of community, churches are built, religious practices are established, sacred traditions of art and literature and music develop. Communities pray together and communities undergo change together (and often resist change!). When they are healthy, communities manifest love and care for their members.

If spirituality is about loving the Sacred, then a loving community is a powerful symbol—an icon in its own right—of the love of God. For all this, however, many of us maintain the commonly held idea that only religion is a community matter, while spirituality is a solitary matter. Such a split, however, limits our understanding of spirituality.

Spirituality involves being in relationship with the Divine; community involves being in relationship with other people. The key to understanding the link between community and spirituality lies in understanding *relationship*—the spirituality of community arises out of the idea that loving one another is connected to loving the Divine. In this chapter we'll explore this connection by considering different models for community, along with several concepts central to a spiritual understanding of community—and a communal understanding of spirituality.

Belonging to the other

A community is more than just a group of persons living or working in the same place. Indeed, despite all of the best efforts of planners and developers, the so-called planned communities of American suburbs are often places where people experience isolation, loneliness, and lack of connection with their neighbors. Community thus involves more than just proximity. For a genuine community to exist, several qualities need to be present among all or most of the people involved. These essential qualities include their belief in the overall vision and purpose of the community, their sense of belonging, and their willingness to relate with others—especially those in the community who seem different from themselves in significant ways.

These qualities are essential to any kind of community, whether it's a military squadron, a small business, a family, or a spiritual community. Issues of belonging and dealing with otherness are universal, applicable in a general way to any kind of community. Issues of vision and purpose, however, are what make a specific community unique. A spiritual community, for instance, would consist of persons united by a common vision of relationship with the Sacred, in accordance with certain shared teachings and traditions.

Belonging may, in one sense, be a loaded concept, since it can imply ownership or control. Just as my car and my computer belong to me, I know that my "belongings" are things I have power over. At its worst, to belong means to be enslaved—just as the African-American slave Sally Hemings belonged to Thomas Jefferson.

This view of belonging suggests that statements like "I belong to the Episcopal Church" have ominous implications. Such a notion of belonging implies that "I" am no longer a person in my own right but am simply a passive subject who waits for decisions to be made for me. "The Episcopal Church" is the active agent, an agent making choices and decisions on my (passive) behalf.

This may seem to be a matter of little or no consequence; however, an implicit sense of ownership reveals itself in subtle ways. For instance, surprising numbers of intelligent people think that if they stop worshiping in the church of their upbringing, they will surely go to hell—or at least, God will be very angry with them and life will take a turn for the worse. The logic runs like this: If I stop obeying the church (which "owns" me), then I will surely be rejected by God. My only hope of appeasing God is to repent—in other words, to resubmit to the authority (ownership) of the church, thereby "assuring" God's favor toward me. Sadly, I believe these kinds of ideas are widespread. Yet no matter how prevalent they may be, they are inimical to a spiritual life centered on love and trust of the Sacred.

Thankfully, such notions of ownership need not be the only ways to understand belonging. Belonging can be viewed in a way that supports the idea of a healthy community. To find this better understanding, we need look no farther than the realm of love and romance. For example, my wife and I believe we "belong to each other." Here, instead of one of us "owning" the other, we have a sense of the rightness and appropriateness of our being together. In this way, belonging is connected with *being in the right place* and with mutual *acceptance*. In contrast to belonging-as-ownership, true lovers relate as equals and as autonomous persons—the relationship is based not on control, but on freely-chosen companionship.

Mutuality is thus an essential characteristic of a healthy love relationship. If I belong to my wife, that she also belongs equally and mutually to me is both healthy and appropriate. Neither of us "owns" the other, but we share a sense that our lives are "right" when we are together. This positive understanding of belonging applies equally well to community. If I belong to a community, that belonging is healthy only insofar as the community equally belongs to me. Seen this way, a healthy relationship with a church (or any community) means that "I belong to the church" is balanced by "The church belongs to me" in a mutual relationship of acceptance, trust, and love.

Probably the foundational relationship involving such mutual belonging is our relationship with God. Spirituality, as the process of loving the Sacred, consists of a relationship in which that sense of mutual belonging can manifest. I believe there is a fundamental rightness about my being in relationship with God—therefore I and the Divine belong together. Because of this "right" foundational relationship of mutual love and trust, the relationships I form as part of my spiritual community also have the potential to manifest the quality of belonging-as-mutuality, rather than belonging-as-ownership.

Otherness is explored by Jewish theologian Martin Buber, who talked about "I and thou" as the essential elements of relationship—and therefore of community. To enter into a relationship with another person or with a group of persons comprising a community requires that my self encounter someone or a group of someones who are other than me. Without a "thou" who is *other* than my "I," no relationship is possible. (Of course, I may talk about having "a relationship with myself," but that is really only a psychological game I play—it requires that I mentally split my sense of self into a separate subject ["I"] and object ["myself"].) To enter into a relationship requires an encounter with one who is truly other.

The more open we are to the "other," the more easily we can be part of a community. Clearly, when the other is a person with whom we have a safe and loving relationship—say, a family member, a spouse, or a trusted friend—we are generally open to the relationship, and it seems to flow effortlessly. But when the other is someone whose "otherness" may be challenging to us, the relationship becomes more difficult. Such "otherness" may mean the person is of a different race, gender, sexual orientation, political or religious belief, or level of income, or is different in some other real or perceived way. Nevertheless, what makes community —especially spiritual community—challenging is that we are not excused from relating to the other, even when we encounter significant differences. The Sacred is the Loving Source for *all* persons and, for that reason, we who claim to love the Source do not have the option to place limitations on what kinds of people we will love and relate with. In other words, on the spiritual journey we learn that we cannot reject people of different races or ideologies, or of a different gender—or those who are different for any other reason—simply *because* they are different.

I am reminded of a humorous message I read on the Internet: "The good news is, God loves you. The bad news is, God loves everyone else, too!" The "bad news" challenges us because it calls us to recognize that divine love does not stop just with people who are like ourselves. Since God loves everyone else, if I am serious about being in a relationship with the Divine, I need to relate lovingly (with fairness, justice, and goodwill) with everyone, not just with the people around whom I feel comfortable.

Belonging (especially in terms of mutuality) and working with issues of otherness (even when doing so is challenging because of differences) are essential aspects of any community—whether it's as large as the billion-member Roman Catholic Church or as small as a one-on-one friendship. A third quality is also necessary: a shared vision. In terms of spiritual communities, whether small or large, the shared vision will entail some form of devotion to the Sacred. This quality of devotion, as part of a shared vision, is what makes a spiritual community distinctive from all other forms of community.

The monk and the murderers

Why is community a necessary part of the spiritual life? Sure, the idea that community shapes culture and belief is very nice, and belonging and relating to the other are laudable characteristics—but prayer requires solitude. In fact, many of the ideas we've considered in this book, from wonder and playfulness to belief and prayer, all seem to be primarily individual experiences and activities. Does a person *need* a community context in order to be spiritual?

We can answer that question in two ways. First of all, solitude and community constitute another polarity of spirituality, just as body/soul, matter/spirit, and openness/discipline are polarities. As is true with these other polarities, both aspects of the solitude/community polarity are necessary for a mature and fully developed spirituality, although every person will have a uniquely appropriate balance of aloneness and relationship.

The other way to look at that question is to consider how, even in solitude, we still participate in a community. An excellent way to explore this is to look at two radically different kinds of person, who both impact community from positions of solitude—murderers and monks.

First, we'll consider murderers. I won't cite one specific example, for we are familiar with the pattern, having seen it emerge again and again. Our society has spawned many kinds of solitary killers—one might live in a remote cabin in the mountains, emerging from the wilderness periodically to mail bombs to his victims; another chooses to live alone in a city, where he lures numerous victims to his apartment for torture and death; yet another lives a quiet, private life until one day he inexplicably leaves his solitude and visits the nearby elementary school, where he murders dozens of innocent children before finally killing himself. The circumstances may have been different with each of these killers, yet one common characteristic is chillingly present—all three craved privacy.

Now let's contrast murderers with monks. To do that, we'll consider a specific monk, Thomas Merton. If anything, Merton was even more of a solitary person than the murderers we've considered. At age 27, he entered the Trappist order, one of the strictest of Catholic monastic communities. He lived the highly structured life of the monastery for about twenty years, until finally he was given permission by his monastic superiors to pursue his fondest dream—to build and live in a hermitage away from the other monks. For the last few years of his short life (he died in a freak accident at 53), Merton lived as a hermit, but during those years he capped off a splendid career as a writer, authoring books that explored not only the spiritual life but also the central political issues of his time (the 1960s), including race relations, peace and nonviolence, and the morality of U.S. involvement in Vietnam.

This monk and the murderers appear to have only one thing in common—they all loved solitude. The murderers' solitude involved a toxic aloneness, a solitude that did not prevent them from acting out their violent compulsions. Merton's monastic solitude was radically different. Ironically, rather than functioning as a way for him to escape from community, it allowed him to be connected and of utmost service to community. He served not only the immediate community of his monastery but that of the entire world as well, contributing intellectually through writing and nurturing society's spiritual health through prayer on behalf of all people.

Indeed, solitude is necessary in the spiritual life—not the toxic withdrawal of a sociopath but rather a life-affirming aloneness, like that of a monk who understands healthy solitude as part of a creative polarity —with an appropriate engagement of community in some form as the other aspect of the polarity. Of course, for all their love of solitude, the murderers each engaged their community on some level—as did Merton even after becoming a hermit. So the crucial questions we have to ask include: Did the solitude that the monks and murderers embrace represent an escape *from* society or perhaps an escape *to* the creativity of the Sacred? Furthermore, did the solitude empower the person to relate to his community lovingly or with hostility?

Merton's spiritually motivated solitude, though genuine, nonetheless depended on other monks, who provided him with food and care. He, in turn, plumbed the depths of his solitude and out of those depths contributed to the monastic community and the global community through his writing. Like Merton, we all depend on our communities, not only for material sustenance but for spiritual sustenance as well. Spirituality may begin as a solitary personal matter, but it cannot end there. To be spiritual means being in relationship, with God and with other people, in the context of community.

Spiritual friendship

To consider community more closely, let's begin with the smallest possible community, the community of two. Relating to another person— one other person—is utterly foundational to all forms of community. A baby first interacts with the world by learning to relate one-on-one with her mother (or surrogate mother). From the time of that primal relationship on, every encounter, every friendship, every partnership, indeed every relationship of any category is, at heart, a one-on-one encounter. The "I" and the "thou" remain at the essence of every relationship.

Recognizing the foundational importance of one-on-one relationships is crucial to the spiritual life, for when we encounter the Sacred, we enter into a one-on-one relationship with God! I suppose we could argue that the relationship between human and God is even more foundational than the relationship between baby and mother, although in terms of *physical* relationships, the maternal relationship certainly is primary. The power of any earthly relationship lies in its potential to reveal something about our relatedness to the Holy. Whenever we gaze into another person's eyes, we run the risk of suddenly seeing the eyes of the Divine in that person's face. Whenever we reach out to help someone in need, we may well be offering our hands to the Sacred, so we become an instrument of divine love for that person. Whenever we vulnerably ask someone for a hug, the embrace we receive may carry in it a love from the Heart of All Things. Just as paintings and trees and buildings can be icons of the divine presence, so also—and perhaps especially—can our encounters with other persons be windows onto our relationship with the Sacred.

One-on-one relationships can take many forms, including such structured forms as parent-child, husband-wife, or therapist-client. But the most basic form of one-on-one relationship is friendship. Even a relationship with a spouse or a sibling is satisfying only insofar as it manifests the qualities of friendship. Unfortunately, our driven meta-culture places too low a priority on friendship. Although we idealize close relationships in the media (for example, the television show *Friends*), the ways we organize our lives seem more focused on career and shopping than on companionship. When a person works fifty hours a week, has a ninety-minute commute, and must fight traffic to get to the crowded mall on Sunday—where is the time to develop meaningful, lasting friendships? We seem to have many acquaintances and "contacts," but few friends.

Poets and artists and philosophers have lauded the joys of friendship throughout the centuries. One philosopher who praised friendship was the twelfth-century Christian monk Aelred of Rievaulx. As the abbot of a Benedictine monastery, Aelred recognized the importance of friendship in the lives of the monks under his guidance. He wrote a treatise called *Spiritual Friendship,* in which he praised the virtues associated with friendship—virtues such as loyalty, proper intention, discretion, and patience—and commented on how the virtues that make friendship meaningful and valuable are the same virtues that characterize the spiritual life. Aelred encouraged his monks to develop close friendships with other monks in the community, recognizing that such intimate human relationships are symbolic of the love that flows between the spiritual seeker and the Sacred.

The call of the Sacred includes, I believe, a call to nurture friendship, even in the midst of a world where friendship sometimes seems almost to be a remote luxury. But like grass that persists in growing through the sidewalk, we can persist in cultivating relationships based on intimacy and vulnerability, especially when we encounter others who share our passion for the Sacred—in other words, others who join us in our faith community, whatever form that may take.

The anamchara, *or "soul friend"*

I began this book by disclosing my hope to write as a sort of literary *anamchara*, or soul friend. This Celtic notion of the spiritual friend has meant much to me over the years, and my understanding of the *anamchara* and the role he or she can play in the spiritual life only deepens with time.

An *anamchara* is a friend who accompanies you in the ongoing journey of your spiritual life—the life of prayer and of seeking relationship with the Divine. I first discovered the concept of the *anamchara* in the writings of Kenneth Leech, an Anglican priest who has authored several splendid books on the connection between prayer and social justice. Leech's *Soul Friend*, a book about spiritual guidance, draws inspiration from the *anamchara,* whom he describes as a kind of spiritual companion, a person whose function may have had its roots in the culture of the ancient Druids. In the days before the coming of Christianity to the Celtic lands, Druids provided counseling and guidance to kings and chieftains. With the arrival of Christianity, this kind of spiritual advisor became known as a *soul friend*—and the function then apparently extended beyond the realm of government. Among monks and nuns, the general belief was that "anyone without a soul friend is like a body without a head." The role of soul friend was not just for priests and monks (although they did take it on), but for women and laypersons as well (Leech 1994, 45-46).

In *Power of Raven, Wisdom of Serpent: Celtic Women's Spirituality*, Noragh Jones describes how an *anamchara* would be a person's friend over the course of life and would also speak a blessing over that person when he or she lay dying. In fact, Jones states that the ancient Celts preferred the blessing of a soul friend at death to the blessing of a priest (Jones 1994, 196-7).

Others describe how the *anamchara* is meaningful as a model for spiritual friendship today. Edward C. Sellner suggests, in *Mentoring: The Ministry of Spiritual Kinship,* that a contemporary *anamchara* would exhibit qualities that foster a spiritually meaningful relationship—qualities such as maturity, compassion, respect, confidentiality, self-disclosure, knowledge, and discernment (Sellner 1990, 76-77). John O'Donohue, an Irish Roman Catholic priest, has recorded a series of tapes on Celtic spirituality called *Anam Ćara: Wisdom from the Celtic World*, in which he considers the poetic qualities of a soul friendship. "Now this friendship was a deep act of belonging and recognition [that] cut across all convention and morality and category . . . the soul was a kind of light that flowed into you, and flowed into the other person so that the art of that kind of belonging brought a deep and special closeness. . . . in this kind of love you're understood as you are, and understanding is a very precious quality, because the place that you're understood, that is the place that you're really at home" (O'Donohue 1996, tape 3).

What is evident from Fr. O'Donohue's descriptions is that a soul friend is one who weaves the qualities of belonging and of understanding the other into the mysteries and possibilities of the spiritual life. A soul friend is one who holds both her relationship with the Divine and her relationship with her friend as sacred mirrors of each other. Truly, as all human love flows originally from the Divine Source of life and love, so all friendships and all relationships also draw their sustenance from the well of Divine Life. A soul friendship is a relationship that actively acknowledges and celebrates this fact.

Today, many kinds of relationships can be friendships of the soul. Formal spiritual relationships, such as those between a priest and members of her "flock," or between a guru and his disciple, or between a transpersonal psychologist and her clients, can transcend the boundaries of the professional relationship and become an intimate friendship grounded in God. In its most formal sense, the ancient Celtic *anamchara* tradition lives on today in a Christian ministry called "spiritual direction," where a person seasoned in the life of prayer offers guidance and mentoring to a novice.

As one matures in his or her own spiritual journey, the need for mentoring gradually gives way to the need for mutual relationships that are deeply infused with prayer and contemplation. While a beginner needs to receive training and instruction, a more mature seeker simply needs companionship. No matter how "advanced" we get in the life of prayer (and great mystics like Thomas Merton caution us to remember that on some level we always are beginners!) and no matter how deeply we explore the mysteries and blessings of solitude, we always continue to need a soul friend. We continue to need such a companion in the spirit, for the journey is long and sometimes arduous, but always it is a journey into the heart of love—and love is meant to be shared.

Even beyond the gifts of companionship and intimacy, a soul friend also provides a "reality check" as we explore the mysteries of the Sacred. Spirituality can be a tricky matter—times of aridity can leave us jumping to the conclusion that God no longer cares, while experiences of mystical depth can be misinterpreted to mean that we have somehow been "chosen" or are in some other way spiritually more important than others. Because misinterpreting the experiences of spirituality is so easy, nothing is more valuable than the humble comfort of a friend who can see through our malarkey and help us be realistic in our assessment of our relationship with God.

How does a person go about finding an *anamchara*? Fortunately, many opportunities exist for making connections with spiritual seekers— through churches, synagogues, and other established faith communities; through workshops and classes and informal spiritual groups; and even through places and situations that don't seem "spiritual" on the surface. Natural-food co-ops and homeless shelters are two places where spiritually-minded persons often may be found. While forming acquaintances does not guarantee that a soul friendship will develop, at least through such acquaintances we can begin to experience spirituality as part of a community, and by the grace of the Sacred, deeper relationships will unfold.

Another strategy for seeking a soul friend is to engage in a formal kind of relationship that incorporates the qualities of the *anamchara*. Therapy and twelve-step groups, while explicitly focused on mental and emotional health, overcoming addictions, and wellness, often carry a spiritual dimension. (Distinguishing between an *anamchara* and a therapist is important, though. An *anamchara* accompanies you in your life of prayer and of seeking relationship with the Divine, while a therapist helps you on your journey toward psychological health and maturity.) Many monks and nuns or other religious professionals will provide one-on-one spiritual direction in return for a fee or for an offering made to their church or monastery. When you are seeking such one-on-one direction, keep in mind the importance of choosing carefully—preferably either someone you know or someone to whom you have been referred. Even a formal relationship of spiritual direction can, like therapy, easily become quite intimate—therefore issues such as confidentiality and respect of boundaries will arise. Forming such relationships only with persons whose spiritual depth and ethical standards are trustworthy is important.

Formal mentoring relationships, like informal relationships with acquaintances, may or may not develop into deep friendships. However, they are valuable because they give us the opportunity to explore intimacy with the Sacred in the context of a close relationship with another person.

As we have seen, a mature soul-friendship is an invaluable part of the spiritual life. It functions as an icon symbolizing that most fundamental of relationships—our individual relationship with God—and it involves community, for a friendship is the basic building block of community. In addition, the great issues that face communities—involving power and conflict, the search for shared values, the tension between the demands of the group and the needs of the individual—are all present in deeply lived friendships.

Promises and agreements

Relationships involve intimacy. When I am intimate with someone, I am close, vulnerable, self-disclosing, open, and available to that person. (Although in our culture we have tended to sexualize the word "intimacy," here of course it refers to emotional intimacy.) The spiritual life likewise invites us to bring intimacy to our relationship with God.

Intimate relationships rely on promises and agreements. This is true whether the "other" in a relationship is God or a person. When I seek intimacy with you, I promise you a number of things, either implicitly or explicitly. These promises constitute the agreements that are the foundation of our relationship. For example, I promise to treat you with kindness and love—although I also promise to be honest with you when I'm angry or hurt. I promise to speak honestly and forthrightly to you and to listen as well as I can when you speak to me. I promise to be honest and fair in my dealings with you. I promise to keep agreements and to let you know when things change.

The appropriateness of these statements may seem obvious, for they are usually the unspoken basics of any kind of relationship. But do we also think of them in regard to our relationship to the Divine? Are we honest with God when we're angry or hurt, or do we pretend that "God isn't interested" in such things? Do we allow our full personality to show when we meditate or pray, or do we insist on only bringing our best behavior to our prayer? Do we really try to listen for the voice of the Divine? Do we follow through on our agreements—or, failing that, are we willing to admit it when we can't or won't?

The beauty of spiritual friendship is that it provides us with a "mirror" in which we can see how we make promises and agreements with the Sacred—and what those promises and agreements imply. If I secretly think God hates me or doesn't care about me or is angry with me over something, such secret beliefs are more likely to be revealed over the course of a close friendship with another prayerful person. When I discover these kinds of limiting beliefs, I can offer them to the Sacred for healing and transformation.

Conflict in spiritual friendship

British author Susan Howatch has written a series of six novels (*Glittering Images*, *Glamorous Powers*, *Ultimate Prizes*, *Scandalous Risks*, *Mystical Paths*, and *Absolute Truths*) that follow the lives of several priests in the Church of England, along with their families, over the course of fifty years, from the mid-1930s to the mid-1980s. Set in the fictional town of Starbridge against the backdrop of sweeping changes in society (the priests in the 1930s argue over the morality of divorce, while their children fifty years later are engaged in a ministry to persons with AIDS), these novels explore the social and theological ideas that shaped the church in each passing decade. What I find particularly interesting is the way Howatch celebrates the Christian ministry of spiritual direction—and spiritual friendship in general—as a key feature in the lives of these priests.

The basic plot of each book is the same, involving a person connected with the church—a priest, a monk, a seminarian, or a bishop—whose relationship with God becomes clouded either by a crisis (such as the death of a spouse) or by misconduct (usually illicit sex—these are novels, after all). Each book takes the reader inside the minds of the central characters, illuminating in detail the thoughts, feelings, and self-deceptions that motivate the characters' behavior. Generally, one misstep after another ensues, and the character typically winds up involved in some sort of mess.

This is when, in each of the novels, a soul friend steps in. In most cases, Howatch portrays the soul friend in the context of spiritual direction, as would have been customary among clergy of the time.

Honesty and dishonesty dance throughout the course of the relationship, as the character in trouble first tries to hide his problems from the spiritual friend, only to disclose the truth eventually, discovering in the process the truth he has hidden even from himself. Over the course of such discoveries, powerful and often spiritually moving transformations take place.

The Starbridge novels tend to dramatic excess, but if we filter out the excesses, these novels are useful for their examination of the dynamics of a deep, intimate spiritual friendship. They reveal the possibilities for growth and transformation inherent in such relationships. At the same time, they show how certain qualities are necessary if soul friends are to create a meaningful relationship:

- *Commitment*—in order for a friendship to develop and mature, both persons need to make the relationship a priority in their lives;
- *Honesty*—speaking truthfully about thoughts and feelings is necessary for intimacy to occur;
- *Willingness to unmask self-deception*—for a friendship to have a meaningful impact on a person's spiritual life, she must be willing to allow her friend to call her on her blind spots, to help her see what she cannot or will not see about herself.
- And most of all, the practice of *prayer*—a friendship intended, at least in part, to foster closer attentiveness to the Sacred must be a friendship in which both persons engage in prayer, both in solitude and together.

Part of what makes the depiction of spiritual friendship in the Starbridge novels so fascinating is the author's deft treatment of conflict in relationships. Conflict is a part of life, and a healthy relationship is not without conflict. Rather it is one in which conflict is dealt with honestly and creatively. This is true not only with friends, but also with humans and the Divine. For instance, the life of prayer is a life in which God may call us to make changes; a soul friend helps us wade through all our perceptions and feelings as we try to discern the real leadings of the Spirit. However, to the extent that my will may differ from the will of God, I am certain to face conflict in my spiritual life. But this conflict is not to be avoided; it is to be recognized, accepted, and worked through.

Soul friends are also valuable helpers when one must work through this conflict—or perceived conflict—with the Sacred. For example, if I believe God's will for me is to lose weight, but I honestly don't want to change my eating or exercise habits, I have a conflict. Or I may insist that

God doesn't care if I keep smoking, even though I keep coughing. Working through my feelings, my beliefs, my denials, the thoughts and feelings I experience while (and after) praying, and my perceptions of the Sacred—all with the help of my soul friend—can help me see the nature of such conflicts and better understand how the Sacred is encouraging me to grow and change. Support from an *anamchara* has implications not only for personal spiritual issues, like diet or prayer or self-esteem, but can also impact the ways I perceive God is calling me in my relationships—in terms of career, family life, and other obligations.

I need to mention one final quality that is significant in relationships with spiritual friends, or indeed in all relationships—*reconciliation*. All of us have relationships that become strained or even broken. Whether the matter is as small as that of two friends refusing to speak to each another after a spat or as mighty as that of two nations at war, conflict without reconciliation leads to destruction. To the extent that we allow unreconciled conflict to overrun our spiritual life, our relationship with the Sacred can also become strained or broken.

A relationship dedicated to the leadings of the Sacred must be one in which fair and just reconciliation is sought, even in the midst of the fiercest conflict. Reconciliation is not the same thing as appeasement, where one party in a conflict passively gives in to the other. Nor does reconciliation involve the resolution of a conflict through struggle, in which a single "winner" emerges. True reconciliation begins with both (or all) involved parties acknowledging and seeking to protect the dignity and worth of the other(s). Reconciliation then involves patient exploration of the needs, fears, hopes, and angers in every aspect of the conflict, on all sides, seeking the leading of Divine Wisdom to challenge everyone involved to move together to a new place, where the conflict is resolved fairly and a new relatedness is possible.

The sweep of human history shows how rarely such sacred reconciliation has been achieved at the political level. Sadly, it is also a rare occurrence even at the interpersonal level. Nevertheless it is achievable, and its rarity does not take away from its inherent worth or sacred quality.

Friends with a purpose

The word "community" comes from the Latin words for "shared tasks," suggesting that a community finds its identity in some form of common purpose. A spiritual community, naturally, derives its identity from the shared task, or common purpose, of worshiping, loving, and relating to the Divine—as those activities are understood by that community. Buddhists, Wiccans, and Muslims all have radically different conceptions of divinity, yet members of each group find a shared understanding with others who are on the same path.

Spiritual communities exist in many different forms. This social aspect of spirituality may or may not create a *religious* community. Generally speaking, though, spiritual communities do exist in order to practice a shared religion—whether they are communities as large and established as the Christian churches, with millions of members worldwide and local congregations that often number in the thousands, or as small and newly formed as a Neopagan group with four or five participants that worship in members' homes. However, spiritual communities may also exist outside the bounds of religion—as in the case of twelve-step groups or the Rainbow Family, communities dedicated to the possibilities of wonder and transformation, but without a set of doctrines or religious practices.

Even for those persons who feel alienated from or unattracted to "religion," a mature and creative spirituality still depends on involvement in some sort of sacred community—some sort of linking together with friends or associates who share the common purpose of the spiritual journey. (Thus, persons who resist the idea that spirituality and religion go together may prefer thinking in terms of spirituality and community.)

Spiritual communities vary not only in size, but also in organizational structure, leadership styles, and focus. Communities can have strong central authority (like the Catholic Church) or diffuse, consensus-oriented authority (such as the traditionalist Quakers, who have no paid clergy). Communities may be organized around sacred teachings (like the Bible), a sacred practice (like Zen), or a strong, charismatic leader (like Mohammed or Buddha). Of course, many communities may have more than one focus of organization. For example, Catholicism derives its authority from the Bible (teachings), the sacraments (practices), and the Pope (strong leader).

The value of community in the spiritual life has been endorsed by various of the major religions. Buddhism and Christianity, for example, emphasize it. Buddhism teaches that the liberation of the ego comes through devotion to the Buddha, the Dharma, and the Sangha—in other words, to the teacher (an icon of the Sacred), the teachings (the foundation of belief), and the community (the supportive network of fellow seekers). Each of these categories is regarded as necessary to the person seeking enlightenment. Jesus promised his followers that "where two or three are gathered in my name, I am there among them" (Matt. 18:20), implying that the quorum for spiritual community is two (the soul friendship would qualify) or three (as would multiple soul friendships). Also, in the early years of Christianity, a strong emphasis on community developed, as exemplified by Paul's teaching that the faith community is "the body of Christ."

For Buddhists, devotion to the Buddha and his teachings is not complete without devotion to the Buddhist community; for Christians, Christ is manifested whenever his followers create a community. Buddha, Dharma, and Sangha, in fact, parallel the Christian concepts of Christ, Gospel, and Church. The message from both religions is clear—to enter into the spiritual community is to enter into a place where the Divine is present.

I suppose by now my feelings about the statement "I'm spiritual but not religious" are clear. While I understand that many people have been wounded by churches and other religious organizations, and I support people choosing to leave communities that are abusive or inimical to spiritual growth, I also believe deeply in the role that community plays in the spiritual life. I believe that people who leave religion in order to nurture spirituality still need some form of community setting in order for their spiritual life to blossom fully.

The Internet: a model for community

What are the characteristics of a spiritually centered community, whether or not such a community is religious in nature? To begin exploring that question, I'd like to look at an emerging technology that has people all around the world thinking about the importance of community —the Internet. One of the exciting developments in the world today, the Internet is the world's largest computer network (actually, a network of networks), literally spanning the world. It is the cornerstone of *cyberspace* —the realm of communication and information sharing that exists among and between networked computers and the minds of computer users. Although it has existed for years as a tool for government, academic research, and communication, business and personal use of the Internet has soared in the 1990s.

Many pundits hail the Internet as an important tool for creating community. In chapter 6, we considered how the Internet, like television, may be the *only* source of "community" for many people. It has been greeted almost as a new messiah, with some observers seeing in it the creation of a global consciousness, perhaps even a collective uniting of human consciousness as the emergent "mind of God." But could this happen? Is the Internet a model for creating community or just the latest techno-fad? What can we learn about the spirituality of community from a worldwide computer network with millions of users?

Personally, I find the Internet to be a fascinating tool for communication. While the current primary means for "conversation" involves typewritten exchanges (e-mail or "chat"), the near future promises real-time telephone conversations or even exchanges via live video. Through the Internet, I've made new friends, reconnected with several old friends, and corresponded with people literally the world over. I've set up a site for contemplative and interfaith spirituality on the World Wide Web (the "multimedia" portion of the Internet), and I've joined numerous topical discussion groups (known as "mailing lists"), in which members communicate through e-mail distributed to everyone on the list. Such discussions can be fascinating and insightful—though they can also be banal.

I find the Internet exciting and useful, and I hope it will become increasingly available to all members of society. Even so, I am skeptical about whether the Internet really provides anything new in the human quest for community. Rather, I have come to believe that the Internet simply reflects, on a global scale, both the promise and the perils of human community that have existed since the dawn of history.

As in any other community, making acquaintances is very easy on the Internet—and forging true friendships is much harder. Finding someone halfway around the world (or just down the street) who shares similar interests with me is exciting. However, as much as I enjoy my online friendships, the limitations of typewritten words, even when such words come from the heart, prevent us from enjoying the wonderful nuances of companionship.

Not surprisingly, conflict online is just as prevalent as it is anywhere else—and just as difficult to face or to resolve. This is particularly so because the anonymity of the computer screen allows many people the safety to discard civility, and once conflicts erupt, resolution often seems elusive—especially since the only medium for communication is the stream of words on the screen. "Flaming," the practice of sending abusive or insulting messages over the Internet, is ample proof that cyberspace offers no magical means for resolving conflict gracefully. As in any other circumstance where people communicate, conflict happens on the Internet, and people vary widely in their ability to resolve differences.

The promise of the Internet lies in its ability to bring people from all over the world together, freed from the limitations of time, place, and cost that impede other methods of communication. To some, the Internet is a place of nearly total freedom of speech, as its global content is beyond the control of national governments. Indeed, most computer users react angrily when issues such as censorship or regulation of the Internet are discussed. But despite the Internet's reputation for being a democratic medium, it is shaped by dominant forces, as is every other area of life. With business now marketing on the World Wide Web, the character of the Internet is rapidly changing from that of an "electronic library" to that of an "electronic shopping center" where the largest and most heavily visited Web sites represent (or feature the advertising of) corporations like Microsoft and IBM. Interestingly, this parallels the dynamics by which the spiritual essence of culture has tended gradually to be eclipsed by the sometimes-too-narrow vision of our profit-oriented meta-culture.

Still, the Internet can be a useful and meaningful tool for anyone, including spiritual seekers. I participate in a small e-mail "roundtable" dedicated to exploring issues relating to spirituality, creation, and community. We regularly offer prayer and support for one another and engage in discussions on issues of importance in our lives. We have Christians, Jews, and "none of the above" in our group, with members who live in widely varied places—from San Francisco to Florida, from Canada to South Africa. For us, the Internet has been a wonderful gift, a medium without which our meaningful spiritual community might never have existed.

But alongside this promise of community is the peril—the potential for abusive or dishonest ways of relating to proliferate. Like any other community, the Internet has its good neighborhoods and bad neighborhoods. Cyberspace is a medium where people can easily remain anonymous. Cloaked by this anonymity, some settle for values that are certain to undermine the leadings and values of the Sacred. Dishonesty on the Internet is easy, falsely representing oneself is easy, and finding access to pornography and racist material is easy. Like any other aspect of human life, cyberspace has a shadow.

While plenty of hype surrounds the Internet as a new tool for human community, nearly equivalent amounts of hysteria have arisen as people have become frightened by the specter of pornography in cyberspace (I myself am much more concerned about racism in cyberspace, and I am amazed that racism has not received nearly as much attention). The truth about this emerging technology seems to lie somewhere in the middle, between hype and hysteria, and it is that the Internet is no more and no less than the latest tool for human communication—and like any tool, particularly a powerful one, it may be used for great good or great harm. It carries much promise for bringing people together and for enriching their lives with new information, new contacts, and sometimes even deep and meaningful friendships. It also carries the realities of the human shadow—realities that can, if we allow them to do so, teach us powerful truths about ourselves. But if we try to repress them, they will merely return to haunt us in indirect ways. Repressing that shadow (as in proposed government legislation that would, in effect, bring censorship to cyberspace) will simply replace the lesser evil of offensive expression with the greater evil of censorship. However, when we allow the shadow on the Internet to teach us, we learn that the latest and greatest forms of technology still have not erased the human capacity to deceive and to exploit, which implies that any and every community must be prepared to deal with issues of conflict and reconciliation, justice and peacemaking.

So what do we learn from the Internet? People naturally seek companionship and community, and will use even the "cold" technology of the computer to find such connectedness. We who are engaged in the spiritual life seek communities because in them we may find ways to support one another in the sacred journey. However, community in itself, whether it's the conventional kind or a hi-tech kind like the Internet, is not a panacea. Just as "shadow issues" of conflict and injustice are real parts of every community, so also are they parts of the Internet.

Whether a group is as small as an intimate prayer circle or as large as the millions who use the Internet, certain qualities seem essential to a spirituality of community—a spirituality that celebrates the promise of community and seeks protection against the perils. These qualities include *covenant* (the establishment of a community's identity and agreements), *justice* and *peacemaking* (the qualities that keep a community focused on unity and fairness toward all its members), *prophecy* (the capacity that some members of the community have to speak the truth of the Sacred to the community), and the notion of the *body* as a metaphor for community. Let's look at each of these topics in turn.

Covenant

Earlier we looked at how promises and agreements are an important, if unspoken, part of friendship—or of any relationship. This is true whether we are making promises and agreements with ourselves (agreeing to nurture wonder in life rather than just holding onto self-protecting and controlling behaviors), with God (agreeing to pray daily and to allow prayer to change our life in creative and healthy ways), or with one another (to belong to one another, to treat others fairly, to choose peacemaking and healing over violence and abuse). Especially in communities with many members, these agreements need to be spelled out. Such agreements, when they form the basis of a spiritual community, are *covenants*.

Covenants, as elements of spirituality, need to be understood as alternatives to *contracts*. While most agreements in society, especially those originating in government or business, are contractual in nature, the spiritual life and spiritual communities are more properly governed by covenants. If I'm making an agreement in which self-protection is a central concern, then I am likely to make contractual agreements designed to provide security for me or my belongings. But for my relationships that are based on wonder and love and transformation, I may wish to form covenant agreements that embody the values I hold sacred.

Etymologically, a contract is a "pulling together," while a covenant is a "coming together." Both words describe agreements, but the connotation is subtly different. A contract pulls together separate and sometimes hostile parties, binding them in an agreement that emphasizes protection and entitlement. A contract makes sure that, to put it bluntly, "no one gets screwed." At its best, a contract fairly protects all involved parties, while setting the ground rules for a transaction to take place. When a relationship or transaction is dominated by the need to protect, contracts are the only reasonable form of agreement.

A covenant, however, is possible only when two or more parties make agreements based on mutual trust, goodwill, and the desire to cooperate to achieve a shared goal. Since spirituality assumes an orientation toward life based on vulnerability, the agreements that characterize spiritually centered relationships are covenantal rather than contractual in nature.

I do not mean to imply that covenants are better than contracts. Just as there is a legitimate place for any other form of security, so do contracts have their place in life. However, a relationship that understands itself as originating in the love of the Sacred will typically seek alternative ways of relating than those involving impulses toward self-protection or entitlement, impulses that are more contractual than covenantal in nature. Because the spiritual life places its trust in God, we who are spiritual seekers can more confidently trust others, even though we understand realistically that people sometimes let us down. We prudently trust others because we know they cannot ultimately hurt us, thanks to the deep safety we find in the love of the Divine (although prudence also means that sometimes caution is appropriate). A contractual relationship can get the job done, but, being limited by the terms of its agreements, it is not meant to do anything more than that. A covenantal relationship, however, can exceed all expectations by nurturing qualities of trust and love among all involved parties, and that love and trust can break down barriers in people's minds and hearts. A covenant relationship is a relationship where the potentials of love and trust are unlimited.

Justice, peace, and prophecy

Love and trust are wonderful, but we know that conflict is real too, even in spiritual communities. Conflicts may arise when one person or group is at fault or is perceived to be at fault. Conflicts may arise when a person or group attempts to achieve increased power or position within the community, whether by ethical means or not. Conflicts do not necessarily indicate wrongdoing, for they can erupt when parties simply have legitimate needs that differ—and clash. Conflict happens, and the strength of a relationship (or a community) is measured not by its lack of conflict but by its ability to find creative reconciliation that nurtures and benefits both (or all) parties.

Although much harm can come from conflict, particularly when it escalates into abuse or violence, conflicts can be valuable in a community's development. They are valuable because they can function as doorways through which a community can move toward greater justice and peace. But justice and peace can materialize only if conflicts are resolved fairly, not according to a win-lose model in which one side defeats the other. Even in situations in which a conflict clearly stems from wrongdoing, the child's proverb "Two wrongs do not make a right" still applies. Redressing an injustice only works when even the wrongdoer is treated fairly.

Spirituality is deeply concerned with peace and justice. To be in relationship with the Sacred means, in terms of a community, to take a stand for healthy situations in which the dignity and worth of all persons is valued and in which both freedom and equality flourish. *Not* to take such a stand may mean allowing unhealthy ideas about community to come between ourselves and God. This reminds me of a priest who once commented on the spiritual life of a racist. He suggested that while a racist may have a relationship with God, it probably is not a very good or close relationship. By contrast, forming a close, loving connection with the Divine means entering a place where peacemaking and justice are mandatory.

Just as countless kinds of communities exist, so also do countless opportunities exist to create peace and justice. Diplomats, for example, work on various fronts to build or maintain peaceful relationships among nations. Closer to home, each one of us can work for a more peaceful and just society in many ways. We can take a stand by getting involved in political causes or volunteering with a charitable agency. Filling a leadership role at work, in a church, or in a civic organization can be a doorway to creating healthier local communities. Perhaps most important is treating family members and friends with fairness and love—an essential part of peacemaking and justice.

In addition to taking leadership roles in our communities or being good team players, sometimes we may be nudged by the Sacred to speak out against situations that are unjust or conflicted. Whether it takes the form of writing a letter to the editor, speaking at an important hearing, or simply confronting a person who is telling a sexist joke, this call to speak out on behalf of sacred values is the call to speak as a *prophet*.

Prophecy is a community function, and a prophet is a person of vision and insight who speaks the word of God to others, usually on matters involving right relationship—whether that means right relationship with the Sacred or right relationship within a community. A prophet belongs both to the Sacred whose message he or she delivers and also to the community that receives the prophecy. Prophecy is a gift from God to the people, a gift related to reconciliation, peacemaking, and justice.

This is not how prophecy is commonly regarded. In everyday parlance, to prophesy means "to foretell the future," as in the "prophecies of Nostradamus." Many psychics who predict the future are called prophets, even though they may never once refer to the Sacred in their predictions. Divination, prognostication, or soothsaying are better words to describe such fortune-telling. By contrast, a prophet is a person who proclaims the word of the Divine—perhaps with regard to the future, but always with implications for the present.

The word *prophesy* literally means "to speak for," and the prophet speaks for God. A prophet is a revisionist—he or she re-visions the relationship between the Sacred and humanity, which may be an invitation to something totally new and unexplored or it may be a call back to a previous way of being. The prophet is an embodiment of prayer, for a prophet, through speaking forth the word of God, enables us to relate with God in transformative, loving ways. Like prayer, prophecy changes things. Prophets are change agents for the Sacred.

One important contemporary prophet was Martin Luther King, Jr. While he may not always have been particularly holy, and while he didn't offer predictions about the future, King did speak mightily for the Sacred, calling on our national community to change old patterns of racism and injustice and to move into the new possibility of a society in which ethnic privilege (or lack thereof) no longer existed. Martin Luther King, Jr. was an outsider—an African-American in racist America—which put him in the tradition of many other outsider prophets, including Jeremiah, Jesus, Francis of Assisi, and Gandhi. The *outsider* is one who lacks political power but who nonetheless speaks the word of God in such a way that the persons in power hear it. Sometimes a prophet may even initiate conflict, for the words of prophecy may not be kindly received by the powerful. But such conflict arises to protest situations far worse than the one that transient conflict creates, situations that need to be made visible and healed through justice and reconciliation.

Because speaking as a prophet is a possible consequence of a prayerful life, we may find that in choosing to be in relationship with the Sacred, we have put ourselves at risk. God may prod us to speak up about something, to prophesy! Or we may be called to hear and respond to the prophetic word spoken by others. One does not have to be a Martin Luther King, Jr. to be a prophet—indeed, fame and power are not prerequisites for being led by the Sacred to become a voice for divine vision and re-vision. One does not have to be a world leader (or any other kind of leader) to be the recipient of the prophetic word. God does not show interest only in those who have power. All of us "ordinary" persons are equally the objects of Divine love and therefore are potential hearers of the Sacred word. And whether we are speakers or hearers of the prophetic word, we are all called to respond—by creating and nurturing relationships based on love, fairness, dignity, peace, and justice.

The body
We've looked at how the spirituality of community involves a range of qualities, including belonging, loving the other, approaching conflict with an eye to peacemaking, and speaking or responding to the divine

prophetic word. All of these qualities of the spiritual life arise out of prayer and wonder, yet they make sense only in terms of community. Community balances out the internal experience of solitary prayer and wonder.

But when we consider the problems that face community—problems of conflict, individualism, injustice, and so forth—this question arises: What exactly would a divine community—a community that is based entirely on spiritual values—ultimately look like? In the Christian tradition, the spiritual community is called the Body of Christ, and I think the notion of "body" is a helpful and valuable metaphor for a healthy and prayerful community.

Bodies are earthy and fleshly, and they exist in the material world of space and time, anchoring the adventurous inner realm of our consciousness in the here-and-now universe of matter and energy. Similarly, living in community anchors the inner realm of spirituality in the physical world. As with communities, bodies consist of many different parts, each with a different function—a diverse group of elements, all necessary, all needing to work together to form a cohesive whole. The power and beauty of the body arises out of firmness (such as the skeleton) balanced with fluidity (such as the dynamics of muscles and the mind). Healthy spiritual communities also require a similar balance of firmness (organizational structure) and fluidity (individual freedom).

Just as our bodies are gifts to us from our parents and the grace of God, so also is a community a gift from the Spirit, who is present in every individual soul of the community. When each person nurtures his or her personal spirituality, that strengthens the community. Just as our souls are embodied in our physical nature, so also a community is the collective embodiment of the souls of its members.

But even beyond that, a spiritual community may *itself* embody the presence of the Sacred. In the early chapters of this book we considered the idea that the universe is God's "body." Now, following the Christian tradition, I want to amend that to suggest that a community united in the Spirit *also* functions as a divine body. Thus, taking care of our communities is as important to our spiritual health as is taking care of our individual bodies. Serving the community is a way of serving the Sacred.

This raises a final question about community: what is the role of *service* in spirituality—and particularly in terms of service to a community? The answer is simple. Part of belonging to a community involves the effort of pitching in and helping out with the common tasks, both the little day-to-day jobs and the larger, visionary work of the community. Even when all members of a community understand themselves as equals, service is still a feature of the common life—people help one another, give of themselves to one another, and make sacrifices for one another. Serving can be as momentous as a lifetime commitment or as simple as giving the cleaning crew a hand. The key issue is that service in a spiritual community is an essential way to express love, care, and belonging. When we offer our service to our community, we simultaneously make an offering to the Divine.

The concept of service is linked with the concept of sacrifice—which, like culture, has its origins in worship and is thus an important part of spirituality, even though the word "sacrifice" is frequently misused and misunderstood. Thus, sacrifice is the topic to which we now turn.

11

Sacrifice

In 1984, the head and torso of a human body were discovered in Lindow Moss, a peat bog near Manchester, England. Authorities determined that the body was ancient, a matter not for the police but for archaeologists. Despite being approximately two thousand years old, "Lindow Man" had been so well preserved in the peat that even what he ate for his last meal could be determined. Forensic analysis revealed that Lindow Man was a healthy male, around thirty years old, and very likely a member of the privileged class (his nails and hair were finely groomed). The cause of death was violent and threefold—he was clubbed and garroted and his throat was slashed. The unsettling evidence suggests that Lindow Man was ritually killed. Scholars now believe that he was a human sacrifice, very likely offered by the ancient Druids.

The idea of human sacrifice seems barbaric and heinous. The Hebrew Scriptures take a strong stand against it but in a disturbing way. The Hebrew Scriptures recount how Abraham thought God was calling him to sacrifice his own son. Abraham methodically prepares for the sacrifice, and only at the point at which he is ready to slay the boy does an angel stop him. The story lauds Abraham for his faithfulness—and it's interesting to note that the angel praises Abraham for his spiritual dispositions: his awe of God and his willingness to make a sacrifice. However, we who read the story today are more likely to feel revulsion that he would be willing even to consider such an act. Abraham offers a ram instead, and the story suggests that this animal sacrifice was pleasing to God—thereby instituting the Hebrew tradition of animal sacrifice (Gen. 22:1-19). Despite this tradition, later prophets argued that God preferred ethical and just behavior instead of the slaying of animals as offerings.

Following the trend set forth by the prophets, Christianity has not practiced violent sacrifice, but for a somber reason—the death of Jesus, in the Christian tradition, is understood as the ultimate sacrifice, sufficient for all time, making any further sacrifices needless. Even today, Catholic Christianity understands its weekly commemoration of Jesus' death (the Mass) to be a ritual reenactment of his sacrifice. And the Episcopal *Book of Common Prayer* describes Christianity as a religion that makes a "sacrifice of praise and thanksgiving" to God (*BCP*, 363).

I'm tempted to write about how advanced Western society is, since it has progressed from human sacrifice to the offering of animals to replacing violent sacrifice with ceremonial forms of sacrifice. While I believe that is certainly a healthy progression, I also believe our society has very muddled ideas about the nature of sacrifice, a confusion that can actually hinder our spiritual growth. Not only do we reject the ancient practice of sacrificing humans and animals, but we have now also reached the point where the very idea of sacrifice in any form has become suspect. Today, we who wish to engage in a devoted relationship with the Sacred need to reclaim an appropriate understanding of sacrifice in order to express our love for the Divine fully.

Defining sacrifice

Traditionally, a sacrifice was anything that was offered to a deity or deities in hopes either of getting something in return, such as favorable weather or a bountiful harvest, or perhaps of simply currying favor. For example, some scholars believe the Druids offered Lindow Man to their gods in exchange for protection against the advances of the Roman empire.

Today, however, our ideas of sacrifice generally do not include any spiritual or religious connotation. In common usage, a sacrifice is merely something given up, often with the implication that pain or loss is involved —and so it can suggest an unhappy experience. For example, a woman who sacrifices herself for her family may give up personal dreams for a career in order to care for others; a youth with a promising talent as a violinist may sacrifice his talent to please his father, who insists that college be devoted to a "practical" discipline such as engineering. Sacrifice as "something given up" can understandably be regarded as a grim or sour concept and is, not surprisingly, an unpopular one—

especially in a society oriented toward personal gratification, mastery, and control. Sacrifice sounds like something we might prefer to avoid or to protect ourselves against.

But "something given up" is not what the word originally meant at all. Sacrifice actually comes from the Latin words *sacra facere*—meaning "to perform sacred rites" or "to make holy." Thus, to sacrifice something originally meant to make it holy.

So what does that mean? How do we make something holy? One traditional way to make something holy is to give it to God—to immerse it in holiness. Therefore, in terms of its original meaning, we see that a sacrifice—making something holy—can be regarded as an act or process of giving something *to God*. For example, when money is sacrificed— such as when it is given out of spiritual commitment to support a homeless shelter—we make it holy, for it is money set apart as a gift to the Sacred. Sacrifice, "making holy," is involved in all the gifts we offer to the Divine, which may include time, money, or efforts to improve ourselves or make the world a better place. Understood in its fullest and richest way, a sacrifice means not only that we give something up, but that we give it up *to the Sacred*—to God—and by our doing so, what we have given becomes holy.

Gifts given, gifts received

Sacrifice, in the way I use it, thus does not so much mean "giving something up" as a unilateral act. Rather, it means offering gifts to God out of a sense of *relationship* and *mutuality*. Mutuality is important—for these sacrificial gifts are given as signs of participation in a loving relationship, a relationship that involves receiving as well as giving. It's rather like Christmas or Hanukkah or Winter Solstice—the joy of holiday gift-giving is really the joy of *exchanging* gifts. Giving may be more blessed than receiving, but receiving is still a blessing! Receiving gifts is a blessing not only because receiving them is fun, but also because it enables others to give.

The Sacred is both far bigger and far more loving than we mortals ever can hope to be. This means that the gifts we receive from the Sacred are generally bigger and more loving than the gifts we give. In return for the gifts we give, *something better* than what we "gave up" inevitably comes to us. Even beyond that, however, the "better gifts" we receive have been coming to us from the moment life began, regardless of what gifts we do (or don't) offer to God. Herein we discover the joyful truth of sacrifice—we give not in order to get something from God, but out of thanksgiving for the many blessings that have been gratuitously showered upon us out of the generous abundance of the Sacred.

While we have no guarantee that our sacrifices will be painless, we need to remember that sacrifice is not meant to be masochistic. A sacrifice has meaning not in terms of the loss we experience as part of a "giving up" but in terms of the gratitude we feel, which motivates us to give as a way of saying "thank you." A sacrifice is my gift to God, given not so much to earn God's favor, but in response to the abundant gifts God has bestowed on and continues to bestow on me.

This holds true even for "sacrifices" that may not be explicitly religious or spiritual in nature. If I sacrifice a percentage of my income for charitable purposes, I am making a gift—not only a gift to the charity I am supporting, but also a gift to the Divine *through* that charity. Although I may feel the pain of a tighter budget, I also will enjoy the gifts I receive in return. I receive the gift of gratitude—whether it's a letter from the charity's director or some other expression of appreciation. Even more important, I receive the "gift" of seeing my money put to good use and of watching the charitable organization make a difference in the world. I am pleased by the knowledge that I am being helpful to others. My sacrifice has a clear, understandable, holy purpose.

Spiritually speaking, the ability to make a sacrifice or sacrifices depends upon this mutuality of giving. Indeed, if I have not received many gifts from the Divine, then I probably lack the strength to make a meaningful sacrifice. If I lack the emotional, mental, and spiritual strength to make my gift willingly, or if I lack the ability to recognize (and receive) the greater good that comes prior to and lies beyond my sacrifice, then my sacrifice may have no meaning to me—other than, perhaps, as a form of spiritual masochism. If I become filled with resentment by giving my money away, I'd be better off spiritually having kept it!

Spirituality in a religious context involves sacrifice in many ways, and certainly beyond conventional ritual offerings of such things as bread and wine or praise and thanksgiving. Many religious groups encourage their members to make sacrifices in terms of their personal habits. Baptists give up drinking and smoking, while Mormons avoid caffeine. Catholics refrain from eating meat on Fridays, while Seventh-Day Adventists give up meat altogether. Orthodox Jews do not drive on the Sabbath, and Muslims fast during the month of Ramadan.

In all these examples, we can see that the sacrifice of a pleasure or a convenience is not only a "giving something up" but is also a "making holy," since these are gifts offered to God. Here also, when we offer a pleasure or a convenience to the Sacred, we may expect to receive gifts in return, even if they are subtle. For example, persons giving up caffeine or alcohol receive two gifts—the sense of having done something pleasing to their God and also, perhaps just as important, the gift of a healthier body.

Another important point to consider is the role community plays in making a sacrifice. The fullest, richest experience of a sacrificial relationship with God seems to be grounded in the context of a sacrificial (grateful, gift-giving) community. The ancient Hebrew animal sacrifices were always offered for the good of the whole nation. Even now, the branches of Christianity that understand Holy Communion to be a form of sacrifice make that sacrifice on behalf of the entire community.

I began this chapter by considering the disturbing, violent phenomenon of ritual killing. I want to end this particular section by honoring nonviolence—a lovely if frequently misunderstood concept, but one closely related to the highest ideals of sacrifice. In *Care of the Soul,* Thomas Moore points out that "the word *violence* comes from the Latin word *vis,* meaning 'life force.' Its very roots suggest that in violence the thrust of life is making itself visible" (Moore 1992, 126). Compare this notion of violence as a "life force" with Gandhi's notion of *non*violence as a "truth force." Gandhi conceived of nonviolence as *satyagraha* ("truth force"), a concept that suggests nonviolence is not weak or passive, but rather is a positive force—thus, very similar to peacemaking. *Satyagraha* represents not the *absence* of violence so much as it represents the *transformation* of "life force" from the capacity for violence into the capacity for peacemaking.

This capacity for peacemaking, or "truth force," becomes available to us when we make our "life force" holy—that is, when we sacrifice our capacity for violence, offering it up as a gift to the Sacred. In return for this sacrifice, we receive a greater gift—the strength and vision to work for justice, forgiveness, and reconciliation.

Because I believe God to be the Source of love and justice, I reject the violence inherent in the ritual killing of animals or humans. However, I believe deeply in the spiritual value of sacrifice, understood as meaning gifts offered lovingly to the Divine. Each of us will likely have many opportunities to offer significant gifts to the Divine—including gifts of our time, our resources, and our abilities. Such sacrifices, whether small or large, are part of the dynamic of being in relationship with the Sacred, and they require courage and willingness if they are to be offered sincerely and lovingly.

The remainder of this chapter will examine several topics, each of which involves some form of sacrifice, some form of gift to the Sacred. *Fidelity,* or faithfulness, is a spiritual virtue connected with sacrificing the changeability of our feelings for the purpose of nurturing strong relationships. When someone wrongs us but asks our *forgiveness,* we have the opportunity to sacrifice our anger and our sense of victimization. When we ourselves do wrong, we have the opportunity to *repent*—in other words, to sacrifice our sense of arrogant pride or self-righteousness. *Obedience* is a difficult action that relates to the sacrifice of willfulness. The *Sabbath* (a day of rest), an aspect of Judeo-Christian culture that is nearly extinct, requires us to sacrifice our workaholism. Finally, *humility* involves the sacrifice of the unrealistic or inflated parts of our self-image. All of these sacrifices are gifts we may offer to the Divine—gifts given for the purpose of nurturing a vibrant relationship with God.

Fidelity

We don't seem to talk much about *fidelity* these days. A generation ago, fidelity was used largely to describe recording technology—"high fidelity," or "hi-fi" as it came to be known. Nowadays perhaps it's most commonly seen in the names of banks and financial institutions—"First Fidelity" and so forth. A word that's probably more common is *in*fidelity, as in "marital infidelity." Is that who we have become as a culture—a people with a much greater inclination to think of and to speak about unfaithfulness than about faithfulness?

Fidelity, of course, means precisely that—faithfulness—and it encompasses much more than merely a marriage without affairs or a bank or a quality sound recording. To be faithful is the basic quality necessary for making a covenant, living in community, or having any kind of adult relationship. A faithful person keeps his or her agreements; an unfaithful person does not.

Keeping agreements is an essential part of all relationships, earthly as well as spiritual. To make an agreement is like a sacrifice, for it is a gift we offer. To *keep* an agreement also involves sacrifice—sacrificing the tendency to allow our changing emotions to dictate our behavior. Agreements, like relationships, involve both "self" and "other." (Even when I make an agreement with myself, one part of me agrees to behave a certain way in order to satisfy the desire of another part of me. I made an agreement with myself to write this book, which means that the part of me who would rather just read all the time made an agreement with the more ambitious part of me.)

When I make a promise to someone else, I choose to behave in a specifically chosen way, as agreed upon by both myself and the other person. The same holds true for my relationship with the Sacred—my spiritual life consists of agreements I make with God, agreements to behave in certain ways (for example, agreeing to pray regularly or agreeing to be compassionate to the poor). For me to be spiritually faithful means for me to keep those agreements. Agreements constitute a rather unglamourous aspect of spirituality, but a really important aspect nonetheless.

Usually, when two parties make agreements, a mutual compromise or some kind of give-and-take is involved. To me, the best example of that is marriage. Thus, my wife and I show fidelity for each other through our agreement to refrain from sexual or romantic liaisons outside the marriage and our agreement to love each other until we are parted by death. Having made these agreements, I treat her with care and goodwill to express my love—and to honor her trust and love for me—day after day. I trust her to behave in a similar way, knowing she also wishes to honor my trust and love. Marital *in*fidelity would occur if this agreement broke down.

On a person's wedding day, lovingly promising to be faithful until death, to forsake all others, and to treat each other with love and honor is easy. But keeping that agreement day by day (even when conflict arises or the temptation to disregard the promise is strong) is what makes the fidelity real—and makes the marriage worthwhile. Unfortunately, getting married is easier than staying married, and keeping simple agreements is often not so simple.

With God, the matter of fidelity works differently. While some people may, and often do, make agreements with the Sacred to earn love or acceptance or favor, that is really a pointless exercise—for Divine love cannot be earned. It is something we simply receive. Like the initial surprise of our birth, God's love is an ongoing, freely given surprise to all of us. We need not make promises to God in order to be worthy of love; we are worthy simply because we exist.

A basic truth of spirituality is that the Divine is ever-faithful to us. In other words, God loves us without fail and unconditionally. We need not be concerned with how we can *make* God faithful—the question we face is how we may best be faithful to God and *respond to*, or to live up to, God's constant faithfulness to us. The Divine fidelity, as something we can count on, is part of God's unconditional love. Our own faithfulness, which is not nearly as reliable, may rise and fall with our changeable human love.

What does being faithful *mean* in spiritual terms? What are our agreements with God? Here is an important place to stop and reflect. Of course, I cannot tell you what your agreements with God are, for every person's agreements are unique. What I *can* tell you is that just about all people, whether they are actively aware of it or not, have some form of agreement with the Sacred, usually stemming from childhood assumptions about God, spirituality, and religion. It may be something simple ("I'll believe in you, God, if you will give me a reason to hope"), it may involve trying to keep God at arm's length ("I'll go to church, God, but I expect you to leave me alone"), or it may be complex ("I'll live the life of a celibate missionary, and I expect you to bless my ministry"). These examples sound as if we are bargaining with the Divine, and indeed, in such cases, that's what we are doing. Most of us do try to make deals with the Sacred that are on our own terms—whatever they may be. The controlling and self-protecting parts of ourselves really do want to strike bargains with God. Alas, such bargains are more like business contracts than sacrificial covenants!

For most of us, agreements with the Sacred involve a mishmash of ideas about spirituality—including our own hopes and fears, the hopes and fears of our family, things we learned in church, and even public or civic notions about God. Out of these sometimes contradictory notions about the Divine, we develop our own individual ways of understanding or imagining God, and—consciously or unconsciously—we form agreements with and make promises to the Sacred. If we don't consciously know what these bargains and agreements are, then we need to get in touch with our unconscious—because that's where the agreements and the bargains are stored when we aren't aware of them. We need to explore the implications of our feelings, our dreams, and our daydreams; we need to strive for honesty and vulnerability in our soul friendships or other close relationships—for it is in such self-examination and vulnerability that the agreements hidden in our unconscious are most likely to be revealed. In fact, to be faithful *requires* our knowing what those bargains and agreements and promises are, which is why unconscious agreements from our past need to be examined and perhaps changed.

The whole matter of forming agreements is a situation in which community is helpful, and most religious traditions have resources to help people in these areas—hopefully on a level above that of mere bargaining. Often, the initiation rites of a religion include promises that are made to God. In the Episcopal Church, for example, new members agree to do such things as loving their neighbors, striving for justice and peace, and persevering in fellowship and prayer (*BCP*, 304-5).

Spiritual fidelity grows out of our daily spiritual practice, just as marital fidelity grows out of two people making the daily choices necessary to keep their marriage vows. Fidelity characterizes a mature spirituality. The joy of a consciousness bathed in the presence of the Holy One parallels the joy of a teenager who is falling in love for the first time. It's an important, lovely experience—though by itself it is incomplete. Just as teen love needs to find fulfillment in a mature, faithful, adult expression of interpersonal commitment, the excitement of falling in love with God needs grounding in a mature, faithful, adult expression of spiritual commitment. That commitment is covenantal and sacrificial in nature. It involves loving agreements and the offering of gifts. No gift means more, in marriage or in spirituality, than the gift of our abiding faithfulness.

Forgiveness

Forgiveness comes from the old English *forgiefan*, which literally means "to give completely." The link between forgiveness and giving seems clearest in the idea of having a debt forgiven—in other words, the creditor simply gives the unpaid amount to the debtor as a gift. Maybe we've lost something in the tendency of banks and businesses nowadays to talk about "writing off" bad debt rather than "forgiving" it.

Usually we use the word forgiveness to describe ceasing to hold people's wrongdoings against them, especially when the wrongdoers themselves have expressed remorse or made reparation. However, to forgive a person is to make a gift of our respect and goodwill, even if—perhaps *particularly* if—the person hasn't expressed remorse, made reparation, or otherwise seems not to deserve it.

The reputation of forgiveness has taken some blows in recent years. Laura Davis and Ellen Bass, authors of a manual for survivors of sexual abuse called *The Courage to Heal*, see no reason why the survivor should forgive the abuser. They point out that the survivor has already given so much to the abuser, why give anything else now? While this logic is plausible enough on the surface, it is a case in which the over-protective-ness of survival-mind is at play.

If we believe forgiveness involves "giving something up"—similar to the popular understanding of sacrifice—then Davis and Bass are right, and everyone (not just abuse survivors) had better carefully hoard their limited "forgiveness resources." If, when I forgive you, you "win" and I "lose," then my forgiveness would be absurd. But seen from the vantage point of divine love, forgiveness is not a scarce resource, and true forgiveness only happens when *both* parties "win."

An old saying about love declares, "The more you give away, the more you have." The same holds true for forgiveness. When I offer my forgiveness to someone who has wronged me, giving him my love and respect whether he deserves it or not, I also enlarge my capacity to receive abundant love and respect from the Sacred, which I know I *will* receive—and more abundantly than *I* deserve! God does not reward us for forgiving others—the love of the Divine is there for us all along. But the act of forgiving clears a space in our consciousness that allows us to receive the gift of divine love more easily.

When I don't forgive, that "space" in my consciousness is filled with my sense of victimization, my sense of my own moral superiority, and my sense of bitterness at the injustices of the world—especially the injustices caused by the person or persons I am blaming! Unfortunately, these are paralyzing feelings, and I may become stuck in my own little drama of having been wronged. My taking any of these positions actually gives a lot of power to the person I am blaming. But when I forgive someone, I say in effect, "You do not have the power to turn me into a victim. My relationship with you, as with all people, stems from my power to choose and my ability to love, which I derive from the Sacred and which is not contingent on the behavior of others."

I think Bass and Davis take an understandable position, given the enormity of the trauma associated with sexual abuse. I certainly do not support any sort of "forgiveness" that allows an abuser to continue hurting others—just as "peacemaking" must never be a code word for avoiding conflict through appeasement. To forgive someone does not extend to pretending that the person may not need to have his or her rights or privileges curtailed legally. To forgive a sexual offender or a violent criminal means respecting that person's humanity and God-given worth—but it does not mean we have to allow that person unfettered physical freedom.

Forgiveness is a *process*, and the larger the wrongdoing, the more complex the process of forgiveness will be. Thankfully, no friend or relative of mine has ever been murdered, but I imagine that the friends and family of a murder victim might find that the process of forgiving the murderer would take a lifetime. That's perfectly understandable—for forgiveness does *not* mean pretending hurts and anger aren't there! Forgiveness may never transcend the struggle to let go of anger and bitterness—but even the struggle to forgive is spiritually crucial, for without it the anger and bitterness could easily be overwhelming. I believe the victims of violence or abuse who struggle to forgive their assailants and only can forgive imperfectly are still light-years ahead of those who nurse their anger and bitterness and allow it to control their lives.

This can be seen most clearly in the feelings that many crime victims and their families experience with regard to perpetrators who are tried, sentenced to death, and executed. Some victims and family members who press for the death penalty for criminals who once hurt them have reported feeling "cheated" by the execution. Of course they feel cheated—they've spent years nursing blame and hatred, and now the object of their hatred is dead! Compare that to victims who choose to forgive their assailant as best they can. Some time ago I read about a devout Amish family whose son had been murdered. The family took it upon themselves to visit the murderer in prison, and they slowly developed a relationship with the man. For them, that was part of the process of forgiveness and part of their commitment to God. They knew nothing could bring their son back and, in the meantime, they knew their own spiritual health depended on whether they viewed the murderer as an unredeemable monster or as a man who had done a terrible thing. By choosing to view him in the latter fashion, they not only healed their own grief more quickly but they also provided the killer with an unlikely way to do some healing of his own. Eventually, the murderer had to face his own remorse and beg the forgiveness of the family—which, by then, they could offer.

So forgiveness is an important sacrifice, not so much because it benefits the recipient, but because it benefits the giver. The mutuality of sacrifice also becomes evident in forgiveness—I give, both to the Sacred and to whomever has wronged me, the gift of my willingness to stop blaming. In return, I receive far more than I give, for I receive a clearer sense of divine love as well as a sense of freedom. When my forgiving is directed toward, say, a perpetrator of violence or abuse, my being freed of having my energy invested in blame and resentment means I am free to move on with my life—which could mean, for example, that I have the energy to work hard to prevent others from being victimized in a similar way. But when I refuse to forgive, no gifts are exchanged and I am left holding onto my bitterness—hardly a spiritual boon.

Repentance

If forgiveness is the gift of changing our attitude toward those who have wronged us, then *repentance* is the gift of stopping our own wrongdoing. With repentance, I sacrifice my self-justification. I stop thinking that my actions are harmless or reasonable. I admit that they are hurtful, either to myself or to others, and I sacrifice those hurtful actions— I give them to God, choosing instead to act more lovingly.

Unfortunately, repentance seems to be an even dirtier word these days than sacrifice. This is because some branches of Christianity have so misused the term that it has come to imply that this important process is based on fear and control—the very opposite of the kind of spirituality that has been presented by Jesus, Buddha, and other spiritual teachers. As it is used by many fundamentalists today, "to repent" seems to imply refraining from anything that is in any way pleasurable; deciding that all human beings are miserable, sniveling worms who deserve to die; and spending the rest of one's life in a self-righteous crusade to get other people to accept these same ideas. This is not repentance but some sort of psychological dysfunction masquerading as spirituality.

To repent essentially means to feel sorry for one's wrongdoing. The use of the term in the New Testament by Jesus and his followers has a slightly richer connotation, though. To repent is not only to feel sorry about one's wrongdoing but also to change one's behavior so the wrongdoing stops. Now, these two shades of meaning both fall well within the scope of spirituality as we have defined it in this book. Being sorry is a natural feeling that anyone who nurtures wonder and openness in her life will spontaneously experience at the moment she understands that her behavior is or has been hurtful. That moment of personal understanding is important, for repentance cannot be manufactured or engineered any more than wonder or awe can be engineered.

After the sense of feeling sorry, the next aspect of repentance involves change—changing one's behavior. Repentance-as-change is easy to recognize in various traditions, not just in Christianity. Buddhists "repent" when they give up the anxieties of the mind for the serene stillness of meditation. New Agers "repent" when they give up the meaninglessness of a materialistic lifestyle for the new purpose found in metaphysical study or inner healing work. Neopagans "repent" when they adopt a lifestyle based less on consumerism and more on practicing the principles of recycling and voluntary simplicity. To repent is to shed an old way of living for the promise found in the spiritual path and a faith community. Repentance means moving into the world of imagination and possibility, the world that offers the promise of divine love.

The repentance that fundamentalist Christians insist on is more of a contractual obligation than an aspect of covenant. Fundamentalists seem to insist that we repent *before* we can receive God's love. This is not a covenant, but a contract, with the emphasis on exchange (exchanging my repentance for God's not condemning me) rather than on relationship. A covenantal model of repentance starts instead with relationship, where repentance flows naturally out of the safety we already have in Divine love. In that loving relationship, God is "family"—and like all family members, God has the right to ask things of us (which God does both through inner leadings experienced in prayer and through callings we may encounter in our relationships with other people or with our faith tradition). When we respond to those sacred requests—in other words, when we offer the gift of choosing new, more loving behavior—we make the sacrifice of repentance.

Obedience

In chapter 7, I talked about transgression and mentioned that a spiritual community emphasizing obedience would almost certainly not support the idea that transgression is a spiritual act. But I did not mean to imply that obedience somehow lacks virtue or that it is only for the fearful, unimaginative, or ultraconservative. In fact, it has a perfectly legitimate place, and as we begin now to explore that other side of things—*obedience* —we recognize that obedience can also be deeply spiritual and that transgression and obedience are simply the opposite ends of a polarity. Like all polarities, both ends of the continuum are necessary for a fully formed life in the Spirit.

"Obedience" is another word that has become loaded with unsavory connotations. It literally means "attentive listening"—to be obedient is to listen. To obey involves listening carefully and attentively—and taking action in response to what is heard. An obedient person listens carefully to—and acts according to—the directions he or she receives from an authority, whether that authority is a human superior or God.

Our society, however, frequently reduces the concept of obedience to the point that it merely means responding to authority compliantly. We think being obedient means responding to the command "Jump!" with the question "How high?" However, this view of obedience is not only incomplete, it's just plain wrong.

But because we do often equate obedience with *compliance*, we have become uncomfortable with responding affirmatively to authority. We tend to regard obedience as a way of behaving that is best reserved for children, military personnel, and monks and nuns—but not other responsible persons.

I think we resist obedience in general because of our aversion to compliance, especially in abusive or toxic situations. (I will henceforth refer to this kind of compliant or submissive obedience as "toxic obedience.") "Obedience" conjures up thoughts of German soldiers carrying out the Nazi program of extermination and genocide, thoughts of a woman in an abusive relationship doing everything her husband asks simply to keep from getting hit, or thoughts of employees of a dishonest boss going along with unethical practices out of fear of reprisal. These examples suggest that toxic obedience, when linked with a controlling or vengeful authority, can become a horrible force in people's lives.

Is there an alternative to toxic obedience? I believe so, if for no other reason than that obedience has played such a significant role in cultural and spiritual traditions. Every organization, whether a spiritual community, military or other government agency, business, or school, requires duly appointed authority to function. Indeed, any situation that inevitably involves authority and rank—such as parent-child, student-teacher, employee-employer, or military or monastic hierarchies—requires healthy obedience for evident reasons. But what constitutes healthy obedience?

When we are in circumstances that require our obedience to another, several qualities should be present. Most important of all, we should offer our obedience just *to those who deserve it*. In spiritual terms, this means being obedient only to people who are themselves deeply obedient to the call of the Sacred in their lives. Even when we are in positions of obedience, we should also have the clear ability to make *choices,* which includes our being aware of any alternatives and their ramifications (this ability to choose is what separates obedience from mere compliance).

Having determined that the situation requiring our obedience is healthy, we must bring to it our own appropriate attitudes in order to manifest healthy obedience. These attitudes include the determination to *listen* (to really hear what is being asked of us and to take responsibility for clarifying points we don't understand or agree with). Finally, we must be willing to *respond* (to make and follow through on our choices, in accordance with the directions we've heard).

While healthy obedience may involve our obeying a human authority, it is only healthy insofar as it is consistent with obedience to the Sacred. The criterion for all such obedience is found in its harmony with our primary obedience to—in our being present to—the call of the Sacred. With this statement, I recognize that I am dancing around a question ("What is the call of God, and how do I recognize it?") that could easily warrant a book of its own. For now, I'll simply suggest that God's call is discerned through the teachings and traditions of our faith community and through understanding our own experiences in prayer, especially when we have the help of a trusted soul friend. Listening for the whispered voice of God is central to prayer—then being willing and able to discern and respond to that voice wherever we find it in our life is what constitutes the spiritual dimension of obedience.

As an act of listening to and responding to God's call, healthy obedience—in its spiritual aspect—entails my sacrificing my own willfulness and my insistence on having my own way. At its best, this healthy obedience is a way I can loosen the grip that survival-mind has on my consciousness. When I obey the adventurous and loving guidance of the Sacred, I sacrifice my need to be in control—I give the control to God —and in return I gain freedom from needing to manage and control every detail of my life. This virtuous, healthy kind of obedience is based on a paradox: that voluntarily limiting my choices actually expands my freedom—just as limiting myself to one romantic/sexual partner when I got married actually expanded my freedom to explore intimacy, vulnera-bility, and fidelity with one trusted person—my wife.

Interestingly, just as obedience has become something of a "non-virtue" in our society, so has *disobedience* (which is similar but not identical to transgression) taken its place and become a virtue. For example, the idea that "good" children ought to obey their parents seems almost to have become extinct in recent years—and for evidence of this trend, we need look no further than recent movies released by that paragon of family entertainment, Walt Disney Pictures. Disney's *The Little Mermaid* and *Pocahontas* both tell the stories of girls who disobey their fathers. Not only is the disobedience accepted in the story but, in both films, the father who has been disobeyed even comes around to see the wisdom of the daughter's actions. How different this is from the Disney films of fifty years ago—consider *Pinocchio*, in which the boundary between being a good boy and a naughty boy is depicted in terms of whether Pinocchio obeys his father! As long as Pinocchio is disobedient, he finds himself in all sorts of trouble . . . unlike the little mermaid and Pocahontas, whose disobedience leads to romance, adventure, and liberation.

If obedience means "active listening," then we can infer that disobedience means simply "not listening." Disobedience can arise out of a holy call to transgress (for example, the civil disobedience practiced by civil rights activists in the 1960s), but it can also be a very unhelpful way of dodging responsibility. So, while transgression is a spiritual virtue that often involves disobeying human authority in order to obey a Divine call (which may involve upset, particularly if we break rules for the wrong reasons), disobedience may or may not be a spiritually mandated act.

Obedience in terms of a spiritual or religious discipline also raises the issue of *choice* in a particularly significant way, for it calls on me to discern, for myself, the relative importance of fidelity and freedom. I want to be faithful to the teachings of my tradition, but I also want to be free to disagree with them. My personal choice in this matter is to choose in favor of fidelity. This does not so much mean giving up my freedom to disobey, but rather choosing to make fidelity more important than that freedom. However, when I obey the teachings of my tradition, I am still acting out of my freedom—I freely choose to obey for the purpose of maintaining my commitment and faithfulness. This may involve some pain. Obeying may be difficult when and if I am inclined to disobey. But to think that my surface inclinations always represent what is best for me is a mistake—as it would be for anyone. A person trying to lose weight who wants a hot fudge sundae has a strong surface-level appetite that does not reflect what his body and soul really need and want. Spiritual obedience separates us from our surface appetites—the domain of the survival-mind—so we may be faithful to our deeper, soul-level longings and desires.

Let us return now to the obedience-transgression polarity. Which is the higher virtue, obedience or transgression? Obedience and transgression both have their place in the spiritual life, so the answer to this question depends entirely upon the context, along with an understanding that the resolution depends inevitably on holding and working with the tension between those two opposites—not so much simply choosing one instead of the other. Disobedience is only a virtuous transgression when it means obeying the Spirit's highest call. Winston Churchill thought Gandhi was seditious because of his disregard for British law. But, in fact, Gandhi was striving to be obedient to what he considered a higher law, that of spiritual truth, which proclaimed freedom to be worth far more than obeying the dictates of a colonial government, whether they represented "the law" or not. Gandhi's struggle to "listen attentively" to the voice of the Sacred led him to struggle for political and social change through nonviolent means—and obeying that call meant disobeying the law. Gandhi's transgression was truly virtuous, but his virtuous civil disobedience derived from his virtuous *obedience* to the higher call of the Spirit.

On the other hand, the 1995 assassination of Israeli Prime Minister Yitzak Rabin does not qualify as an obedient form of transgression by the assassin, even though he believed he was obeying God. Here, the assassin's desire to control the political future of Israel got in the way of his ability to be obedient to the Sacred. Even if God wanted Rabin's policies to be stopped, God would not have called someone to break the divine law against killing. The Sacred is consistent—a transgression must still obey the highest laws in order for it to be holy.

Few of us are called to the level of extreme obedience that Buddha or Jesus or Francis of Assisi manifested. For that matter, few of us are called to the dramatic level of transgression and protest that marked the lives of Martin Luther King, Jr. and Mohandas Gandhi. For most of us, the spiritual life involves balancing the polarity of transgression and obedience in terms of our various everyday relationships, especially our relationships with authority.

We are all called to the possibility of listening actively for the "still, small voice" of the Divine Presence and then responding (obeying) to the best of our ability. As we do, we may not change the course of history, but we will assuredly find real changes occurring in our lives—changes in the ways we relate to other persons, changes in the ways we relate to work and leisure, changes in the ways we relate to money and possessions, changes in the ways we relate to pleasures and pastimes. Our obedience to God can lead us to lessen our attachments and addictions, making us spiritually free.

Sabbath

The Sabbath, a weekly day of rest, is also a kind of sacrifice—a sacrifice of time. When a community sets aside a specific amount of time for leisure, rest, and worship, it offers that period of time to the Sacred. In the Jewish and Christian traditions, this "sacrifice of time" is called the *Sabbath*. The Sabbath is thus an interruption of ordinary time, usually the kind of time that is otherwise controlled by survival-mind. In the Sacred "pause" created by this interruption, spiritual-mind may come out and play.

Because I grew up in the South, my earliest memories of the Sabbath are linked with what were commonly called "blue laws"—ordinances that kept most businesses closed and prohibited the sale of alcoholic beverages on Sundays. (I still remember my mother explaining to me why drugstores and grocery stores could be open on Sundays, but toy stores couldn't!) By the time I was a young adult, however, most of that had changed. Nevertheless, Georgia still prohibits the sale of alcohol on Sundays, and a few local governments here and there have managed to retain stricter codes. But the blue laws are mostly gone. Nowadays, the malls are as crowded on Sundays as they are on Saturdays, and churchgoing people spend their money on Sundays as fast as everybody else.

As a person opposed to laws that favor one particular religious tradition over another, I have long been troubled by the blue laws. In fact, since I thought the blue laws were wrong, I never developed much interest in the idea of the Sabbath. Even as a practicing Christian, I tended to view the injunction to "remember the Sabbath and keep it holy" as an ancient rule that, like many of the precepts of the Hebrew Scriptures, simply did not apply anymore, at least not to me.

But several years ago, I moved into an Orthodox Jewish neighborhood, and my attitude toward the Sabbath started to change. Almost immediately, I noticed that the Orthodox Jews walked to and from the synagogue on the Sabbath. That seemed natural enough, since Orthodox Jews consider driving to be a form of work, meaning that it is forbidden on the Sabbath. Then, as the months went by, I eventually came to respect what I first rather condescendingly considered "quaint." The blasts of winter or torrential rains never deterred my neighbors from their commitment to let their cars rest during the Sabbath observance.

Further, my favorite local restaurant is a kosher vegetarian deli—which, like numerous local businesses, closes on Friday afternoon (the Jewish Sabbath begins at sundown on Friday) and does not reopen until Sunday. As I got to know some of my neighbors, I learned that Friday evenings and Saturdays were times of shared meals and joyful socializing among the members of the synagogue. Sabbath was not only a time of rest, but it was also a time of recreation—of re-creating the bonds of family and community that held the tiny Orthodox Jewish community together week after week, year after year, generation after generation.

I still disapprove of the blue laws, and I'm not looking into converting to the Orthodox Jewish faith. Yet my respect for my Jewish neighbors is now deeply rooted—and centers on my appreciation for their fidelity to the Sabbath. Thanks to their example, I've come to recognize for myself the sacrificial beauty that this sacred pause in the rhythm of the week represents.

The creation story in the Hebrew Scriptures describes the first Sabbath as a day of rest, which God took after the initial work of creation. Since God took six "days" to create the universe and the seventh "day" to rest, observing the seventh day of the week (Saturday) as a resting day became the model for the Jewish Sabbath—a model that Christians adapted by shifting the Sabbath forward so it coincided with Sunday, the day of the resurrection.

Part of the beauty of the Sabbath comes from its being a communal event. We've noted how spirituality, both in terms of traditional religion as well as New Age or alternative spiritualities, has increasingly become private and individualistic: "My spirituality is between me and God." Yes, of course it is, but it's also between you and every person you relate to. A Sabbath time honored by one's spiritual community provides a way for all to pause together and nurture their connections with one another—and with God.

The communal side of the Sabbath has economic and political implications along with its spiritual purpose. To observe the Sabbath is not the same as merely taking a day off, as the Sabbath represents a time of leisure for the *entire* community. As a day when everyone rests, it's a safeguard against burn-out and also can function to slow down exploitation, whether of people, the environment, or even oneself. It undermines the notion that we must keep pushing and struggling to survive; in the hours of Sabbath rest, we have the opportunity to replace the anxieties that dominate the workaday world with a spiritually nourishing alternative— with faithful openness and wonder. The Sabbath interrupts routines of control and self-protection, creating the space for belief and prayer to be cultivated in people's minds and hearts.

Unfortunately, blue laws represent the Sabbath at its worst—reducing it to a legal restriction imposed on people, which presents the Sabbath in terms of a set of rules that begin with "you can't" ("You can't open your store," "You can't buy a drink," and so forth). Jesus was impatient with this kind of religious legalism and more than once broke the Sabbath laws himself, remarking that the purpose of the Sabbath was to serve humanity, not the reverse.

Yet we need to consider that problems exist at the other extreme as well. If the alternative to the blue laws is a society increasingly given over to hypercompetitive, frenzied business activity, in which the anxiety of the marketplace reigns for seven days a week and no one can afford to take a day off anymore, perhaps it means that when we threw off the shackles of the legalistic Sabbath, we also lost something precious. In losing the spiritual opportunity of the Sabbath, when the community freely rested and responded to the inner need for stillness, perhaps our society became less free than it was when the blue laws were in effect.

Of course, since we now live in a religiously pluralistic world, we cannot and should not bring back the legislated kind of Sabbath that was epitomized by the blue laws—a Sabbath of contract, not covenant. But no matter what our faith tradition may be, we have the choice to be inspired by or even to follow the example of Orthodox Jews, *voluntarily* setting aside a day of rest, not just for ourselves but for our families as well. While a privately observed Sabbath does not have the same power as a Sabbath observed by an entire community, it is still a step in the right direction—a choice to allow the slow rhythms of this alternative time to undo some of our work-related preoccupations and anxieties and to create cracks in the armor of our survival-mind, cracks where the wonder of life can enter. Honoring Sabbath time means to take a breather—to create a space for the Spirit to fill our hearts with joy and love.

Humility and simplicity

Humility, the last of our concepts related to sacrifice, is just as misused and misunderstood as repentance or obedience. It's also as important as any concept we've examined so far. Humility is traditionally considered a supreme virtue, at least in the traditional religions. Contemporary society, however, seems uncomfortable with the word "humble," uncomfortable enough to want to upgrade a word like "simple" to take its place. Most people, for example, think "humble living" sounds dreadful, whereas they consider "simple living" a wonderful alternative to our hectic urban lifestyle. But what is simple living other than a humble way of living? And why does humble living sound so unappetizing—kind of the spiritual equivalent of boiled spinach?

Just as obedience has been confused with compliance, so humility has often been confused with *docility*. To regard humility in this way suggests that being humble means never questioning authority, never attempting to better oneself, never challenging the powers that be. Humility has thus been considered synonymous with submissiveness, passivity, and self-abnegation. To be humble according to this image is either to be someone with no personal desire and ambition or someone who is actively suspicious or contemptuous of his or her own desires and ambitions. In this brand of humility, loving oneself is improper—humble persons are those who seem to have no interest in caring for themselves or who, perhaps, even actively hate themselves.

We have rightly jettisoned such constricted, unhealthy ideas as toxic and inimical to the soul. However, by rejecting *toxic* humility, we have tended also to lose sight of spiritually valuable, *constructive* humility. Fortunately, though, words like "simple" are used to preserve at least part of what is truly good about humility.

Toxic humility is actually an inverted form of hubris. *Hubris* is usually defined as *pride*, but I want to avoid using that word in a pejorative sense, since pride, when defined as "loving self-respect," has an appropriate place in every person's life. But hubris, which really is *excessive* pride, is not the same as "self-love" and is more akin to arrogance or to a sense of excessive self-importance.

Hubris is capable of inverting itself, of slyly masquerading as the self-loathing, self-negating of toxic humility. This pseudo-humility may be built on a recognition that self-love and self-power and self-comfort are all somehow impediments to successful living and thus must be denied or negated by adopting the external characteristics of humility. The resulting kind of "humility," though, is likely to be marked by strong overtones of self-consciousness. Hubris always reveals itself in terms of self-importance or self-inflation, whether that self-importance plays itself out in arrogance (excessive self-love) or as a self-conscious version of toxic humility (excessive self-denial or self-contempt).

Constructive humility involves sacrificing our sense of self-importance to the Sacred. We don't have to negate ourselves or treat ourselves like worms to be humble. We simply must learn to take ourselves less seriously, which means celebrating our good qualities, admitting to our foibles, and maintaining a balanced and honest self-image. It's not an easy task! But when we offer our self-importance as a gift to the Sacred, we receive the greater gift of honest self-knowledge in return—and genuine love for ourselves as the earthy creatures we are.

One way to explore the dynamics of constructive humility is by considering the root word of humility, *humus,* which means "of the earth." Healthy humility is part of materiality as much as it is part of spirituality. Humble persons are earthy persons—in other words, persons who are unafraid of the messiness of life, who are willing to get their hands dirty to get a job done. Humble persons are marked less by how much they love or hate themselves (all of us are complex mixtures of self-love and self-criticism) than by such things as their sense of humor, their willingness to make mistakes, and their courage to admit it when they don't know an answer or they need help. Humble persons are probably pretty realistic about themselves—they know they have some gifts and talents and are probably pleased about that, but they also have an honest awareness of their shortcomings.

Humility, like all the sacrificial characteristics we've considered, has a community dimension. My self-image—which includes my sense of self-importance or lack thereof—is problematic only insofar as I am anxious about the opinion others hold of me, the place I occupy in society, or how I look in comparison to others. Hubris is meaningless as far as a hermit is concerned, since a life lived all alone includes no one whose approval or admiration matters. While hubris derives its power from what others think, constructive humility can transform our relationships, leading us from the anxieties of self-importance to a position of light-hearted self-acceptance. Humility allows us to be in relationship with other persons starting from the spiritual position of vulnerability and playfulness, rather than from the controlling positions of hubris or preserving our reputation.

Humility is a necessary component of a spiritual community, since only in our realistic, down-to-earth appraisal of ourselves can we relate to one another out of honesty and love. To the extent we can do that—that we are honest and humble and loving with one another—we are able to co-create the web of relationships within a community that will serve our ultimate goal: to be, as individuals and as a group, lovers of the Sacred.

I began this section by considering how simplicity has become a code word for constructive humility, so I'd like to finish up with a closer look at simplicity, which is a spiritually valuable quality in its own right. Spirituality is often concerned with a simple rather than a complex view of things. "God is love," "Prayer changes things," and "Life is to be celebrated!" are really quite simple notions, yet they are the stuff of spirituality.

To live humbly can involve a number of simple choices—seeking simpler ways of managing money, simpler ways of managing time, simpler ways of building and enjoying community with family and friends. Such simple, humble living is truly an alternative to the sophistication and drive that characterize the central values of our society—and yet, in this alternative way of living, we allow a spaciousness in our bodies and souls for the love of the Sacred to take root.

Gifts received, gifts given

A Benedictine monk named David Steindl-Rast has written a book called *Gratefulness, the Heart of Prayer*. It's a wise book, and the title captures some of that wisdom, but I'd like to expand on the wisdom of that title and suggest that *two* qualities, gratitude and sacrifice, are what constitute the heart of prayer. We are surprised and thrilled by the many gifts given to us, including our life, our lovely universe and wonderful planet, our many meaningful relationships with so many different kinds of people. Even the struggles and conflicts of life may be regarded as gifts, given to us for the purpose of learning, in Blake's splendid words, "to bear the beams of love." As we cultivate the skills of peacemaking, community building, and intimate friendship, we truly learn the way of love.

So much has been given to us, and gratitude is the heart-level response we can bring to our prayer. Saying "thank you" to the Sacred is one of the most profound spiritual acts anyone can undertake. Yet to respond to the call of sacrifice is to embody those words—to put our gratitude in action. Out of the much we have been given, we are free to give to others. Because we have been given so much, we choose to give in return. We offer gifts, either directly to the Divine or indirectly through what we give to others in the name of the Divine. Such sacrifices are truly acts of prayer, for they all constitute ways of showing our appreciation to the One who loves us beyond all bounds.

12

Fruition

Spirituality involves choices, choices arising out of the splendor of the encounter with the Sacred. The scope of the spiritual life includes a wide range of actions, behaviors, and commitments—ranging from the innate, preconscious choice that every person makes to keep breathing all the way to world-shattering transformations such as Buddha's choice to attain enlightenment or Gandhi's choice to initiate a nonviolent revolution.

Our meandering journey through the various themes of the spiritual life has given us an opportunity to consider some of these spiritual choices for our own lives. Spirituality begins with the fundamental choice to trust life's wonder rather than to fear life's risk. It includes the choice to live life with a greater emphasis on vulnerability and playfulness than on control and inflexibility. Then there's the choice to be open to belief, the choice to pray and meditate with imagination and dedication, and the choice to respond to prayer in ways that bring about change, or at least allow change to occur gracefully. We have also considered the choice to embody spirituality in such practices as community building, peacemaking, and sacrifice.

In the life of prayer and wonder, some choices are better, wiser, more Sacred, or simply more wonderful than others—in other words, some choices contain more value. Every tradition of spirituality has identifiable values, and every religion encourages its followers to make choices based on the tradition's values. Even if a community claims to be "value-free" (as is the case with some spiritual groups), theirs probably is merely a system of masked values—beneath the surface, the community's

211

perspectives might include such unspoken values as "tolerance is good" or "liberalism is good." And when people change religions, often they are motivated to do so by a sense that their personal values do not, or do not any longer, match up with the values of the religion.

In the choices that are considered praiseworthy or holy by the adherents of a tradition, we find the values of that particular tradition. If I choose to follow a specific spiritual path, then the choices I make will be influenced at least to some extent by the culture of my chosen path. In the process of making choices that match the values of my spiritual tradition, I will gradually take on the character of those values. I—and all of us— may not be able to make ourselves good, but by the grace of the Divine, we can choose to *do* good and we can course-correct when we make unwise choices. As we make more and more good choices, we ourselves become increasingly good (in a relative sense, of course, for only the Sacred is pure goodness). By choosing to *do* good, we slowly and gradually *become* good.

The Christian mystical tradition asserts that the spiritual journey is a process of becoming "participants of the divine nature" (2 Peter 1:4). However, we do not ourselves create this sacred nature; it is given to us. God transforms us and conforms us to the divine nature. God does the forming, although we cooperate with that process by the choices we make. We experience this *spiritual formation* in and through the many choices, big and little, we make in response to God's loving guidance and the inspirations of prayer—choices we make to practice our spirituality in a loving way.

As we begin to manifest this process of spiritual formation—this process of being formed, transformed, and conformed in the Sacred—we begin to take on the nature and stamp of God's presence in our lives. Our lives manifest the values and qualities of the spiritual life, not unlike the way a tree bears fruit. Indeed, "the fruits of the spirit" is a Christian term, but I think it applies nicely to all traditions of spirituality. A Neopagan who begins to take seriously a commitment to recycling and organic gardening and permaculture and who makes choices in her life to live in harmony with her values is manifesting the fruits of Neopaganism—just as surely as Christians who devote their lives to peacemaking and serving others are embodying the fruits of the Christian way.

The fruits of spiritual living are not easily or blithely attained. The Christian fruits of the spirit include love, joy, peace, patience, kindness, generosity, faithfulness, gentleness, and self-control. None of these values is manifested at the snap of a finger. Indeed, people make jokes about the difficulty of attaining them ("I want patience and I want it now!"). How, then, does the spiritual practitioner reach the point of fruition? By choice, of course—by praying for the gift of bearing the fruit of the spirit and, just as importantly, by taking the time to make simple, undramatic choices over and over again that embody the desired values.

For our Neopagan friend, whose spiritual fruits may include living in ecological balance with the Earth, the process of prayer, of "asking" for the values of ecological harmony, may begin with a course of action as simple as studying permaculture and organic agriculture. Along with her prayer and study come the daily, undramatic choices: choosing to recycle, to ride the bus instead of driving, to make sure food scraps go into the compost. The many little decisions are, spiritually speaking, as important (or perhaps more so) than dramatic decisions like choosing to convert the entire house to solar electricity. As we all have seen only too well in our own lives and the lives of others, making a dramatic decision without the little daily decisions to support it is a sure recipe for failure. Buying an expensive exercise machine does not make us exercise. Only the un-glamourous, daily use the machine will get us into shape. Similarly, someone who has a dramatic vision of God and then immediately rushes off to join a monastery without first taking the time to establish a daily regimen of prayer and simplicity may very well be doomed to fail as a practicing monk.

Let's take a look at some of the ways in which various traditions understand the mature, fruit-bearing spiritual life. We'll consider notions such as *insight, holiness,* and *enlightenment,* notions that carry rich connotations of spiritual maturity—notions of a life lived in appreciation of the Sacred, a life filled with the desire to embody wonder, a life lived with choices made carefully and lovingly, a life thereby becoming full with meaning—a meaning that even transcends the boundary of life that we call death.

Insight

Insight, or "in-sight," is an umbrella term that encompasses many spiritual experiences. Wonder and awe, intuition, the sense of the presence of God or of union with God, the sense of being called to make changes in life—these are experiences that all originate in what can be called inner sight. "Sight," of course, does not refer here to physical vision but to pure and immediate inner perception.

Insight comes in many ways. Sometimes it is unbidden, as in the example of a young person who takes a walk through the forest, only to be suddenly inspired to go to Europe to study art, even though she has never considered such an option previously. Parents and family may not understand what's going on, but for the youth who receives the insight, not to follow through would be tragic.

Insight involves more than just unbidden experiences, however. In fact, one of the purposes of spiritual disciplines such as contemplation and keeping the Sabbath is to create conditions in life that make us more receptive to insight. This "cultured" insight, like a cultured pearl, is just as beautiful and just as deep a source of knowledge and wisdom as its "natural" counterpart.

Here's an example of insight from my own experience. I believe God loves me and that God loves all beings. This belief came to me as a result of reading sacred texts that support such beliefs, but the ideas from the texts became *real* to me as a result of having an insight—a direct, unquestionable, inner understanding and perception of myself as loved by the Creator. That experience was so powerful that it made the love of God "real" to me, not only in terms of how I'm loved, but also in a way that enabled me to comprehend God's love for others. I remember the day this insight occurred. I was home alone, praying about something in my life I was unhappy about (I can't even remember what it was). I sensed God inviting me to forgive myself thoroughly—and as I considered what it truly meant to forgive myself, my awareness became flooded with a sense of unearned love, the love of the Sacred, truly enabling me to see how unimportant my self-criticism really was in the context of Divine love!

The power and impact of such an insight may be fleeting or long-lasting; it may be gentle or overwhelming; it may come during a time of prayer or, although triggered by prayer, it may not come for hours or days afterward. Or, as in the case of the future art student, it may come as a bolt from the blue.

The different religious traditions of the world have many names and descriptions for various kinds of extraordinary "peak" insight experiences. A yogi might speak of *samadhi*, while a Zen Buddhist seeks *satori*. The Pentecostal looks for *Baptism with the Holy Spirit*, while a Catholic or Orthodox monk may seek *illumination* or *mystic union*. Are such peak experiences of insight essentially the same experience, apprehended in culturally relative ways? I certainly lack the knowledge to say. I am not suggesting that these different religious terms do (or do not) point to the "same" experience. In my opinion, what's important is not whether the Buddhist in a state of satori is experiencing the same thing as a Pentecostal being filled with the Holy Spirit. Maybe they are, and maybe they aren't. For that matter, how do we know that two Pentecostals have the same experience when both receive the Spirit Baptism? While we cannot identify or evaluate the similarities or differences in these experiences, we do know that *some* kinds of experiences are occurring—these seekers are all having moments of brilliant insight. And when the splendid radiance of the moment passes, something will have changed. It may not be a dramatic change (a person may receive a perfectly wonderful insight into something as simple as how better to stack the old newspapers), but it is a change nevertheless.

Insight is similar to prayer, for it is also a starting point for Sacred change. When I experience insight, something about me becomes different. Perhaps I undergo a change in my values or my behavior; the change inspired by insight might be a simple inner shift or it might involve my being inspired to participate in actions that affect the entire world. While I may not be able to explain the dynamics of my insight experience itself, I can show the fruits of the insight in terms of how it has made a difference in my life.

The theological term for this insight-driven change is *metanoia*. Like the sun bursting from behind the clouds in a glorious rush of morning light, the moment of metanoia ("conversion") suddenly casts everything in a new light, and what formerly was hidden suddenly becomes impossible to miss. Conversion, incidentally, is not a "one time only" proposition. The spiritual life brings metanoia over and over again. Life is a process filled with change; to grow spiritually is to be transformed (or converted or conformed to the calling of the Holy One) continuously.

Because insight is often linked with genuinely extraordinary experiences, we need to be careful about any temptation to try to engineer or to create experiences of insight. While disciplines such as prayer and meditation are meant to foster *receptivity* to insight, they don't involve actually trying to engineer the experience. Spirituality may lead us into a world of transformative (and possibly very extraordinary) experiences, but the *goal* of spirituality is a relationship with God, not the pursuit of extraordinary phenomena. Spirituality may involve unbidden wonders, including dramatic, life-changing insights, but attempting to control the Spirit for the purpose of being entertained by ecstasies is never useful.

Why? Because when we attempt to control the Sacred, survival-mind, not spiritual-mind, is at work. Survival-mind is great for making sure there's enough food on the table, but when the time comes to encounter the Sacred, we need to give survival-mind a rest and approach the Holy with wonder and vulnerability. Efforts to seek out (or create) experiences of ecstasy or mystic union tend, by nature, to be ego-driven rather than spiritually inspired, and thus they are likely to lead, at best, simply to abandoning the effort or, at worst, to frustration, confusion, and even self-delusion. The wisdom of the mystics regarding spiritual experiences tends to emphasize these two points: don't seek out such experiences and, if you have them, learn from them but don't take them (or yourself) too seriously.

Enlightenment

Whereas spiritual insight refers to a moment of brilliant, divinely inspired perception, *enlightenment* suggests a stable, ongoing sense of living in the Sacred presence. Enlightenment means, of course, "to be filled with light." The ultimate goals of many different spiritual traditions seem to be remarkably similar in this regard, and they have similar words for the enlightenment experience, including *ascension*, *illumination*, and *mystical union*, all of which imply an extraordinary state of spiritual awareness.

The Gnostic traditions, which flourished in the early years of the Christian era, taught that spiritual enlightenment was not only the goal to be attained, but also was a goal that only few *would* attain. Enlightenment was nevertheless a goal toward which the average, ordinary spiritual seeker—who was "unenlightened"—should aspire. This notion of aspiring to enlightenment still looms large on the spiritual landscape. Visit a metaphysical bookstore and scan the literature on "ascension"; the basic themes do not seem all that different from the Gnostic teachings of two thousand years ago.

This Gnostic idea of enlightenment seems to suggest a spiritual "elite" —and thus it goes somewhat against the grain of the egalitarianism of the postmodern world. Many of us today tend to be much more comfortable with the ideas of someone like George Fox, founder of the Religious Society of Friends (the Quakers), who taught that there was "that of God" in *all* people, an "inner light" that knows no hierarchies, no elitist system of spiritual privilege, no distinction between the enlightened few and the unenlightened many. Rather than believe in some kind of two-tiered system of spiritual elitism and privilege, many of us would prefer to believe in the divine egalitarianism of the Quakers.

Is there such a thing as spiritual enlightenment, and if there is, does it imply a difference between the spiritual "haves" and "have-nots"? Or is that just a fabrication of spiritual hubris? What is the relationship between enlightenment and egalitarianism on the spiritual journey? Which way is more fully true—the Gnostic way or the Quaker way? Or is it more complicated than a mere either/or choice?

Is the goal of enlightenment *both* a quality that requires attainment and mastery *and* a quality of the spiritual life in which everybody already shares? Theologically speaking, this involves a polarity between *grace* and *works*. Grace is the unearned gift of divine love, while works refers to acts of spiritual or religious merit that a person may perform in response to Divine favor.

A spirituality that emphasizes the necessity or even the value of attaining enlightenment is a spirituality that stresses the need for "works." Depending on the tradition, those works could be anything from grueling physical and mental effort (such as the regimentation of ascetic monks) to a singular, transformational process (like being "born again").The underlying belief is that, without having completed the works, a person simply has not "arrived" spiritually.

By contrast, a spirituality centered on grace emphasizes that Divine favor is so far beyond human control that nothing a person can do could ever make any difference to the splendid abundance of God's love. This emphasis, taken to its logical conclusion, suggests that everybody is already fully enlightened, but most people just haven't realized it yet.

I lean toward the "grace" view of spirituality, but both approaches to enlightenment have their problems. A theology of works seems to reduce the Sacred to a mere "Santa Claus," or a puppet pulled by the strings of human effort, who dispenses enlightenment as a spiritual goody, not unlike toys at Christmas given to those who are well-behaved or otherwise worthy. On the other hand, the spirituality of grace may emphasize God's power by downplaying works, but if everyone is enlightened, why does a difference seem to exist between persons who have realized it and others who have not? So some form of "work"—some form of human effort— still seems to separate the enlightened from the unenlightened.

These apparent problems with grace and works are what signal to me that a polarity is involved and that unearned grace and attained enlightenment are both real and significant parts of the spiritual life. The Sacred loves us all, unconditionally, and in that love is pleased to offer us grace and light that we cannot control and cannot earn. And yet, not wanting to force something on us, the Divine leaves us the freedom to choose, meaning that we really are able to determine the level of spiritual maturity we reach. Only, lest we destroy ourselves with spiritual pride, we must remember that the love of God precedes and remains greater than our efforts to accept that love. We may achieve enlightenment, but all we really have done is cooperate with the Divine. All we have done is merely allow ourselves to receive.

Once enlightenment is reached, regardless of whether or how we come to it or it comes to us, what then? Is the point of the spiritual life simply to while away the years in a blissed-out state of ecstasy? Although that may seem an attractive goal for persons who are unhappy with their lives, the facts seem to be that the process of moving toward enlightenment itself includes making peace with one's life. Spiritual enlightenment is not an escape from the pain of an unfulfilled life; on the contrary, paradoxically, to achieve enlightenment requires accepting such a life even with all its lack of fulfillment. The process of seeking enlightenment includes this irony—if we want spiritual happiness, we must first learn to accept and even celebrate life without it—although learning to do that makes ecstasy or any other external source of happiness less necessary.

Furthermore, while being bathed in God's love may be its own reward, we should not assume that enlightenment is a state of carefree bliss. Union with the Sacred surely carries its own callings and urges. The journey that begins with longing to receive the love of God often leads to a new place, a place with a new longing—only this time, it's a longing to *give* the love of God away—a longing to share Divine love in a sacrificial way with others. Such giving is likely to manifest itself in some form of service to others, which may be as humble as ladling soup in a homeless shelter one evening a week or as heroic as Mother Teresa's many years of service to the poor of Calcutta. Service to others may be a simple matter of maintaining high ethical standards in the workplace and treating one's family with loving care and respect. Granted, a person does not need to be "enlightened" to expend effort in service to others. But once a person is enlightened, no other choice seems to be possible with regard to how time and effort are spent. The enlightened person feels great gratitude—and expresses that gratitude through service to others.

Holiness

The word "holy" means "to be set apart for the purposes of God." If we think about maturing in the spiritual life as a process of spiritual formation, of being formed in the image and likeness of God, then the idea of holiness may be a particularly useful concept for understanding what the mature spiritual life is like.

The Sacred, as the source of love and generosity and creativeness and grace, is by nature the source of giving. Enlightenment, as attractive as it seems to be, still has a sense of being something "received." If my goal is only to attain enlightenment, I still am approaching spirituality with a bit of the "What's in it for me" attitude, rather than with a sacrificial "What may I do to help" attitude. I'm not sure that is entirely bad, for we are, after all, creatures of the Earth, and survival depends on our ability to look out for ourselves and make sure our needs get met. So I do not wish to call the quest for enlightenment bad or mistaken or even incomplete, but I do want to suggest that once one climbs to the summit and attains enlightenment, one will find that beyond that highest peak, yet another mountain beckons us to climb it. This mountain beyond enlightenment is the mountain of holiness.

Holiness is the state of being set apart for God. It's a state of *being*— the culmination of all the transformations of the formative life. But holiness is not just a culmination, for holiness is also present in the acts and choices we make *to become* holy. The journey is the destination. And since God's nature is one of self-giving love, holiness means the state of setting life apart in the service of, and the emulation of, that self-giving love. (Self-*giving* is not the same as self-*denying*, although sometimes a self-giving love may include acts of denial.)

When we give ourselves lovingly, to whom should we do the giving? That is a loaded question, since, for example, some spiritual teachers have abused the notion of holiness by suggesting that women are holy when they sacrifice their will to their husbands and children or that spiritual aspirants become more holy by fully surrendering their will (not to mention their financial assets) to the control of the spiritual teacher. But self-giving love is not a form of masochism or even a form of self-diminishment, and we are only called to give ourselves to the Sacred through those who honor our love or those who are less fortunate than we are. The call to holiness may involve a call to be vulnerable with a caring spouse or to be generous with persons who suffer in poverty—but it is not a call for us to accept the abuse of those who would hurt us. Even a sacred commitment to peacemaking (as embodied, for example, by Gandhi or Martin Luther King, Jr.) makes sense only in terms of nonviolent *resistance* to abuse or injustice.

So as we prepare to climb the highest mountains or to plunge into the very heart of God, we see that love and sacrifice (i.e., giving) emerge as the two deepest treasures of the spiritual life. To nurture spirituality means to nurture the qualities of loving and of offering gifts. And as we grow spiritually, our capacity to receive blossoms into a related capacity—the capacity to give, even as we receive, because we have received so much from God. This capacity to love and serve and give to others marks our entry into holiness, the fruition of the spiritual life. At the same time, since holiness also includes the process of making holy choices, holiness is not just a goal of the spiritual life. A tree does not bear fruit only when it is old, but indeed bears fruit from its early life onward. Similarly, the gifts of a holy life are ours to give from the earliest stages in our spiritual journey. My suggestion that a mountain of holiness exists beyond the mountain of enlightenment means that holiness, as a process, is ongoing—though it is never fully achieved, since new opportunities for loving sacrifice and giving will always exist. We scale one mountain and we discover a new adventure in the distance.

As I write this extravagant celebration of giving these words, my practical survival-mind just can't keep quiet. "But people who give of themselves and who are generous and loving get taken advantage of! If we all lived like that, life might be nice, but the truth is, we don't! For me to be vulnerable like that would be a recipe for disaster!" True enough. The spiritual life really *does* involve taking risks. The sacrificial nature of holiness carries the potential for vulnerability with it—yes, *vulnerability*, one of the qualities necessary to spiritual living at any stage of the journey!

If we allow ourselves to be vulnerable to others, we *are* likely to get hurt. But we choose vulnerability because we believe spiritual vulnerability is a doorway into a more deeply lived life. "Life!" sneers the voice of survival-mind again. "I'm trying to *protect* life in every way I can—but this silly idealism about love and vulnerability and sacrifice is what's putting life in danger. Not only will people take advantage of you, but they will also kill you—if not literally, then spiritually and emotionally. If you are open and vulnerable and loving, you are going to die."

I cannot argue with the concern these words express, and I include this dialog between the "spiritual" and "survival" parts of myself, because I

want to be clear that spirituality is not an attempt to deny the reality of
suffering, pain, wounding, and even death. To be vulnerable really means
to be in a position where we can get hurt or even get killed, at least
metaphorically.

Spirituality, however, makes a bold claim at this point. Two bold
claims, actually.

- The first: "A life lived from a position of wonder, belief, openness, and
holiness is a happier, more meaning-filled life, even if suffering ensues
because of it—and if suffering does ensue, despite that suffering."
- The second: "Even in death, we cannot be separated from the love of
God."

Certainly, the beliefs set forth in these claims, or similar beliefs, must
be what enabled Jesus to find meaning in the crucifixion and are probably
what inspired the faith of countless martyrs and others who have been
willing to lay down their lives for a purpose higher than just that of self-
protection and survival.

Thankfully, few of us will ever face the trauma of dying for our faith.
However, the call of holiness may nonetheless beckon us to give a gift
larger than we think we are capable of giving. Spirituality calls us to live
in vulnerability and openness, in sacrifice and love, because the Divine
makes the bold claim that even in vulnerability we are safe—yes, even in
death we are safe—in Divine love. Death is not the end. This is true both
for symbolic deaths (like the end of a relationship or getting fired) as well
as for physical death, the great mystery that we all shall someday face. In
either case, spirituality assumes that there's more to come. But before we
consider what that "more" might be, we have to face the mystery of death
itself.

Death

We are approaching the end of our exploration of spirituality, and our
final topics, appropriately enough, are related to death. To live spiritually
involves vulnerability and surrender, and death can be nothing other than
the ultimate surrender. To enter the spiritual life is to enter into silence and
the unknown—and death is the greatest of all silences, the greatest of all
unknowns. To encounter the Sacred is to touch the borderlands of eternity,
and death, according to the testimony of spiritual traditions the world over,

is a doorway into some sort of an eternal state. Thus, dying appears to be a profoundly spiritual act.

The various religions offer various theories about the meaning of death, as well as stories designed to explain what happens after we die. Theories of heaven and hell, nirvana, reincarnation, and other states of existence dance through the mythologies and cosmologies of the world's spiritual traditions. Some traditions see the survival of the human personality occurring beyond death; others suggest that we cast off our ego but that our soul lives on. Yet others look for the resurrection of the body —or perhaps of a new body—to occur.

In the final analysis, all persons of all spiritual persuasions, regardless of the depth of their convictions, must admit that death is an ultimate mystery, for we cannot penetrate the unknowing that lies beyond death. Death is the greatest silence of all.

Death is the final trump card, the final message to humankind, telling us that no, we are *not* in control, no matter how much we wish to be. Indeed, beliefs about death and what lies beyond death (whether they involve heaven and hell, reincarnation, or some other state—that is, any dogmatic statement about death) are veiled attempts to control death, but death cannot and will not be controlled. Ultimately, our theories are nothing more than theories. We have stories about what the afterlife is like, with many lovely images from different cultures, like the Greek notion of the Elysian fields and the Celtic notion of Tir na Nog—two examples of heavenly states of eternal youth and blessedness. But in the end, the theories are just theories, the stories are just stories, and we cannot truly plumb the mystery. The map is not the territory. When we die, we move into a place where, I suspect, our theories will matter very little and may aid us not at all.

On top of the vastness of our unknowing about the adventure at life's end, we have a similar vastness of unknowing regarding *when* that end may come for each of us. Not only is death a mystery, but it is also unpredictable and always possible. The careful work of my survival-mind may reduce my risk of death and actually prolong my life, but the day will surely come when death will triumph over my strategies to live. Death, ultimately, is stronger than I am.

But this image of death's strength reminds me of one of my favorite images from the Hebrew Scriptures. In the Song of Solomon—a collection of lyrics about love—the power of love is acknowledged in the proclamation that "love is strong as death" (Song of Sol. 8:6). Death may be stronger than I am, but even when I do surrender to death, I can trust in love. The writer of the Song of Solomon is declaring that human love is as strong as death, and I think it is reasonable to believe that Divine love is even *stronger* than death. In that strength we can find our trust and our safety.

We saw early on in our exploration of spirituality that death is a matter of breathing one's last. So death brings completion to our rhythms of breath—and so, as is common in the realm of the spirit, we come full circle, to finish not far from where we began. We are spiritual beings in that we are beings of breath. Through our lifetime we have a spirit, and while we live we look to the Sacred Spirit for guidance and, most of all, for love. When our days come to a close and our breathing finally stops, we can, I believe, exhale one last time in the assurance that the winds of God will take up our breath and carry it on, into eternity. Beyond that, my words fail. You and I will someday find out for ourselves what the adventure of death is like.

Thinking about death can be scary or unsettling, for it is the final transgression—the boundary crossing from which no one returns. Yet that is the way it must be. But I believe the best antidote for the fear of death is the celebration of life. Until the moment actually arrives, death remains only an abstraction in the future. The present, however, is all we truly have anyway, and the more fully we live in the present, the less fearful the uncertainties of the future become. I believe that the more fully we live and celebrate our life, the more likely we will be prepared to meet the coming of death with serenity and even with gratitude.

The person who walks the path of the spirit with integrity, devotion, and commitment discovers that, regardless of what the future holds, the spiritual path contains incalculable present value. We are called to live fully and vulnerably here and now, believing the Sacred is with us whether we feel that presence or not. Spirituality offers wonders enough to give life more radiance and value than we might ever have been able to imagine or realize. This radiance and wonder, beyond the limits of our dreams, is truly a gift of love from God.

Resurrection

I am writing these words on Easter Sunday, and there seems no better time to talk about *resurrection* than today. The word "Easter" comes from the name of the Celtic Goddess of the dawn, *Eostre*, who is the goddess not only of new mornings but also of springtimes and other times in which life springs forth in newness from a previous "death." So Easter means not only the celebration of resurrection in the Christian tradition, but the word itself also carries vestiges of an earlier Pagan celebration of natural resurrection through the coming of spring.

Easter could only have come about because of a death. Just as the resurrection of spring follows the "death" of nature in winter, so the resurrection of Christ followed his death. This is the way it is with all of us—our "resurrections," our new beginnings, our second chances, and our times to start over are follow-ups to times of "death"—metaphorical deaths, of course, but no less real. Losing a job, getting a divorce, going though a time of illness, moving from one residence to another, and just about all other major transitions—not just painful ones or changes outside our control, but also the joyful ones and the changes we've chosen—involve some sort of death, some sort of ending . . . which opens up the possibility of a new beginning. That's the way the world works. To me, thinking that bodily death also works like that is both plausible and comforting.

I believe in resurrection. Evidence all around me demonstrates that resurrection is a fact of life, and many of the spiritual traditions of our planet proclaim it to be a fact of death as well. The Song of Solomon declares that "love is strong as death," and for me, an essential aspect of spirituality is my conviction that God's love is *stronger* than death. As with the archetypal fairy tale in which the prince and the princess live happily ever after, spirituality testifies to a love so deep and so real that no tragedy, not even the finality of death, can ultimately extinguish it. In the heart of God, we can—ourselves—live "happily ever after."

For us in our bodies as they currently exist, to live forever is simply impossible. But in a universe where little resurrections happen all the time on this side of the grave, we are capable of envisioning a grander resurrection on the other side as well. How does it happen? I do not know. Why does it happen? Because God's love is stronger than death. In this I place my trust. Beyond the resurrection, I believe life really *is* "happily ever after," in a depth of love and wonder—a depth of love and wonder that truly is beyond our wildest imaginings.

Epilogue:
Cultivating the Practice

Throughout this book we have considered that spirituality involves a number of inner characteristics, such as vulnerability, openness, and playfulness. We have seen that through cultivating these inner characteristics we will, hopefully, find the presence of the Sacred within us.

We have also alluded to ways in which spirituality involves specific choices—the choice to live life out of wonder rather than self-protection; the choice to be open to believing in God; the choice to nurture a relationship with God through prayer; and the choice to engage in community building, peacemaking, and sacrifice. Spirituality, we have come to understand, involves a marriage of inner characteristics of consciousness to outer choices and actions that are intended to foster the life of wonder.

In chapter 3, I further suggested that we need to cultivate a "discipline of wonder." Such a discipline consists of choices we make and actions we take in response to God's call to us. The disciplines and practices we choose help, in turn, to create an internal environment in which our developing a deeper sense of the Sacred is possible. Thus, for the person who wants to become "more spiritual," I encourage him or her to work on some or all of the suggestions in this epilogue.

None of these steps will guarantee a mystical experience—that is, a conscious encounter with the Sacred or any sort of spiritual consolation. That's part of the mystery of spirituality—it cannot be predicted in that kind of neat and tidy way. Relating with God cannot be reduced to a magic formula: "Do this to experience that." All I can say is that these practices are designed to foster a sense of wonder and openness and an awareness of the Sacred presence. Your spirituality, your adventure with the Divine, will be unique and absolutely yours—and only you and God can co-create that mutual relationship.

Here, in no particular order, are my suggestions for a discipline of wonder—for nurturing the spiritual life within yourself:

1. *Pray or meditate daily.* Make it a priority! Most of us have time to watch TV or play computer games or do some sort of mildly pleasant but wholly unnecessary activity for hours every week. So you must be clear about the priority you give to prayer. That's not to say you can no longer do useless, fun stuff like watching TV. You simply need to cultivate a balanced life, which includes attending to the Sacred in silence and solitude until the process becomes habitual and feels as natural (and necessary) in your day as brushing your teeth.

2. *Engage in spiritual reading and study.* If you are an adherent of a specific religion, start with the sacred texts of your faith. Beyond those sacred texts, reading the writings of saints and mystics tends to be fruitful for the spiritual life. Having some guidance from a soul friend or a faith community is helpful in selecting study material. The important thing is to get into the habit of actually doing the reading. Reading also serves as a wonderful entry into prayer—read a story from a sacred text and then devote time to meditating on the story's meaning for your life.

3. *Find an* **anamchara.** A soul friend may be a mentor who can teach you about the ways of contemplation or just a companion, available for mutual sharing. I strongly recommend that this person be someone other than a spouse or family member. To help you explore your life in the Sacred, your *anamchara* relationship probably ought to have—and will benefit from—a certain distance. A spiritual guide or friend helps on several levels, for the relationship provides a sounding board, an opportunity to explore issues of concern or uncertainty, and it can even provide challenge when your soul friend sees through your malarkey! A soul friend helps you experience spirituality in terms of community—even just a community of two.

4. *Join a healthy faith community.* Consider the values we have discussed—openness to wonder, a willingness to pray, a balanced approach to community and individualism, a sense of God as loving rather than controlling, a commitment to peacemaking and caring for others. If your current faith community does not embody these values, please be aware that others do! If you are not already a member of a faith community, I recommend that you learn about and visit a variety of groups before making a specific commitment—but make the commitment!

5. *Cultivate beauty in your life.* A simple but important part of living spiritually is choosing to create or appreciate beauty in life. If you have an

artistic talent, devote time to it. Other talents embody their own forms of beauty—so whether your talent involves athletics, cooking, or throwing a wonderful party, cultivate it! Use your gifts to make your life and the lives of others more beautiful. Pursue excellence simply for the wonder and joy of the pursuit. If you think you do not have a talent, at least set aside time to appreciate the beauty that is created through the talents of others. Become a regular at an art gallery or take time to enjoy lovely music—simply for the wonder of it.

6. *Engage in some sort of personal improvement program.* We all have ways in which we wish we were different. We all have choices we can make and ways we can change ourselves, options we often and too easily allow to lie dormant. Whether it's stopping smoking, reducing the fat in our diet, exercising regularly, or even choosing to follow through on committing to a challenging spiritual discipline, making an effort to improve ourselves is a way of embodying the spiritual mandate to love—by loving ourselves.

7. *Tithe.* If the thought of giving ten percent of your income makes you break out in a cold sweat, start with just three percent, which is three percent better than nothing. One important point to remember—do not give money away for the sake of the recipient; give it away for your own sake. We tithe not because we're so special or because others need us so much, but because doing so is a way to grow spiritually. Tithing is a sacrifice, a gift offered to the Sacred; beyond that, it is a discipline for cultivating the characteristic of generosity in our lives.

8. *Honor some form of Sabbath.* Take a breather! Work is good for the soul but work is also related to survival, and constant work over-stimulates the survival-mind's tendencies toward self-protection and control. Not only that, but excessive work is physically and emotionally taxing, hardly useful for the larger purposes of the spiritual quest. To take a Sabbath break, to interrupt the impulse to keep working, allows us to lessen our self-protective consciousness by attending to silence, solitude, and openness—which, in turn, can lead to deeply felt prayer.

9. *Relate charitably to those who are needy.* This is not the same thing as tithing. In fact, one danger of giving away money is that it can tempt us to cut corners on this other kind of opportunity to give. Relating to persons less fortunate than ourselves means just that—*relating*. It means finding opportunities to work together, play together, and get to know one another. Volunteer as a Big Brother or Big Sister. Feed homeless persons.

Take meals to persons with AIDS. Be in contact with real human beings—and don't let your charity end with writing a check.

10. ***Actively seek political solutions to complete the ministry of charity.*** There is a difference between putting a bandage on an open sore and curing a disease so the sore goes away. When we feed the homeless or do literacy training, we need to be asking what kinds of political, economic, and social policies can help to solve such problems. What can we do to make sure that tomorrow's children are better off than today's? If this seems more political than spiritual, be mindful of the fact that spirituality is also a material process. Working for social change is a profound way to discover wonder and the presence of God in life.

11. ***Seek ways to interact with persons from other traditions.*** While following one particular path with commitment and fidelity is important to learn the lessons associated with community, we need to avoid thinking "Our way is the only way" or "Our way has it all." We learn much from those who differ from us. Pluralism is here to stay, and the good news of pluralism is that every one of us can connect with a person of a different spiritual tradition than our own. Consider these examples: if you are a Methodist, take a class at a Buddhist center. If you're a Baptist, study the Greek Orthodox tradition. If you're Jewish, learn about Native American religion. Whenever you can, create or nurture a friendship with a practitioner of an alternate tradition—but if that is not possible, at least take a class or make the effort to study. Learning about another path does not take away from your own. On the contrary, your "home" path will be enhanced.

12. ***Maintain equilibrium and a sense of humor regarding your discipline.*** This last point may be the single most important one on my list. Anyone who tries with a burst of gusto to make sweeping changes in life in order to master these points or any similar program of spirituality is probably in for a major disappointment. Taking on too much all at once is a temptation associated with the desire to control rather than to be open and vulnerable. Be playful—have fun with the choices you make and the covenants you create. Remember to be gentle with yourself, for transformations do not happen overnight. Try to make spiritual changes in your life through many small choices rather than through one or two big, dramatic choices. A small choice made today can have major repercussions five or ten or fifty years from now, while a dramatic choice made today to start a spiritual practice could easily lead to a very *un*dramatic decision to abandon the practice in a week or two. Beware the fate of the

person who, in a burst of excitement over getting in shape, buys an expensive exercise machine, only to let it gather dust!

Finally, in regard to the foregoing list of suggestions as well as to every other list or book that's filled with spiritual advice and guidance, keep this in mind: do not confuse spiritual goals with the spiritual life. A goal provides something worthwhile to strive for and to organize efforts around. But spirituality is not lived in the future; it is lived in the present. Don't think that spirituality is something you'll "achieve" when you reach your goals; rather, it's something you embody in your life today. If your goal is to contemplate for half an hour every day, do not put it off until after you are "perfectly organized." (For one thing, without God's grace, you may *never* get your schedule organized, and if you cannot find God now, in the stolen moments of the day, you probably will still have difficulty finding God tomorrow—even though tomorrow you may have thirty minutes of quiet.) We live our relationships not through terrific planning but simply by being present with the ones we love. This is as true whether the loved one is another person—or God.

Spirituality is a breathing in of the life of the Sacred. To be spiritual is to be present to our patterns of breathing. Follow your path, relate compassionately with others, and keep breathing. Choose to be present with the Sacred today. Be vulnerable and open, dare to believe, and announce to God that you are willing to enter a place of mystery, wonder, and maybe even awe. Blessings to you as you choose this. You are entering into the journey of a lifetime—and beyond!

Shalom. Namasté. Blessings.

Bibliography

Abbreviations

In citing works, the following abbreviations have been used:

BCP   *The Book of Common Prayer*

COED   *Compact Edition of the Oxford English Dictionary*

Adler, Margot. *Drawing Down the Moon*. Rev. ed. Boston: Beacon Press, 1986.

American Heritage Dictionary of the English Language. 3rd ed. Boston: Houghton Mifflin Company, 1992.

Armstrong, Karen. *Visions of God: Four Medieval Mystics and their Writings*. New York: Bantam Books, 1994.

Backhouse, Janet. *The Lindisfarne Gospels*. London: Phaidon, 1993.

Bamford, Christopher, and William Parker Marsh, eds. *Celtic Christianity: Ecology and Holiness*. Stockbridge, Massachusetts: Lindisfarne Press, 1987.

Barnhart, Robert, K., ed. *The Barnhart Concise Dictionary of Etymology*. New York: HarperCollins Publishers, 1995.

Barry, William A., S.J. and William J. Connolly. *The Practice of Spiritual Direction*. San Francisco: Harper & Row, 1982.

Berchholz, Samuel, and Sherab Chödzin Kohn, eds. *Entering the Stream: An Introduction to the Buddha and His Teachings*. Boston, Shambhala, 1993.

Blake, William. *Blake's Poetry and Designs*. Ed. Mary Lynn Johnson and John E. Grant. New York: W. W. Norton & Co., 1979.

Bloom, Anthony. *Beginning to Pray*. New York: Paulist Press, 1970.

The Book of Common Prayer. New York: Church Hymnal Corporation, 1979.

Brennan, Barbara Ann. *Hands of Light: A Guide to Healing Through the Human Energy Field*. New York: Bantam Books, 1988.

Buber, Martin. *I and Thou*. New York: Macmillan Press, 1970.

Burnham, Sophy. *A Book of Angels*. New York: Ballantine Books, 1990.

Carr-Gomm, Philip. *The Elements of the Druid Tradition.* Shaftesbury, England: Element Books, 1991.

———, ed. *The Druid Renaissance.* San Francisco: HarperCollins, 1996.

Carter, Stephen. *The Culture of Disbelief: How American Law and Politics Trivialize Religious Devotion.* New York: Anchor Books, 1994.

Compact Edition of the Oxford English Dictionary. Oxford: Oxford University Press, 1971.

Conze, Edward, trans. *Buddhist Scriptures.* London: Penguin Books, 1959.

Cross, F. L. and E. A. Livingstone, eds. *The Oxford Dictionary of the Christian Church.* 2nd ed., rev. New York: Oxford University Press, 1983.

Danielou, Alain, ed. *The Complete Kama Sutra: The First Unabridged Modern Translation of the Classic Indian Text.* Rochester, VT: Inner Traditions International, 1995.

Dass, Baba Ram. *Be Here Now.* New York: Crown Publishing, 1971.

Davis, Laura, and Ellen Bass. *The Courage to Heal.* San Francisco: Harper & Row, 1985.

Dawood, N.J., trans. *The Koran: With a Parallel Arabic Text.* London: Penguin Books, 1991.

Day, Dorothy. *Selected Writings.* Ed. Robert Ellsberg. Maryknoll, NY: Orbis Books, 1992.

De Mello, Anthony. *Sadhana: A Way to God.* New York: Doubleday Image Books, 1978.

Douglass, James W. *Resistance and Contemplation, the Way of Liberation: The Yin and Yang of the Non-Violent Life.* New York: Doubleday Books, 1972.

Edwards, Tilden. *Living in the Presence: Disciplines for the Spiritual Heart.* San Francisco: Harper & Row, 1988.

Ellis, Peter Berresford. *Dictionary of Celtic Mythology.* New York: Oxford University Press, 1992.

———. *The Druids.* Grand Rapids, Michigan: William B. Eerdmans Publishing Company, 1994.

Fox, George. *The Journal of George Fox.* Ed. John L. Nickalls. Philadelphia: Religious Society of Friends, 1995.

Fox, Matthew. *On Becoming a Musical Mystical Bear.* Paulist Press, 1976.

———. *Original Blessing: A Primer in Creation Spirituality.* Santa Fe, New Mexico: Bear and Company, 1983.

———. *Whee! We, Wee All the Way Home.* Santa Fe, New Mexico: Bear and Company, 1981.

Gandhi, Mohandas K. *An Autobiography: The Story of My Experiments With Truth.* Boston: Beacon Press, 1993.

Goss, Edmund. *Jesus Acted Up.* San Francisco: HarperCollins, 1993.

Hardinge, Leslie. *The Celtic Church in Britain.* London: S.P.C.K., 1972.

Holy Bible, People's Parallel Edition: King James Version and The Living Bible. Wheaton, Illinois: Tyndale House Publishers, 1981.

Howatch, Susan. *Glittering Images.* New York: Alfred A. Knopf, 1987.

———. *Glamourous Powers.* New York: Alfred A. Knopf, 1987.

———. *Ultimate Prizes.* New York: Alfred A. Knopf, 1987.

———. *Scandalous Risks.* New York: Alfred A. Knopf, 1987.

———. *Mystical Paths.* New York: Alfred A. Knopf, 1987.

———. *Absolute Truths.* New York: Alfred A. Knopf, 1987.

Johnson, Sonia. *From Housewife to Heretic.* New York: Doubleday Books, 1981.

Jones, Cheslyn, Geoffrey Wainwright, and Edward Yarnold, S.J., eds. *The Study of Spirituality.* New York: Oxford University Press, 1986.

Jones, Noragh. *Power of Raven, Wisdom of Serpent: Celtic Women's Spirituality.* Edinburgh: Floris Books, 1994.

Joy, W. Brugh, M.D. *Joy's Way: A Map for the Transformational Journey.* Los Angeles: J. P. Tarcher, 1979.

Julian of Norwich. *The Revelation of Divine Love in Sixteen Showings.* Trans. M.L. Del Mastro. Liguori, Missouri: Triumph Books, 1994.

Kavanaugh, John F. *Following Christ in a Consumer Society: The Spirituality of Cultural Resistance.* Rev. Ed. Maryknoll, New York: Orbis Books, 1992.

Kavanaugh, Kieran, O.C.D., and Otilio Rodriguez, O.C.D. *The Collected Works of St. John of the Cross.* Washington, DC: Institute of Carmelite Studies, 1991.

Keats, John. *The Complete Poems.* New York: Viking Press, 1977.

Kelsey, Morton. *The Other Side of Silence: A Guide to Christian Meditation.* New York: Paulist Press, 1976.

King, Martin Luther, Jr. *I Have a Dream.* New York: HarperCollins, 1993.

Langemeyer, Georg, "Culture," in *Handbook of Catholic Theology*, ed. by Wolfgang Beinert and Francis Schüssler Fiorenza. New York: Crossroad, 1995.

Leech, Kenneth. *Soul Friend: Spiritual Direction in the Modern World.* Rev. ed. London: Darton Longman and Todd, 1994.

———. *True Prayer: An Invitation to Christian Spirituality.* San Francisco: Harper & Row, 1980.

————. *Experiencing God: Theology as Spirituality*. San Francisco: Harper & Row, 1985.

————. *The Eye of the Storm: Living Spiritually in the Real World*. San Francisco: HarperCollins, 1992.

Lesser Feasts and Fasts. New York: Church Hymnal Corporation, 1991.

May, Gerald G., M.D. *Will and Spirit: A Contemplative Psychology*. New York: Harper & Row, 1982.

McGaa, Ed, Eagle Man. *Mother Earth Spirituality: Native American Paths to Healing Ourselves and Our World*. San Francisco: HarperCollins, 1990.

McGinn, Bernard. *The Foundations of Mysticism*. New York: Crossroad Press, 1992.

————. *The Growth of Mysticism*. New York: Crossroad Press, 1994.

Meehan, Bernard. *The Book of Kells: An Illustrated Introduction to the Manuscript in Trinity College Dublin*. New York: Thames & Hudson, 1994.

Merriam-Webster's Collegiate Dictionary, Electronic ed. Springfield, MA: Merriam-Webster, 1995.

Merton, Thomas. *Contemplative Prayer*. New York: Doubleday Image Books, 1971.

Moore, Thomas. *Care of the Soul*. San Francisco: HarperCollins, 1992.

Metzger, Bruce M. and Roland E. Murphy, eds. *New Oxford Annotated Bible with the Apocryphal/Deuterocanonical Books*. New Revised Standard Version. New York: Oxford University Press, 1991.

Nh'at Hanh, Thich. *Living Buddha, Living Christ*. New York: Riverhead Books, 1995.

O'Donohue, John. *Anam Ćara: Wisdom from the Celtic World*. Boulder, Colorado: Sounds True Audio, 1996.

Panichas, George A., ed. *The Simone Weil Reader*. Wakefield, Rhode Island: Moyer Bell Limited, 1977.

Rey, Hans Augusto. *Curious George Rides a Bike*. Boston: Houghton Mifflin Company, 1952.

Ruether, Rosemary Radford. *Sexism and God-Talk: Toward a Feminist Theology*. Boston: Beacon Press, 1983.

————. *Gaia and God: An Ecofeminist Theology of Earth Healing*. San Francisco: HarperCollins, 1992.

Sapphire. "Wild Thing," from *American Dreams*. New York: Vintage Books, 1996.

Sellner, Edward C. *Mentoring: The Ministry of Spiritual Kinship*. Notre Dame: Ave Maria Press, 1990.

Spangler, David. *A Pilgrim in Aquarius*. Findhorn, Scotland: Findhorn Press, 1996.

Spretnak, Charlene. *States of Grace: the Recovery of Meaning in the Postmodern Age*. San Francisco: HarperCollins, 1991.

Starhawk. *The Spiral Dance: A Rebirth of the Ancient Religion of the Great Goddess*. San Francisco: Harper & Row, 1979.

Steindl-Rast, David. *Gratefulness, the Heart of Prayer*. New York: Paulist Press, 1986.

Teresa of Avila. *The Interior Castle*. Trans. Kieran Kavanaugh, O.C.D. and Otilio Rodriguez, O.C.D. New York: Paulist Press, 1979.

Thornton, Martin. *Christian Proficiency*. London: S.P.C.K., 1959.

Trungpa, Chögyam. *Cutting Through Spiritual Materialism*. Boston: Shambhala, 1973.

Underhill, Evelyn. *Mysticism: A Study in the Nature and Development of Spiritual Consciousness*. New York: E. P. Dutton & Co., 1961.

———. *Concerning the Inner Life*. London: Methuen & Co., 1926.

———. *The Mystics of the Church*. Cambridge, England: James Clarke and Company, 1925.

———. *The Golden Sequence*, New York: E.P. Dutton & Co., 1933.

Walker, Alice. *The Color Purple*. New York: Pocket Books, 1984.

Walker, Susan, ed. *Speaking of Silence: Christians and Buddhists on the Contemplative Way*. New York: Paulist Press, 1987.

Wakefield, Gordon, ed. *The Westminster Dictionary of Christian Spirituality*. Philadelphia: Westminster Press, 1983.

Wallis, Jim. *The Soul of Politics*. Maryknoll, New York: Orbis Books, 1994.

Watts, Alan. *In My Own Way: An Autobiography*. New York: Pantheon Books, 1972.

———. *Myth and Ritual in Christianity*. New York: Farrar, Straus and Giroux, 1968.

Wilber, Ken. *A Brief History of Everything*. Boston: Shambhala Publications, 1996.

Wolters, Clifton, trans. *The Cloud of Unknowing*. London: Penguin Books, 1978.

Wood, Ernest. *Zen Dictionary*. Rutland, Vermont: Charles E. Tuttle Company, 1972.

Zaehner, R. C., trans. *Bhagavad-Gita*. New York: Oxford University Press, 1969.

———, ed. *Hindu Scriptures*. New York: Everyman's Library, 1992.

Zukav, Gary, *The Dancing Wu Li Masters*. New York: William Morrow, 1979.

World Wide Web sites devoted to spirituality

Here is a sampling of the many spirituality resources available on the Internet. Unfortunately, the World Wide Web changes constantly, with sites frequently being created, deleted, or moved to a new address, so a printed list such as this will soon be outdated. If you cannot access a site listed below, use a Web directory such as Yahoo (http://www.yahoo.com) or Altavista (http://www.altavista.com) to search for other similar sites.

African Traditional Religions.
    http://users.iol.it/cdi/
Celtic Christianity.
    http://www.shsu.edu/~lib_maa/celt_christ.html
Christ in the Desert Monastery.
    http://www.christdesert.org
Contemplative Outreach.
    http://www.io.com/~lefty/COHome.html
Covenant of the Goddess.
    http://www.cog.org
Dharmanet International.
    http://www.dharmanet.org
Firewatch: Information on Thomas Merton and Religious Contemplation.
    http://140.190.128.190/merton/merton.html
Foundation for Shamanic Studies.
    http://www.shamanism.org
Gay Men's Spirituality.
    http://www.the-park.com/barzan/main.htm
Global Hindu Electronic Network.
    http://www.hindunet.org
House of Breathings: A Virtual Sanctuary for the Contemplative Way.
    http://www.anamchara.com
Islamic Resources.
    http://www.latif.com
International Association of Sufism.
    http://www.ias.org
Judaism and Jewish Resources.
    http://shamash.org/trb/judaism.html
Mysticism in World Religions.
    http://www.digiserve.com/mystic/
Order of Bards, Ovates, and Druids.
    http://www.obod.co.uk/obod

Order of Buddhist Contemplatives.
   http://www.OBCON.org
Orthodox Christian Icons.
   http://www.mit.edu:8001/activities/ocf/icons.html
Rainbow Family of Living Light.
   http://welcomehome.org
Redhawk (Native American spirituality).
   http://www.redhawk.org/
Religious Atheism.
   http://www.hypertext.com/atheisms
Religious Society of Friends.
   http://www.quaker.org
Sikhism Home Page.
   http://www.sikhs.org
Under Shekhina's Wings: Cross-cultural Women's Spirituality.
   http://www.geocities.com/Athens/1501/
www.interfaith.org.
   http://www.interfaith.org

Credits

The author thanks the publishers who granted permission to reprint material copyrighted or controlled by them.

Index

240

Pluralism, 18, 228
Pneuma (Greek), 9
Pocahontas (film), 201
Polarity, 68, 147
Pope, 76
Pornography, 179
Postmodernity, 121
Power of Raven, Wisdom of Serpent (Jones), 169
Practicality, 151
Pranayama, 9
Prayer, 83, 146, 174, 226
   contemplative, 93
   conversational, 97
Prayer, forms of
   adoration, 98
   confession, 98
   intercession, 98
   petition, 98
   thanksgiving, 98
Presley, Elvis, 7, 33
Pride, 207
Promise Keepers, 7
Promises, 172
Prophecy, 182, 183
Purple Heart, 44

Qi Gong, 9
Quaker, 76, 158, 159, 161
Quakers, 16, 216
Qu'ran, 74

Rabin, Yitzak, 203
Racism, 179, 184
Rainbow Family, 17, 69
Ramadan, 158
Rave Mass, 123
Reconciliation, 175
Reiki, 69
Repentance, 198
Resurrection, 223
Rippers (in *Tank Girl*), 84

Ritual, 157
Roman Catholic Church, 69
Roper, Skid. *See* Nixon, Mojo, and Skid Roper.
Rosary, 96
Ruach (Hebrew), 9
Russian Orthodox Church, 134

Sabbath, 156, 203, 206, 227
Sacra facere (Latin), 189
Sacrament, 143
Sacred pipe, 74
Sacrifice, 79, 188
Saints, 72
Santa Claus, 59
Sapphire, 136
Satyagraha ("truth force"), 191
Self-deception, 174
Sellner, Edward C., 170
Serendipity, 51
Service, 185
Sex Pistols, 136
Shadow, 180
Shenandoah National Park, 131
Silence, 88
Simon, Paul, 7
Simplicity, 206, 208
Social change, 228
Solitude, 91, 166
Song of Solomon, 138, 222, 224
Songs of Innocence (Blake), 48
Soul friend, 169
Soul Friend (Leech), 169
Spirare (Latin), 9
Spirit (defined), 9
Spiritual direction, 170, 173
Spiritual formation, 212
Spiritual friendship, 167
Spiritual Friendship (Aelred of Rievaulx), 168
Spiritual-mind, 148
Spiritualism, 128

ABOUT THE AUTHOR

Carl McColman is a freelance writer. He received his B.A. in English Literature from James Madison University and his M.A. in Professional Writing and Editing from George Mason University.

He was born in Alexandria, Louisiana, in 1960. His childhood experiences of spirituality were centered in his family's involvement with the Lutheran Church. As an adult, he developed a wide-ranging interest in alternative spiritual perspectives, including the charismatic renewal, medieval mysticism, shamanism, and Goddess worship. At the Shalem Institute for Spiritual Formation in Washington, D.C., he underwent training in the practice of Christian meditation and contemplative prayer and began his intensive practice under the guidance of a spiritual director (mentor). In 1986 he became a member of the Episcopal Church, and in 1993-94 received additional training in spiritual direction from the Institute for Pastoral Studies in Atlanta.

He now regularly teaches courses on spiritual formation and contemplation, and, as a practicing Christian strongly committed to interfaith dialogue, he incorporates elements of Buddhism and Neopaganism into his spiritual practice. He is interested in the Internet as a medium for spiritual training and networking and, in 1996, began developing a World Wide Web site, the *House of Breathings* (www.anamchara.com), as a resource for persons wishing to cultivate the practice of contemplative spirituality.

Carl McColman lives in Atlanta, Georgia, with his wife and stepdaughter.

Other outstanding books from North Star Publications

FISHING BY MOONLIGHT
The Art of Choosing Intimate Partners
Colene Sawyer, Ph.D.

"From healing past pain to preparing for a healthy mate, this book is filled with useful insights."
—John Gray, Ph.D.
Author, *Men Are From Mars, Women Are From Venus*

DANCING IN THE DARK
The Shadow Side of Intimate Relationships
Douglas & Naomi Moseley

"A+✓ [TOP RATING]. This book is not for the faint-hearted, but it is for those who want to take their relationship to a glorious level—and are willing to do the work in the shadows to get there."
—*Marriage Magazine*

"Bravo! Brava! Finally a book with real solutions for real relationships . . . a must-read for individuals, couples, and helping professionals."
—Pat Love, Ed.D.; co-author, *Hot Monogamy*

RIDING THE DRAGON
The Power of Committed Relationship
Rhea Powers & Gawain Bantle

"A radically fresh, challenging and inspired path into vastly expanded personal and mutual development attainable through a committed relationship."
—W. Brugh Joy, M.D.; author, *Joy's Way, Avalanche*

BEYOND BLAME
Reclaiming the Power You Give to Others
Alex & Gayle Lukeman

"Excellent! A clear explanation with step-by-step examples. I heartily recommend it."
—David Spangler; author, *Everyday Miracles*